Introduction to Computer Programming for the Social Sciences

Introduction to Computer Programming for the Social Sciences

PETER B. HARKINS
University of North Carolina

THOMAS L. ISENHOUR
University of North Carolina

PETER C. JURS
The Pennsylvania State University

Allyn and Bacon, Inc.
Boston

Oct. 18, '73

Library of Congress Catalog Card Number: **72–89238**

Printed in the United States of America

1785086

To
The Missing Left Parenthesis

or

If $\qquad f(x) = \dfrac{1}{2\pi x^3}\, e^{\frac{-1}{2x}}$

Does $\qquad$ FX=(1/((2.0*PI)*X**3))*E**((−1)/(2.0*X)))

CONTENTS

Preface

The increasing application of computer technology to the social sciences is a common phenomenon throughout higher education today. It is no longer unusual for graduate programs to accept competence in computer skills in place of one of the more familiar languages such as German, Russian, French, or Spanish. Our primary objective in writing this book was to assist the social science student in acquainting himself with a research tool that will become increasingly important to him during the present decade.

Our choice of FORTRAN IV as the particular computer language for this book was not arbitrary. It is, and almost certainly will remain for years to come, the ubiquitous language in campus computer centers. We felt a thorough discussion of FORTRAN would be superior to a brief introduction to each of several computer languages. Similarly, we chose to emphasize IBM conventions of FORTRAN IV and we used examples of IBM machine conventions whenever a specific, machine-dependent example had to be employed. By the most conservative estimates over two-thirds of all installed computers are of IBM manufacture. This does not imply, by any means, that users of non-IBM equipment cannot use this book. Indeed, approximately one fourth of the programs presented here were developed on a Raytheon 706 and then converted to IBM conventions. As indicated in the text, local manuals must be consulted for implementation of these programs on any specific machine. However, we have attempted to maintain compatibility with as wide a variety of popular machines as possible.

Our desire was to develop a text that would permit students on all levels of social science to acquire the skill of computer programming from a social scientist's viewpoint. For this reason we have avoided segregating subject matter under separate headings such as programming language, statistics, social science methodology, etc. wherever possible. Instead, in the first three chapters we have presented what we feel to be the necessary background for a beginning programmer in any field. Then we immediately launch into the main portion of the book, consisting of example programs that solve social science problems and that progress in difficulty of concepts, mathematical models, and programming operations. We feel that the student by working through these problems, studying the listings, flow diagrams, etc., and by trying them himself will rapidly become a competent programmer.

Hence, the student should approach this book by reading through the first two chapters on "Introduction to Digital Computers" and "Computer Logic, Programming, and Flow Charts", and then by studying thoroughly the main portion of Chapter 3 on FORTRAN IV. (The latter portion of Chapter 3 on "Additional Capabilities of FORTRAN IV" should be deferred until the student has had considerable experience with simple programs.) Then the student should go directly to the problems and refer to the text and appendices as necessary. He should by all means copy these programs, run them on the computer, and compare the results to the text examples; he should modify them, preferably with simple modifications at first, and then with more complex ones, and try out the modifications; and he should write his own simple programs, and as quickly as these work, more complex ones. In the final analysis, programming is the only way to learn to program.

This work was completed while the senior author was director of the Division of Data Analysis, Institute for Research in Social Science at Chapel Hill. Without his staff's understanding, forbearance, and especially Ronni Meltzer's frequent refilling of the coffee pot, we would still be debugging the examples.

Finally, special acknowledgement is due Mark and Diane for making this possible, and Mini for making it necessary.

January 1972   Peter B. Harkins
                                     Chapel Hill, North Carolina

                                     Thomas L. Isenhour
                                     Chapel Hill, North Carolina

                                     Peter C. Jurs
                                     State College, Pennsylvania

PART 1

Basic Computer Concepts
and
FORTRAN IV

1

Introduction to Digital Computers

Computers are drastically altering our lives. In the modern world their use enters and affects virtually every aspect of man's activities. The ordering of automobile parts and butchers' aprons, the predictions of elections and of the weather, the scheduling of baseball games and cross-country buses, and even the redistricting of congressional delegations and reapportioning of state legislatures are all problems which are routinely approached with computer analysis. The average individual has his church contributions and life insurance billed by computer; his child's college curriculum and his television set designed by computer; and his paychecks and obituary written by computer-generated instructions.

Unfortunately, undesirable results from computer usage seem almost as frequent as desirable ones. To wit the phrases: "Your check will be three weeks late because the computer made a mistake," and "Official Memo 163—Grades must be submitted three days earlier this year because University Central Records office has a new computer to increase efficiency."

The reason for the seemingly inconsistent effects of employing computers may be found by considering the computer as an intelligence amplifier. If stupidity is the negative of wisdom, then it follows that computerizing any process will only result in an amplification of the success or failure level to be expected of the programmer without a computer.

The computer is changing many aspects of the sciences. The social sciences are not being excepted from the general revolution now underway. To the modern social scientist, a user's knowledge of the capabilities of the high speed digital computer is rapidly becoming indispensable. Computers are used in a great variety of ways, but the major scientific applications may be summarized as follows:

1. Computers can routinely and conveniently perform numerical calculations more rapidly and accurately than if performed by hand. (A second generation computer of the IBM 7090 class can perform approximately the equivalent of a man-life of calculations every two hours. For third generation computers this time is reduced to minutes.)

2. Computers can produce answers which would be useless if the time for hand calculations were required. (For example, the necessary calculations for correcting the trajectory of a spacecraft must frequently be accomplished within a limited time. By the time a hand calculation could be done the answer might be only academic.)

3. Certain types of problems may be optimized or simulated by computer calculations. (For example, redistricting congressional delegations and reapportioning state houses and senates may be accomplished with a minimum of partisan political overtones through a computer simulation. The growth and development of metropolitan areas may be simulated decades into the future, a powerful tool for both planners and politicians.)

4. Computers are routinely used for information storage and the retrieval, organization, management, and presentation of large data banks. (For example, thousands of source documents may be searched for certain key words or concepts. The questions asked in a hundred or more surveys, along with a frequency distribution of their answers, may be catalogued in such a way that an investigator could access all questions bearing on "the cost of living" or "attitudes toward the Supreme Court.")

5. Computers can be used to gather data from experiments as these data are produced (in real time); and they can often be incorporated into experimental apparatus so that they direct the experiment as it actually takes place. (For example, intensive care units in hospitals continuously monitor patient physiological signs by computer.)

6. Computers can be programmed to display intelligence by learning to perform tasks while improving their success as their experience increases. (Some advocates of machine intelligence go so far as to

say that computers are essentially a new life form with nearly limit-less possibilities.)

While the above list shows that computers are capable of a wide range of scientific activities, the emphasis in this book will be on the first category, numerical methods. This is because the use of computers for performing calculations is the foremost use in beginning program-ming, and it is in many ways the easiest type of programming to discuss because of the concise nature of mathematical formulations. However, the emphasis on numerical examples and problems should not be con-strued to mean that computers are limited to such uses.

A modern, general-purpose, digital computer is an awesomely complicated electronic-mechanical assemblage. Everyone who has seen a large computer must admit to being impressed—at least on his first encounter—with the variety of complicated behavior including various flashing lights, spinning magnetic tapes, disks, and drums, noisy high-speed printers and typewriters, clacking card readers, and the implication of thousands or even millions of hidden electronic circuits rapidly per-forming various complex operations.

Fortunately, one need not understand the internal operations of a computer to make good use of its capabilities. The computer can be treated in the same "black box" fashion that we treat many everyday mechanical and electrical devices. For example, an extremely complex apparatus which is used almost exclusively from a black box viewpoint is the ordinary television set. Few operators, or even repair men, clearly understand the concepts of intermodulation distortion or image rejection, but the average five-year-old can routinely operate a TV.

Thus, it is apparent that a working knowledge of the internals of many devices is not required for adequate, or even efficient utilization of the device. However, the truly necessary knowledge is the relationship between the inputs and the consequent outputs of the device.

In keeping with this discussion, we hasten to point out that the ma-jority of computer programmers, many of whom might be classed as experts, have little or no knowledge of the internal workings of a com-puter. Our approach to programming will assume that the reader has virtually no knowledge of the computer beyond that of the black box concept. Hence, we will deal exclusively with methods for obtaining desired responses, such as answers to calculations we wish to perform. For the interested reader, the next few pages of this introductory chapter give a brief, simplified look into the internal construction and organiza-tion of computers in general. It should be realized, however, that an understanding of this subject matter is in no way necessary for successful progress throughout the rest of the book.

Internal Organization of Computers

The fundamental property of a digital computer, indeed the source of the term digital, is that it operates by changing from one discrete state to another. We may make a comparison of the computer to an electric lamp, the simplest of which has two states, *off* and *on*. If we define *off* to represent the number zero and *on* to represent the number one, then an electric lamp becomes a computer capable of adding one to zero or subtracting one from one. The lamp's input is in the form of a bistable (two position) switch, its memory is the position of the switch, and its output is the light (or lack of it) produced. Hence, if the lamp is in the *off* state, representing the number zero, one may be added to zero by advancing the switch one step. On the other hand, if the lamp is in the *on* state, representing the number one, one may be subtracted from one by advancing the switch one position. (This next step of the switch returns the lamp to *off*, the zero position; hence, the effect of subtraction has been accomplished.) Such a single binary device constitutes the simplest digital computer. If we enlarge the machine by adding a second such stage it will have an increased capability. For example, there are now four possible different states: both *off*, 00 (binary zero); one *off* and the other *on*, 01 (binary one); one *on* and the other *off*, 10 (binary two); and both *on*, 11 (binary three). Now it is possible to carry out more extensive calculations and deal with larger numbers. This discussion may be extended to show that the number of discrete states of any binary digital system is equal to 2^n where n is the number of individual binary components.

The process of addition in this binary system would be accomplished by adding one bit at a time to binary device a, and connecting the devices so that when device a is switched from *on* to *off*, it adds one to device b. However, when device a switches from *off* to *on* it would not affect device b. Counting would then proceed:

	Device a	Device b	Binary Value	Decimal Value
	off	off	00	0
add 1	off	on	01	1
add 1	on	off	10	2
add 1	on	on	11	3

An analogy may be drawn between this system and the reels of an automobile odometer (mileage indicator). They function in the base ten number system (see Appendix A for a discussion of number systems), but they are connected together in the same manner as the simple two-digit binary illustration above.

The working components of digital computers are largely electronic devices which deal with physically realizable voltages, currents, and magnetic fields. Many of these operations may readily be utilized in binary, or bistable, devices because of the phenomena upon which they are based. Hence, virtually all modern digital computers are internally binary machines. (This is not fundamentally necessary since currents, magnetic fields, etc. do have intensities and could be made to operate at several levels. However, it is normally much easier and quicker to detect the presence or absence of a current, or the orientation of a magnetic field rather than their magnitudes. Furthermore, a very high degree of reliability can be realized in this manner.) By combining many binary components, the computer is capable of assuming a large number of discrete states. These discrete states are actually the combination of the physical states of many thousands of electronic circuits or magnetic elements. The detailed discrete state of the computer at any particular time is usually not fully known, but in principle it could be described fully. This property is in contrast to continuous systems which are not quantized and accordingly have an infinite number of states. (However, it must be realized that any real system has noise, bandpass, and sensitivity limitations which limit it to a finite number of distinguishable states.)

Digital computer components, therefore, assume discrete states that represent coded information in a binary form which symbolize both numbers and the instructions for operating on them. These symbols are then manipulated internally to produce the desired calculations. *It is the extreme speed with which this is done, and the combinations of manipulations possible, that allows the digital computer to perform complex operations.*

The discrete nature of digital computers logically leads to some interesting and important consequences. The statement that computers are arithmetic does not mean computers are merely fast adding machines. They are actually universal information processors. This universality is evidenced by the basic observation that any computer is a manifestation of an abstract universal information processor; as such it does not differ from other computers in abstract capacities, but only in practical ways. Much artificial (machine) intelligence research depends on the abstract information processing abilities of computers.

Digital Computer Components

The major components of a digital computer are the main storage, the central processing unit (which includes the arithmetic-logic unit, the control unit, and the registers), the input units and the output units. These components, which are shown schematically in Fig. 1.1, are discussed individually in the following pages.

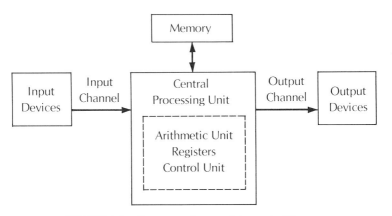

FIGURE 1.1   *Computer System Schematic Diagram*

Main Storage. The main storage (memory, core) of the digital computer works in close conjunction with the Central Processing Unit (CPU) by storing and feeding back information to the CPU as instructed. This memory unit must be distinguished from storage on magnetic tape, disks, or other devices which constitute longer term storage. The memory is divided into sections, or cells, each of which can store one "word" in a binary representation and each of which has a unique address associated with it. A "word" may theoretically consist of any number of bits (binary digits) but is usually between 8 and 64 bits, depending on the particular computer design. The term "word" is used because the quantity being stored can be a binary representation of a number, a letter or series of letters, a combination of letters and numbers, or a coded symbol for an instruction. The main storage not only stores numerical information such as data or intermediate results of a computation, but it also stores the sequence of instructions constituting the program which the computer is executing. Hence, the CPU repeatedly calls on the core memory for the next instruction to be executed.

Each bit of each word is physically stored on a tiny doughnut-shaped, ferrite element. These ferrite rings are strung on wires in a three-dimensional array. Any ferrite ring can be put into either of its two stable states (with magnetic field pointing in one of two directions) by sending a current through two of the three wires which pass through that ring. A correspondence is set up between the direction in which the ring is magnetized and the binary symbols 0 and 1. Thus, binary numbers, or other symbols in binary representation, can be placed into the memory, saved there, and retrieved for later use.

Actual computer memories consist of banks of these ferrite rings strung on wires and divided into memory cells. Memories are usually classified by the number of memory cells (words) they contain; large computer systems may have several million memory cells, i.e. many tens of millions of bits. In order to be used by the computer, each word has a unique address whose use allows the contents of that particular memory cell to be retrieved. Because the contents of any memory cell can be reached independently, the main storage is a *random access* device. (Magnetic disks and drums are also random access devices.) This feature is in contrast to magnetic tape which is an example of a *sequential*, or *serial*, *access* device. A measure of the speed and sophistication of a computer is the rapidity with which any word stored in the memory can be retrieved by the CPU for possible action. This is known as the *access time*. It varies between thousandths of a second, or milliseconds, for the earlier, slower computers down to a few hundred billionths of a second, nanoseconds, for the latest generation of computers. These computers are becoming so fast that the speed of light limitation is governing their physical size. Of course, the access time of a computer has a direct bearing on the overall speed with which it can perform a calculation.

It should be noted that the technology of computer manufacturing is progressing at a fantastic rate and that newer, better methods of constructing main storage units are being studied and implemented. Within the next few years, solid-state memories requiring no internal wiring may well be commercially available.

Central Processing Unit—CPU. The CPU directs and coordinates the overall functioning of the computer and contains the circuitry that actually executes the program instructions. The CPU has the following sub-units:

1. The *control unit,* which is able to address main storage in order to store or fetch information and to sequence instructions in the desired order.
2. The *arithmetic-logic unit,* which performs arithmetic or logical processing of data.
3. Many *registers* for short-term memory or storage of intermediate results of arithmetic instructions.

The part of the computer that actually performs the arithmetic and logical operations is called the arithmetic-logic unit. It contains electronic circuitry for performing addition and subtraction in the binary number system and for performing elementary logical operations. Larger computers have circuitry that performs multiplication and division; small computers often perform these operations by executing simple programs involving repeated additions or subtractions. In actual practice arithmetic or logical operations can be reduced to the two simple logical operations of (a) negation and (b) conjunction, which can both be conveniently implemented with electronic circuits. This is discussed in more detail in Appendix B.

The CPU contains a set of registers, which are readily accessible temporary storage and can be used to store (a) the numbers being handled by the arithmetic circuits of the machine, or (b) the address of the next instruction to be executed. An accumulator register (often called the AC or ACC) is used to store the sum or difference in addition or subtraction operations. A multiplier-quotient register (often called the MQ) may be used as well as the AC for multiplication and division. The MQ contains the multiplier or quotient, respectively, where the AC stores the product or dividend, respectively, during multiplication or division. Large computers have many registers; for example, a UNIVAC 1108 may have as many as 128 registers incorporated into its CPU.

The CPU also contains the control unit which directs the sequence of operations to be performed by the computer. The various units of the computer are electronically linked by transmission lines that can be used to transmit information from one unit to another. The control unit is wired to respond to a repertory of basic instructions calling the other units into action as necessary. Typical instructions are as follows: Store the AC contents in a certain memory location, perform some operation on the contents of one of the registers, fetch the contents of a certain memory location, etc. These instructions are executed by activating the transmission lines in the correct sequence from electronic logic circuits in the control unit. Thus, the control unit is the executive of the computer organization.

Input.   There are many alternative methods for communicating with a modern digital computer. Input devices include punched cards, magnetic tape, punched paper tape, magnetic disk, magnetic drum, electric typewriter, teletypewriter, and others. Each of these devices has its unique advantages and disadvantages, and the choice of which to use in a particular case depends on many circumstances. Table 1–1 lists the most common input/output devices along with some typical characteristics.

The input medium most widely employed by computer users is the

TABLE 1–1. Input/Output Device Chart

Device	Transmission Rate	Storage Capacity	Sequential or Random Access	Physical Phenomenon
Core Memory	10^6 word/sec	up to $\sim10^8$ bits	R	magnetization of ferrite core
Magnetic tape	10^5–10^6 char/sec	200 mega bits/ 2400 ft. reel tape	S	magnetization of film on substrate
Magnetic disk	$\sim10^5$–10^6 bytes/sec	10^8–10^{10} bits	R-S	magnetization of film on substrate
Magnetic drum	10^6 bytes/sec	4×10^6 bits	R-S	magnetization of film on substrate
Typewriter	15–25 char/sec	—	S	
Teletypewriter ASR-33	10 char/sec	—	S	
Punched cards	300–2000 cards/min 10^2–10^3 char/sec	80 char/card	S	holes in paper
Punched paper tape	300 char/sec	—	S	holes in paper
Line Printer	2000+ lines/min 10^3 char/sec	120–132+ char/line	S	

punched card. Punched cards are produced on keypunches which have keyboards similar to standard typewriters. Decks of punched cards are convenient to handle, cards may be inserted or deleted easily, and they can be quickly processed by high-speed card readers. Magnetic tape is commonly used where information is repeatedly input in volumes too great to be easily handled by cards. Tapes are normally not produced directly by the user, as are cards, but are the result of some previous computer operation. One standard 2,400 foot reel of one-half inch wide magnetic tape can contain an enormous amount of information—approximately thirty million English language words, for example (or about sixty times the entire vocabulary of the English language). Paper tapes are employed mainly in conjunction with smaller computers where the relatively low initial cost of paper tape reading equipment more than compensates for their slow operating speed. A distinct disadvantage of paper tape is that correction, insertion, or deletion of information from a previously prepared paper tape requires remaking the entire tape. Punched cards, magnetic tape, and paper tapes are examples of sequential information sources because the information contained on them is in a distinct serial arrangement that must be handled in a prescribed, fixed order.

Magnetic disks and drums, on the other hand, are examples of random-access devices which allow access to any information without the necessity for processing preceding information first. They are widely used for storing information that is needed repeatedly. Most large computer systems have disks and/or drums which can be considered an extension of core memory and on which are stored information the computer must repeatedly access as it performs its duties, e.g., accounting information about the users of the computer. Disks and drums store information in the same manner as do magnetic tapes, by selective magnetization of the iron oxide coating on a support material. Disks physically resemble a stack of phonograph records with interspersed spacers, drums are cylindrical with the coating on the surface.

Electric typewriters are used for inputting information in several special cases. They are normally built into the computer console and are used by the computer operator to communicate with the computer while it is running. Electric typewriters are also widely used in time-sharing systems where one computer is simultaneously accepting input from many users. Time-sharing systems also often incorporate teletypewriters as input devices. Teletypewriters are frequently used in conjunction with smaller computers for the same reasons as punched paper tape—their low initial cost more than compensates for their relatively slow operation. Some special computers systems are capable of using large cathode-ray oscilloscope screens for inputting information by sensing the position on the screen where the user directs the beam of a small flashlight called a light pen.

Output.   The devices used for the output of information include all those listed for input plus some important additions. The most widely used output device is the line printer. This device prints information on paper one entire line at a time at the rate of up to 2000 lines per minute. All large computer installations have one or more line printers for handling output. Punched cards are used for output when relatively small quantities of information which are to be used for input for later programs are involved. Magnetic tapes are used for outputting large quantities of information. Most computer users do not output information for long term storage onto disks or drums, although at some large computer installations space on these devices may be leased.

Special output devices, which are used when applicable, include a wide variety of plotters that (along with their necessary support programs) can directly produce graphical presentation of output, and also cathode-ray oscilloscopes. Such oscilloscope screens allow computer programs to draw visual output which may be photographed or viewed by the programmer, thus allowing him to judge how well the program is doing and then to affect its further activities, if necessary.

Useful Characteristics of Digital Computers

Digital computers have several important characteristics which lead to their versatility and usefulness. Four of these will be discussed: high precision, extremely rapid execution rate, low error rate, and the ability to execute stored instructions.

The ability to define virtually any number of bits as the word length in a digital computer (at least at the time the computer is designed) leads to an almost unlimited *precision* with which numbers can be stored and retrieved. However, a specific amount of memory must normally be set aside for the overall organization of the machine to be effective; this mitigates in favor of a fixed word length.* For the IBM System/360 operating in the FORTRAN IV mode, the word length is usually 32 bits. This means that there are 2^{32} or 4,294,967,296 possible discrete states for any given word. If however we use the leftmost bit to signify the condition positive or negative, we can represent any number from -2^{31}

---

* There are some computers for which the word length may be defined by the programmer. Furthermore, there are means of varying word length within certain limitations on some computers. These methods will be discussed later. For this section of the book it will be assumed that the word length is fixed.

through $2^{31} - 1$, or a total of 2^{32} numbers including zero in a 32 bit word. All integers from -2^{31} through $2^{31} - 1$ may be *exactly* represented by a 32 bit word. The rub comes when we need to work with larger absolute quantities or with fractional values. To allow a wider permissible range of numbers, to work with fractional values, and to facilitate certain arithmetic processes, numbers are often represented in a "floating point" or "real" notation wherein some of the bits comprising the word are used to store significant digits (mantissa) and the remaining bits represent an exponent of the appropriate base (characteristic). In the case of the IBM System/360, twenty-four bits are used for the mantissa, one bit for the sign, and the remaining seven bits are used for the characteristic and its sign. (This particular system is hexadecimal, or base 16.) Hence numbers having a precision of 1 part in 2^{24} or about seven decimal significant figures ($2^{24} \cong 10^7$) and ranging from 10^{-78} to 10^{75} can be represented in this fashion. The twenty-fifth bit is the uncertain one in every case; hence, every number is represented with approximately the same degree of precision. Other machines have different word sizes and real number conventions.

For ordinary applications this degree of precision seems unnecessarily high, but it is required for the following reason. Not all fractions can be exactly converted from decimal to binary. Furthermore, because computers are arithmetic, they can only perform the elementary arithmetic operations such as addition and subtraction. Therefore, the values of all trigonometric, logarithmic, and other functions must be calculated by arithmetic approximations which usually result from evaluation of series. The number of basic operations needed to compute a final result is known as the arithmetic depth of a calculation. Roundoff errors accumulate rapidly as the arithmetic depth of computations increases, and high precision is therefore necessary in order that the final result be at all precise. However, it should be pointed out that incorrect numerical results can certainly be obtained by unwisely coded algorithms.

A second important characteristic of digital computers is the *very high speed* with which they can perform calculations. Operation speeds as high as hundreds of thousands of floating point multiplications per second are obtained. As pointed out earlier, this is useful for all computations because computational speed is one, and perhaps the best, direct measure of the overall capability of the machine. Doubling the compute speed of a machine can nearly double its productivity. (The reason for qualifying this statement is that in input/output limited operations, where compute speed is not the limiting factor, increasing the compute speed may not improve the capability of the machine. Most situations are some compromise between the two extreme cases.) For certain calculations, however, the high compute speed is absolutely necessary. These are situations where the results of the computation are useless if not available within a certain time. (A posthumous pardon from the Governor is of little utility.) Thus, a whole realm of experimentation is made possible because of the extreme speed with which calculations can be performed. Space exploration programs provide excellent examples in that they depend completely on the ability of computers to function quickly as well as correctly.

The third desirable feature of computers is their very *low error rate,* that is, the rate at which mistakes are introduced *by the machine* during the processing of information. This feature is in distinct contrast to the calculation of functions with great arithmetic depth by humans, where the error rate is quite significant. One carefully considered estimate placed the *minimum* error rate of human data manipulators at about one error per thousand operations. Most people would readily admit to a much greater rate for ordinary calculations. However, the present undetected error rate — there are certain redundancy and parity checks which indicate the occurrence of many types of errors in computers — of high speed computers is almost vanishingly small. Indeed, if it were not, the results of most computations would be gibberish.

The fourth, and perhaps the most important, of the major characteristics of high speed digital computers, is their ability to *execute sequences of stored instructions.* For this reason it is not necessary to build a separate computer for each different calculation, or even rewire or modify the computer in any way other than inputting a new set of instructions. Hence, the execution of any program proceeds according to that set of instructions, and it is not dependent on previous history. The instructions are executed in order (although it is possible for the instructions themselves to define the order) and thus carry out the desired sequence of steps. The computer must have a memory capable of storing the instructions and the intermediate results. But once it has such a memory, it needs only one electronic circuit for each basic operation, and the entire operation can proceed at electronic speed without slow human supervision. Additionally, and this is probably the most important point of all, the sequence of execution of the stored instructions can be modified during execution. Thus, a computation can proceed according to intermediate results. This feature, therefore, allows digital computers to make decisions while executing sequences of stored instructions. A great deal more will be said about this ability later.

2

Computer Logic, Programming, and Flow Charts

Computer Logic

As previously stated, modern digital computers use the binary number system because of certain basic characteristics of electronic circuits. Because the fundamental operations of the machine amount to binary choices, it is understandable that the basic machine logic is binary; that is, computer logic consists of decisions or branches that can have one of two outcomes.

From combinations of the most primitive binary logical operations, the basic arithmetic operations are developed. These then are combined to form specific detailed lists of machine instructions which, when taken as a whole, constitute the fundamental capabilities of the machine. These basic instructions are then combined in various fashions, to form specific sets of instructions, called algorithms, which accomplish specific calculations. We will use the term algorithm repeatedly throughout this book to denote a set of unambiguous operations which result in a given calculation.

Therefore, in order to accomplish a given calculation, it is necessary to first know a mathematical or logical algorithm for solving the problem. This algorithm must then be rewritten in the form of a computer program composed of instructions that are compatible with the given computer. This computer program is stored in the machine memory and causes the computer to carry out the necessary steps to arrive at the desired result. For the greatest simplicity in programming, it is obvious that the computer instructions should be as close to normal mathematical notation as possible. We shall discuss this point in detail in a later section of this chapter.

Example A. *Calculating the area of a circle.* A mathematical formula for the area of a circle is

$$A = \pi r^2,$$

where A is the area and r is the radius.

From this formula it is seen that one algorithm for calculating the area would be to measure the value of the radius, square it, and multiply the result by pi.

An algorithm for such a calculation is

Step 1.   Look up r.
Step 2.   Look up π.
Step 3.   Calculate $A = \pi r^2$.
Step 4.   Output A.

The next step of converting the logical algorithm into actual computer acceptable statements will be the subject of Chapter 3.

The most crucial point in the development of the computer algorithm for solving any problem is that it must be totally unambiguous and explain with complete accuracy what operations are to be carried out. This does not mean that the program cannot have built-in options. It does mean, however, that those options must be precisely defined; and that furthermore, at the time of execution each option must be reduced to a single path. (We shall later see how very flexible programs can be written without introducing any ambiguities.) The next example shows an algorithm for another problem.

Example B. Determine the difference in actual cost between leaded and unleaded gasoline.

Assume a given car gets X miles per gallon with regular leaded gasoline, and Y miles per gallon with regular unleaded gasoline. If the leaded gas sells for 39.9 cents per gallon and the unleaded for 41.9 cents per gallon, which is actually less expensive to use? (All questions of ecology aside.)

The mathematical equation for determining the difference in cost is

$$D = \left(\frac{39.9}{X} - \frac{41.9}{Y} \right) \text{ cents/mile.}$$

If D is positive, then the unleaded gas is actually cheaper to use than the leaded.

An algorithm for calculating D is given by

Step 1.   Look up X and Y.
Step 2.   Calculate $D = (39.9/X - 41.9/Y)$.
Step 3.   Output D.

There are several types of computer instructions. Instructions such as those above deal with the data itself. They might obtain the data or perform calculations upon it or upon intermediate results. Another type of instruction controls the program itself. This type of instruction is used to cause a program to branch according to conditions existing at the time the branch is reached. The program above, which is used to calculate the difference in cost between two gasolines, can be rewritten using this second type of instruction in a more general form.

Example C.

Step 1.   Look up the cost per gallon of the leaded gas, CPGL, and the cost per gallon of the unleaded gas, CPGUL.

Step 2.   Look up the number of gallons of leaded gas used over a given period of time, NGL, and the miles driven during this time, NML.

Step 3.   Look up the number of gallons of unleaded gas used over a given period of time, NGUL, and the miles driven during this period, NMUL.

Step 4.   Look up the miles per gallon obtained by using leaded gas, X, and the miles per gallon obtained using unleaded gas, Y.

Step 5.   If X and Y were measured, go to step 9.

Step 6.   If NGL, NML, NGUL and NMUL were measured, go to step 8.

Step 7.   Go to step 1.

Step 8.   Calculate $X = $ NML $\div$ NGL
                     $Y = $ NMUL $\div$ NGUL

Step 9.   Calculate $D = $ CPGL$*X - $CPGUL$*Y$.

Step 10.   Output D.

This program proceeds through the above steps one instruction after another until it reaches the control statements at steps 5, 6, and 7. These statements cause control to transfer elsewhere, but the exact action taken depends upon circumstances at the time the particular instruction is executed. Notice that if neither NML, NGL, NMUL, and NGUL, or X and Y were measured, control returns to step 2 again. If these data were never measured, control would keep cycling around the loop consisting of instructions 2, 3, 4, 5, 6, 7, 2, 3, 4, 5, 6, 7. . . . This illustrates a possible pitfall in computer programming; one must be careful to anticipate all possible sequences of action or to provide alternatives when undesired situations occur.

Flow Charts

In order to help organize the necessary instructions for accomplishing a given calculation, flow charts are often used. These diagrams consist of a standard set of symbols that can be combined to represent or outline lists of instructions. The flow chart is the equivalent of a schematic diagram for a computer program and is useful not only to help the programmer organize his thoughts but also to show others what he has done. The symbols to be used for flow charts in this book are given in Fig. 2.1.

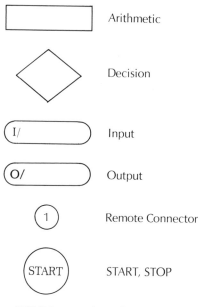

FIGURE 2.1   *Flow Chart Symbols*

These symbols are connected by lines with arrowheads that denote the direction of flow through the program. A rectangular box denotes an arithmetic operation, e.g., addition, multiplication, or the evaluation of a function. A diamond-shaped box denotes a decision. Normally there are either two or three possible paths exiting from a decision box. The operations of either input or output are denoted by the oblong figures with rounded ends with the symbol I/ denoting input and O/ denoting output. The small circle with an enclosed number is a remote connector whereby distant parts of a flow chart may be connected without drawing a line from one point to the other. The beginning and end of a program are denoted by a larger circle enclosing the word "START" or "STOP."

Several examples of flow charts follow. Figure 2.2 is a flow chart for Example A, the algorithm for computing the area of a circle. Fig-

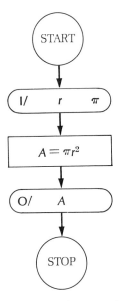

FIGURE 2.2   *Flow Chart for Example Algorithm A*

ure 2.3 is a flow chart corresponding to Example B, the algorithm for computing the difference in actual cost between two gasolines. This algorithm contains no branches, so control passes straight through the sequence without deviating. Figure 2.4 is the flow chart corresponding to the algorithm of Example C. This flow chart contains diamond-shaped decision elements which allow the program to proceed according to the situation encountered. Figure 2.5 is a flow chart for an algorithm which calculates the mean of n given numbers, $x_1, x_2, \ldots, x_n$. It contains a loop in the center of the flow chart. The first $(n-1)$ times the decision box is reached the answer to the question "Is $i = n$?" is no, and so the *No* branch is taken, and thus the sum is accumulated. The nth time the decision box is reached, the *Yes* branch is taken, the average, $\bar{x}$, is calculated and is output.

In developing more complex programs it is often convenient to work

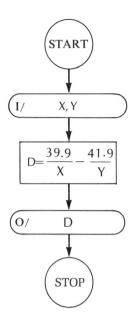

FIGURE 2.3   *Flow Chart for Example Algorithm B*

out the flow chart first in order to organize the overall problem. In explaining a program to someone else, it is sometimes easier to use a flow chart rather than the program itself. Some of the problems which form the second half of this book contain a flow chart as well as the program for the particular calculation.

Programming Languages

There are several levels of programming languages. The most basic, of course, consists of the actual machine instructions, which are in binary code. While writing programs in the fundamental binary machine instructions certainly offers the maximum flexibility and potential efficiency in machine usage, this task is so difficult that it is normally avoided. The instruction set of the IBM System/360 includes more than 100 basic instructions of the most fundamental nature. Examples of such instructions include: "Add accumulator contents to register A" and "Clear accumulator,"—each of which would be represented as a string of binary digits. A simple arithmetic operation such as required in the earlier calculation of the difference in cost between two gasolines (Example B) would require several dozen machine instructions.

To overcome the arduous task of writing programs directly in binary

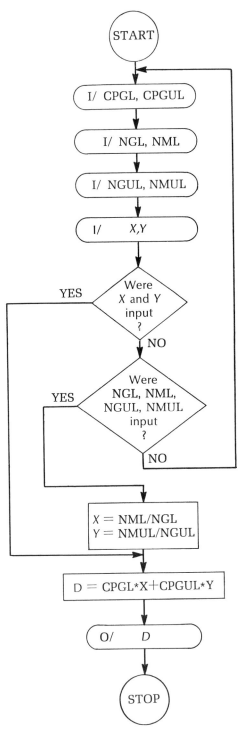

FIGURE 2.4 *Flow Chart for Example Algorithm C*

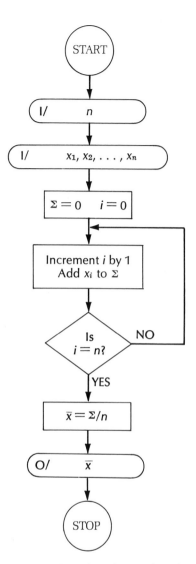

FIGURE 2.5   *Flow Chart for an Algorithm to Calculate the Mean of n Numbers*

notation, a second level of language, called assembler language, was developed. An assembly program consists of virtually the same set of operations available in the basic machine code, but written in an alpha-betic-numeric code which is far simpler to code. For example, the instruction to store uses the mnemonic "ST" in IBM System/360 Assembler. The completed assembly program is submitted to a special program, the assembler, which is written in basic machine code. This master program reads the assembly instructions and converts them to basic machine instructions, thereby saving the programmer the necessity of working directly in binary machine language.

However, assembly programming still requires a high level of knowledge of the basic computer capabilities and is also restricted to the available instruction code of the particular machine. If all programming were done in assembly language, it is a safe bet that not ten percent of the present programmers would have taken the trouble to learn programming. (The situation is analogous to restricting all radio transmission to Morse code. It's doubtful that radio would have become a commercial success under those circumstances.)

The third level of programming languages is designed to bridge the gap between machine level instructions and the type of representation familiar to the average user of mathematical operations. These languages are called compiler level languages and can certainly be credited with having made the computer accessible to a much wider range of potential users. Compiler languages use a pseudoalgebraic, English code to describe the problem instructions in a manner that can be translated into machine code by a master program called a compiler. In this case the programmer can write in terms relatively familiar to him; though some flexibility and efficiency are lost, he can avoid having to learn the basic logic of the machine. Furthermore, compilers can be written for various machines in order that the same statements are translated into the basic instructions for the particular computer. Thus, compilers are also the first approach to a universal computer language.

Typical compiler languages include FORTRAN, BASIC, APL, ALGOL, COBOL, LISP, and PL/1. These languages are designed for user convenience and often with special purposes in mind. For example, while FORTRAN is designed for scientific computing, COBOL is designed for business applications.

A program written in a compiler level language is called a source program. When a source program is translated by the compiler into machine language, an object program is obtained. Under certain circumstances the object program is produced in the form of punched cards or on magnetic tape and then saved in this form to be reused as often as necessary. Other systems store object programs in temporary storage as an intermediate step in carrying out the calculation; compilation must, therefore, be done each time the calculation is made.

Various generations and versions of many compilers exist. The original FORTRAN developed by IBM has now evolved into a variety of forms of FORTRAN IV which have so much in common as to be considered dialects rather than separate languages. FORTRAN compilers exist for virtually every major machine manufactured and, furthermore, exist in various versions for the same machine. One of the authors has noted (to his horror) the conversion to newer versions of IBM FORTRAN IV four times within one year at his local computation center. In general, the specific version of a language such as FORTRAN which can be used on a particular computer depends on (a) the computer, (b) the manufacturer, and (c) the compiler type. Luckily, things are not as bad as they might seem, because within FORTRAN there has been considerable standardization and there is a large subset of statements which are acceptable to many different computers with different versions of FORTRAN compilers. However, the user should be prepared to consult the specific reference manuals for the particular machine and compiler that he is using.

3

FORTRAN IV

FORTRAN is a user-oriented language for symbolic communication with a suitable computer. The significance of the word "symbolic" in the previous sentence should not be overlooked. Always remember that FORTRAN statements have no intrinsic meaning but are simply strings of symbols which the computer, or more specifically the compiler, must translate into machine code. In recognition of this, the word "FORTRAN" is a contraction of the words "formula translation." The symbolic nature of FORTRAN dictates that the punctuation and syntax rules of the language are totally inflexible. You can communicate in most languages using incorrect punctuation (most of us do) but not in FORTRAN. The compiler scans each statement looking for one of a relatively small number of ordered symbol sets. If a statement does not perfectly satisfy one of the symbol sets expected, no action is possible. Furthermore, close doesn't count. Programs written in FORTRAN consist of sets of statements which, when translated into machine language and linked together, form a list of specific instructions that the computer can execute.

Several generations of FORTRAN exist. This chapter will introduce features of the language that are common to most versions of FORTRAN. Where necessary the conventions used by IBM System 360 computers will be used. As noted previously, the incompatibilities that exist between various FORTRAN systems occur, generally, in the more advanced capabilities of the language and should create few, if any, problems for the beginning programmer. In order to write programs for a specific computer, it is necessary to become familiar with (a) the version of FORTRAN in use, and (b) the specific conventions for the computer. These data will normally be available from manuals and publications by the computer manufacturer and the computer center.

There exists a specially designed compiler for FORTRAN IV, called the WATFIV compiler, which is meant for student programming. It is compatible with IBM FORTRAN IV, but has three distinct advantages for introductory programming:

1. The diagnostic messages are unusually concise and understandable.
2. It has default input/output statements which are easier to use than ordinary FORTRAN IV input/output statements.
3. Programs compile significantly faster under WATFIV than standard FORTRAN IV compilers.

The unique input/output capability of FORTRAN IV under WATFIV will be discussed later in the chapter.

The first section of this chapter introduces the basic features of FORTRAN, specifically the characters used in FORTRAN, the types of constants and variables and the formation of FORTRAN expressions. The second section gives the necessary statements of FORTRAN with which many useful programs can be written. A third section discusses some of the more advanced capabilities of the FORTRAN language. Section 3 is of less importance to beginning programmers, and the detailed consideration of it should be put off until the contents of the first two sections of this chapter are thoroughly understood. Finally, FOR-TRAN requires a relentless attention to detail. As you read the following chapter these details will seem to pile up. Rather than give up, take comfort in the fact that no one ever learned to program by just reading a book. The proper approach is to study this chapter, learning enough elements of the language so that you can start to experiment with the programs found in the final section of the book. By experimenting with these programs and writing your own, the seemingly endless detail will take care of itself.

3–1.   The Basics of FORTRAN IV

The basic components of FORTRAN IV will be presented in the first section of this chapter. These basics include the character set, constants, variables, and expressions that are used in FORTRAN IV.

Character Set

A limited set of symbols, the character set, are used in FORTRAN.

1.   26 alphabetic characters: ABCDEFGHIJKLMNOPQRSTUVWXYZ
2.   10 numeric characters: 0123456789
3.   12 special characters: $* / + - . , ( ) \$ = ' b$

The lower case "b" is used to represent a blank space. The combined alphabetic and numeric characters—but not the twelve special characters—are referred to as the alphanumeric characters. In writing FOR–TRAN statements, members of the FORTRAN character set are combined into strings that resemble English words, statements that resemble algebraic expressions, and combinations of symbols that have meaning only in FORTRAN.

Constants

Constants are quantities that are fixed in value. The two most basic types of constants in FORTRAN are integer constants and real constants. Integer constants are strings of decimal digits with an algebraic sign but without a decimal point. The decimal point is always assumed to be on the right end of an integer constant, which leads to the terminology "fixed point" for this type of constant. Unsigned integer constants are assumed to be positive. Some examples of valid integer constants are:

$$\begin{array}{ccc}
1 & 62914 & 1970 \\
+21 & 0 & 3 \\
-739 & -7 & -42
\end{array}$$

There is a maximum size for integer constants in any computer. For the IBM System/360, the largest positive integer is $2^{31} - 1$, the largest negative number is -2^{31}; for the IBM 7040 or 7090 the largest positive value is $2^{35} - 1$, the largest negative, $-2^{35} + 1$. For the IBM 1130, the largest negative and positive integers are -2^{15} and $2^{15} - 1$, respectively.

For the IBM System/360, System/370 and 1130 computers the standard precision for real constants consists of one to seven significant decimal digits with or without a sign. The movable nature of the decimal point leads real constants to be called "floating point." Some real constants without exponents are:

123.4	7094.3
−0.017	0.0
3.14159	−72.0

Unsigned real constants are assumed to be positive.

Real constants that include an exponent must adhere to the prescribed form, which contains the number with a decimal point, followed by the letter E and then a signed or unsigned one- or two-digit integer constant. Examples of such real constants and their equivalents in mathematical notation are as follows:

Real Constant	Mathematical Notation
1.00E−06	1.0×10^{-6}
−0.033E−12	-0.033×10^{-12}
1947.0E3	1947.0×10^{3}

Real constants have a range of magnitude; for example, for the System/360 they must remain within the range 10^{-78} to 10^{75}, and for the IBM 7040, 7090 or 1130 they must lie within the range 10^{-38} to 10^{38}. This range of magnitude is fixed for each of the computer systems discussed so far. The *precision,* however, is alterable. *Extended precision* in 1130 systems will produce up to *ten* significant decimal digits; for System/360, *double precision* will allow approximately *seventeen* significant decimal digits; and under System/370, it is possible to obtain *thirty-four* decimal digit accuracy.

Variables

Variables are quantities that can assume different values, according to conditions during a program's execution. They are similar to algebraic variables, and their names are formed from combinations of alphanumeric characters. As with constants, there are two types of variables — integer variables and real variables (also known as "fixed-point" variables and "floating-point" variables). Integer variable names are formed by combinations of one through six (five for IBM 1130 systems) alphanumeric characters beginning with one of the letters I, J, K, L, M, or N. The remainder of the integer variable name can contain any of the alphanumeric characters (but no special characters), yielding valid integer variable names such as the following:

J	JUNIOR
L32	I8QP
KAPPA	I

Real variables are variables that can assume real values. Real variable names are formed by combinations of one through six (five for IBM 1130 Systems) alphanumeric characters beginning with an alphabetic character other than the six reserved for integer variable names. As with integer variables, the special characters may not be used. Some valid real variable names are as follows:

X	SQUARE
B23	Y1
SUM	GARY
ROOT1	FLO

In writing programs it is often helpful to choose integer and real variable names that convey meaning to the programmer and to other readers.

Variables, either real or integer, are of two classes, scalars and arrays. A *scalar* is simply a single-valued variable, such as X or IJAG. At any time during the execution of a program using either of these variables, X and IJAG can have one and only one value. An *array* is a set of scalars having the same "family" name. Each element of an array has its own storage location. Remembering basic algebra, we use subscripts on array variables to denote which of the "family" members, which element of the array, we are using. For example, if one has five values for a variable, X, and he wishes to retain all five values during the execution of his program, he could use five different scalars, e.g., X1, X2, X3, X4, and X5, or he could use the single-dimensional array X(I), where I would range from 1 to 5 to represent each of the five different values. Back to basic algebra: X_1 represents the first element of the array X; X_4, the fourth element, etc. In FORTRAN instead of setting off subscripts by dropping them half way below the line, we enclose them in parentheses: thus; X_1 becomes X(1), X_4 becomes X(4), X_i becomes X(I), and so on.

The following table gives the several forms for subscripts which will be accepted by most FORTRAN compilers. Much more complex expressions are allowed by the FORTRAN compilers of many larger computer systems.

Form	Example
constant	7
variable	ISUB
variable + constant	IJ+27
variable − constant	IKL−1
constant times variable	3*MSUB
constant times variable + constant	4*K+20
constant times variable − constant	14*LM−5

Note that the variable must be an unsigned, nonsubscripted, integer variable. The subscript must, when evaluated, be greater than zero and less than or equal to the bounds of the array. The exponentiation and divide operator are not permitted within a subscript. Finally, the order in which constants and variables are given in the table is crucial. The expression K*3 is often not a valid subscript, while 3*K is permitted.

The extension of this approach to two or higher dimensional arrays is straightforward. Thus $x_{i,j}$ in mathematical notation becomes X(I,J) in FORTRAN. In general, one variable may have up to seven different subscripts. Again, the subscripts themselves are positive integer constants (not including zero), integer variables, or integer expressions (to be defined in the next section), which are formed according to the above rules and when evaluated have non-zero, positive values—separated from each other by commas. Examples of valid subscripted real and integer variables are

A(I)	Z(KJR,3,LK)	J(L,K)
XSUM(3,4)	G(NSUM)	DODO(N,M)
BETA(M,L)	I(J)	KSUM(L)

To summarize: Variables may be of two types—integer or real. Their names are formed from combinations of up to six (only five on some machines) alphanumeric characters, with integer constants, integer variables, or integer expressions as their subscripts. They may be single- or multi-dimensional.

Expressions

An expression is a sequence of variables or constants or a combination thereof with interspersed operator symbols which specify a series of mathematical operations to be executed. The arithmetic operators of FORTRAN are:

+ addition
− subtraction
* multiplication
/ division
** exponentiation.

Arithmetic expressions are formed when constants and/or variables are combined with these five operators in a manner much like algebra. Some simple algebraic expressions and their FORTRAN equivalents are as follows:

Algebraic Expression	FORTRAN Expression	Type
$x + y$	X+Y	REAL
$a - bc$	A−B*C	REAL
$3d^2$	3.0*D**2	REAL
$k_i(n + m)$	K(I)*(N+M)	INTEGER
$\dfrac{a_{12} - a_{11}}{a_{33}}$	(A(1,2)−A(1,1))/A(3,3)	REAL
$x - k(y - z)$	X−K*(Y−Z)	MIXED

Expressions have type; they are either integer or real depending upon the type of their components. Many FORTRAN compilers require that expressions contain only one type of constant or variable; more recently, some FORTRAN IV compilers allow a mixture of types within an expression. Parts of mixed mode expressions involving only integer variables will be evaluated according to the rules of integer arithmetic. Parts of such expressions involving only real variables, or real and integer variables, will be evaluated according to the rules for *real* arithmetic. In the case of integer and real variables forming a part of an expression, the integer variables are converted automatically to real form before computation.

As the examples show, an expression can be enclosed within parentheses. Additionally, expressions within parentheses can be connected by operators to form larger expressions, although two operators may not be placed in sequence, e.g., A*−B is incorrect. The correct form for this expression would be either A*(−B) or −B*A. Ambiguity in the formation of expressions can be avoided by including parentheses to specify the sequence in which the operations are to be executed. Redundant parentheses are permitted: X+1, (X+1), and ((X+1)) are all valid and equivalent expressions. For complex arithmetic expressions, several sets of parentheses may be required. When parentheses are included, the order of execution of the statement is by steps from the innermost set to the outermost set of parentheses. The following examples illustrate the use of parentheses.

Algebraic Expression	FORTRAN Expression
$(a_i + b_i)^2 c$	(A(I)+B(I))**2*C
$(b^2 - 4ac)/2a$	(B**2−4.0*A*C)/(2.0*A)
$a_1 + a_2 x_i + a_3 x_i^2$	A(1)+A(2)*X(I)+A(3)*X(I)**2
$\sqrt{x^2 - x}$	(X**2−X)**0.5
ze/r^2	(Z*E)/(R**2)

In these examples, single letters have been used for variable names for simplicity; in practice any valid variable name may be used.

The order of execution of expressions that have no parentheses, or of expressions contained within parentheses, is as follows:

1. Exponentiation, left to right. In the case of sequential exponentiation operators, execution is from right to left. Given: $X**Y**Z$, $(Y**Z)$ will be evaluated first. Then "X" will be raised to the power $(Y**Z)$.
2. Multiplication and division, left to right.
3. Addition and subtraction, left to right.

The first example above would be evaluated in the following manner:

1. Form the sum $a_i + b_i$.
2. Square the result to obtain $(a_i + b_i)^2$.
3. Multiply the result by c to obtain the final result.

The second example is executed as follows:

1. Square "b" to obtain b^2.
2. Multiply 4 times "a" and that result times "c" to obtain 4ac.
3. Subtract 4ac from b^2 to obtain $b^2 - 4ac$.
4. Multiply 2 times "a" to obtain 2a.
5. Divide $b^2 - 4ac$ by 2a to obtain the final result.

In forming expressions blank spaces can be included anywhere in order to improve clarity. In exponentiation, integers can be raised only to integer powers, but real constants or variables can be raised to either integer or real powers. When performing multiplication and division, the maximum permissible size for variables must be kept in mind, because if the maximum is exceeded the computation will not progress as desired. Division by zero must be avoided, of course.

Performing division with integer quantities can give unexpected answers because the integer result cannot be a fraction. The computer changes fractions into integers by dropping all the digits to the right of the (understood) decimal point. This process is known as truncation. For example, division of two real variables, $X = 9.0$ by $Y = 6.0$, gives $X/Y = 1.5$. But the same division with integer variables, J=9 by K=6, gives J/K=1 because both J and K are integer variables, causing the expression J/K to be integer. Thus truncation can lead to unintended results in the division of integer quantities.

3-2.   FORTRAN IV Statements

The first section has introduced the basic components of FORTRAN. This section will introduce the statements from which FORTRAN IV programs are assembled. The discussion will include arithmetic statements, control statements, input and output statements, format statements, and the use of subprograms, both subroutines and functions.

The Arithmetic Statement

In FORTRAN the general form of the arithmetic statement is a=b, where "a" represents a subscripted or unsubscripted variable, and "b" represents a constant, a variable, or an expression. The equal sign does not carry the same meaning as in algebra. In FORTRAN this statement means that the value of the constant, variable, or expression on the right-hand side is to be calculated and the result of that calculation is to be assigned to the variable on the left-hand side. Some examples of arithmetic statements follow.

$$I=J$$
$$X(I)=Y(I)**2-YAV$$
$$BSUM=BSUM+W(K)*V(L,J)$$
$$KR=KR+1$$

In each case the execution of the statement proceeds by calculation of the value of the expression on the right side of the equal sign and assignment of that value to the variable on the left side.

There are four combinations of type that can occur, and the combination can affect the results of the operation. When both sides of an arithmetic statement are of the same type—integer and integer, or real and real—nothing special occurs. However, when the variable on the left side is real and the expression on the right side is an integer, then the type of the expression is changed upon execution of the statement, but its value is not changed. For example, the arithmetic statement $X=I$ if executed when I has the value of 4 would cause X to have the value of 4.0; the type has been changed but not the numerical value. However, when an arithmetic statement has the form $I=X$, where the right side of the statement is real and the left side is integer, then the value of the expression on the right side is truncated to an integer and assigned to the variable on the left. This, of course, can change the numerical result if the real expression has a fractional value. For example, if X equals 4.83 and the statement $I=X$ were executed, the value of I would be 4. If it is desirable to round off a positive number instead of truncating it, then such rounding can be achieved by the arithmetic statement $I=X+0.5$, or the two statements:

$$X=X+0.5$$
$$I=X$$

In either case the rounded-off value may be returned to real mode by the statement $X=I$. (For rounding off a negative number, subtract 0.5 before truncation.)

It should be emphasized that the FORTRAN character "$=$" signifies replacement, not equality, and a statement such as $I=I+1$ means to take the present value of I, add 1 to it, and replace the previous value of I with this new value.

Coding FORTRAN Statements

Most programs written in FORTRAN are first punched into cards one statement per card. The setup of a FORTRAN card is generally inflexible, and all FORTRAN statements put into cards must follow the prescribed format.

A conventional computer card has eighty columns. Into any of the columns can be placed one and only one symbol by using a keypunch, which punches the correct combination of holes in the card for the desired symbol. Most keypunches also print the characters on the top edge

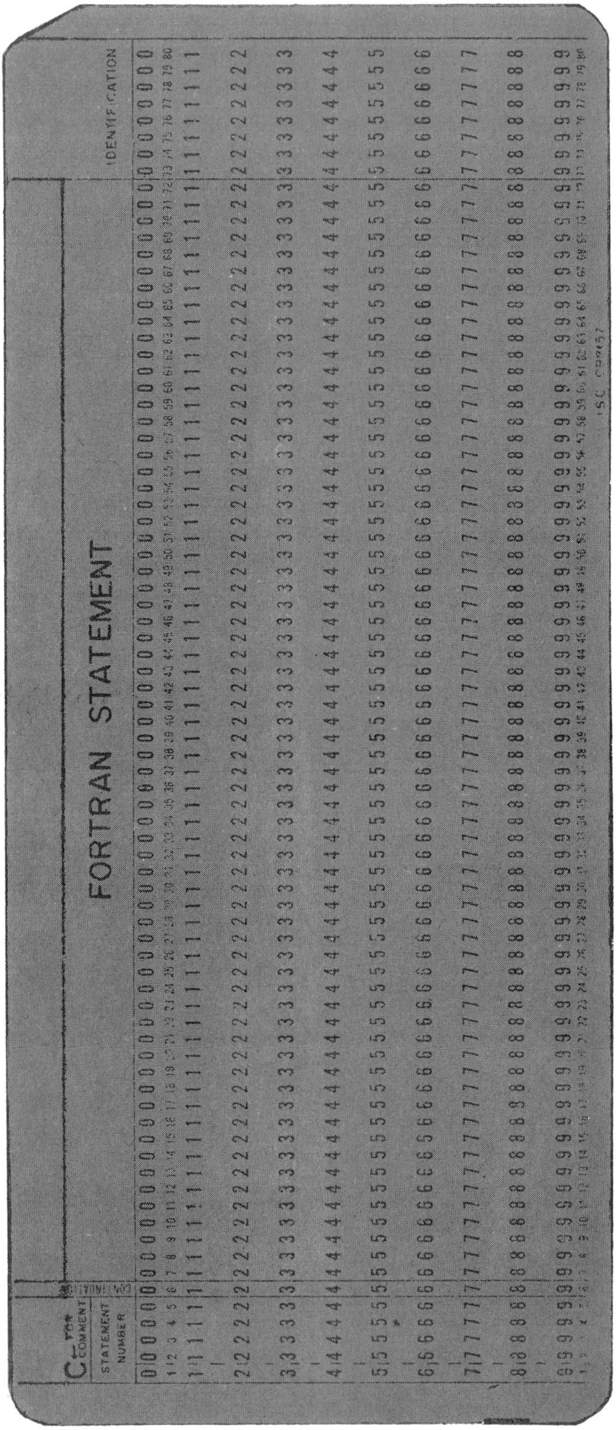

FIGURE 3.1   *FORTRAN IV* Card (Courtesy of Information Supplies Corporation.)

of the card for convenience in reading what has been punched. One statement is punched into each card in the specified format — a group (deck) of cards taken together may then constitute a complete program.

The format for FORTRAN cards and statements is as follows:

Column	Use
1	"C" for comment cards, or
1–5	Statement number
6	Statement continuation designation
7–72	FORTRAN statement
73–80	Not used by FORTRAN. May contain identification information.

A "C" is punched in column 1 when that card is not part of the FORTRAN program but is to be used as a comment — a note to the programmer. Columns 1–5 are used for statement numbers, which are normally given to a few statements in a program. Statement numbers may appear anywhere in the statement number field, columns 1–5. These columns are left blank for statements which carry no statement numbers. Column 6 is used only when the FORTRAN statement of the previous card was too long to fit in columns 7 through 72 and had to be continued over onto another card. In that case a character other than zero is punched in column 6 and the statement is continued. This can be repeated to form very long statements on a series of cards. All other cards except continuation cards and comment cards must leave column 6 blank. Columns 7 through 72 contain the FORTRAN statement itself; when short statements are used, most of the card remains blank and unpunched. There is no requirement that the FORTRAN statement begin in column 7. It may be punched anywhere in 7–72. The final eight columns are not used in FORTRAN but may contain identification and/or a sequence number to insure that if the card deck is dropped it can be collated easily. Figure 3.2 shows a common type of FORTRAN card with a numbered statement punched in it. Coding forms which follow the format of the FORTRAN computer cards are available; use of these forms can help eliminate errors in the writing of FORTRAN programs.

Example 1.

With the introduction of the arithmetic statement, a sufficient subset of FORTRAN has been introduced to enable a simple but complete program to be written. The following program sums the three values of X and divides by three to obtain their average. The FORTRAN statements are written on a FORTRAN coding form in Fig. 3.3.

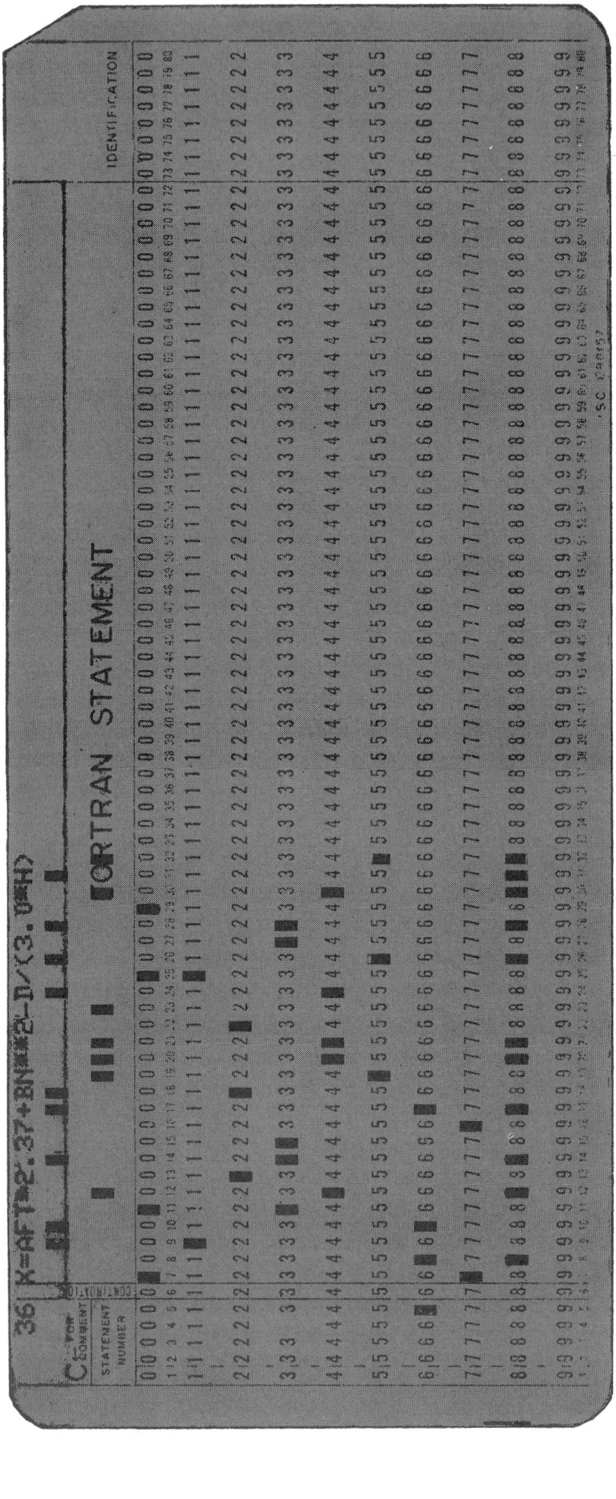

FIGURE 3.2   *FORTRAN IV Statement Punched into a Card* (Courtesy of Information Supplies Corporation.)

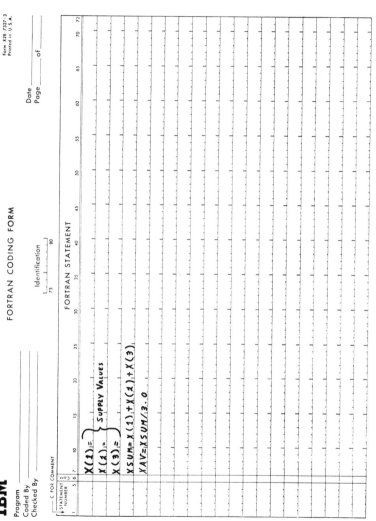

FIGURE 3.3   (Courtesy of the International Business Machines, Incorporated.)

Example 2.

This example program will calculate the weight of a cylinder given the diameter (DIA), the length (EL), and the density of the material of construction (DEN). It is coded on a FORTRAN coding form in Fig. 3.4.

Control Statements

One of the major advantages of digital computers is that the order in which statements are executed during a computation can be altered by conditions existing at the time of execution. For example, a computer program can compute an intermediate result from data that it is given, and then perform one of several subsequent operations depending on the magnitude and sign of the intermediate result. Such decisions are implemented by using control statements to specify the order of execution of the statements forming a program. Because statements are often executed in an order differing from that in which they were read into the computer, the control statements refer to statement numbers in order to transfer control. These control statements include the unconditional GO TO, the arithmetic IF, the DO, the CONTINUE, the STOP, the RETURN, and the END.

This section introduces the basic, necessary control statements of FORTRAN.

GO TO Statement.   The GO TO statement, called the unconditional GO TO, has the general form

$$GO\ TO\ \mathbf{n}$$

where **n** is the number of another executable statement in the program. When the GO TO statement is reached during the execution of a program, control will always transfer to statement number **n**. This statement allows direct branching to any executable statement in the program.

.
.
.

$$
\begin{array}{ll}
13 & X=Y**2 \\
   & GO\ TO\ 15 \\
14 & F2=F2+7.0 \\
15 & F3=F3+1.0 \\
16 & Z=Z**2.0
\end{array}
$$

.
.
.

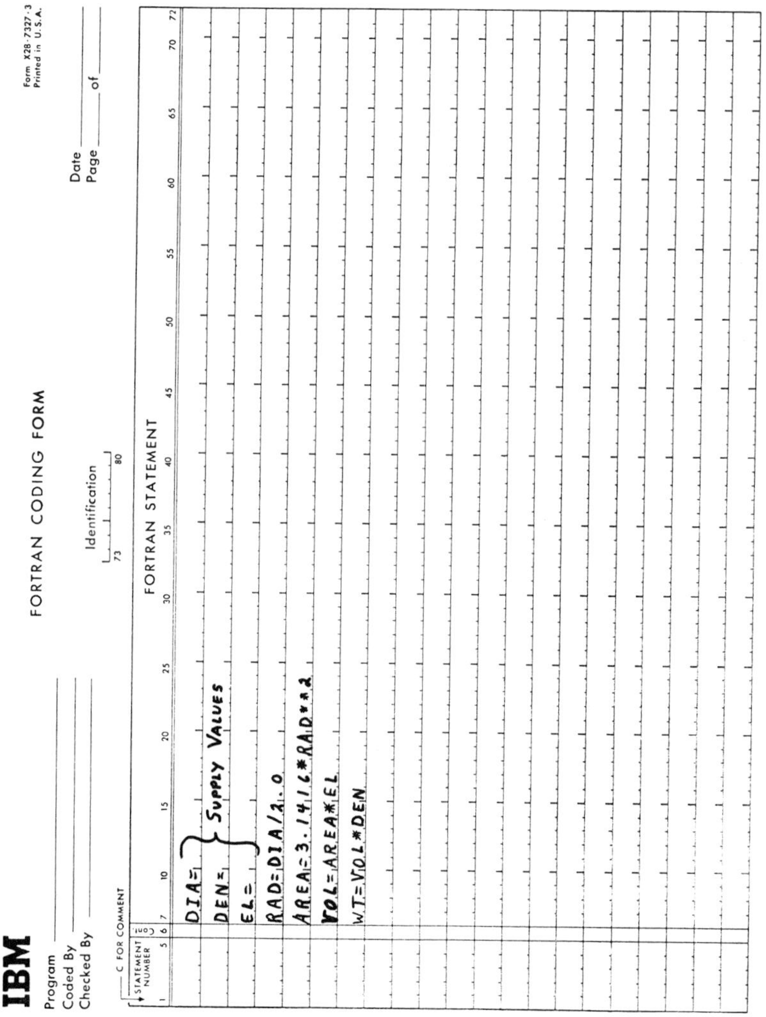

IBM FORTRAN CODING FORM

Form X28-7327-3 Printed in U.S.A.

Program ______ Coded By ______ Checked By ______

Identification 73 80

Date ______ Page ____ of ____

C FOR COMMENT

STATEMENT NUMBER | CONT. | FORTRAN STATEMENT

```
      DIA=  }
      DEN=  } SUPPLY VALUES
      EL=   }
      RAD=DIA/2.0
      AREA=3.1416*RAD**2
      VOL=AREA*EL
      WT=VOL*DEN
```

FIGURE 3.4 (Courtesy of the International Business Machines, Incorporated.)

This program sequence executes statement 13 and then statement 15 before going on to statement 16 and the rest of the program. Statement 14 can only be reached from some other part of the program by the execution of some other control statement. (Notice that F2 and F3 are *not* the second and third members of an array, as would be F(2) and F(3). They are simple floating-point (real) scalar variables.)

IF Statement.   The arithmetic IF statement allows branching within a program according to conditions at the time it is executed. The general form of the IF statement is

IF (expression) n1,n2,n3

where an arithmetic expression (either real or integer) is contained in the parentheses, and "n1", "n2", and "n3" are the numbers of executable statements in the program. When an IF statement is encountered during execution of the program, control is transferred as shown below.

Value of Expression	Control Transferred to
Negative	Statement "n1"
Zero	Statement "n2"
Positive	Statement "n3"

An example of an arithmetic IF statement is

IF(Z)21,22,23

This statement, upon execution, transfers control to statement 21 if Z is negative, 22 if Z is zero, or 23 if Z is positive. An IF statement with an expression to be evaluated is

IF(N−4)50,60,60

This statement transfers control to statement 50 if the expression (N−4) is negative and to statement 60 otherwise. Such an IF statement is employed in the following example which sums the values of X(1), X(2), X(3), and X(4) and finds their average.

.
.
.

N=0
XSUM=0.0

```
50   N=N+1
     XSUM=XSUM+X(N)
     IF(N-4)50,60,60
60   XAV=XSUM/4.0
```
.
.
.

In this example, the program proceeds until the IF statement is encountered and then control is transferred back to statement 50. The second and third times the IF statement is encountered, control is transferred back to statement 50; the fourth time N equals 4, the expression $(N-4)$ equals zero, and control is transferred to statement 60 and the program proceeds. The program is said to have gone through a loop four times.

The IF statement can be used in conjunction with GO TO statements in order to take one of a series of branches as in the following example.

.
.
.

```
     IF(N-2)2,3,4
2    X=Y**A
     GO TO 5
3    X=Y**B
     GO TO 5
4    X=Y**C
5    Z=X**2
```
.
.
.

When the IF statement is encountered, control is transferred to statement 2 if $N < 2$, to statement 3 if $N = 2$, or to statement 4 if $N > 2$. Thus the current value of Y will be raised to the power A,B, or C depending on the value of N when the IF statement is executed. Regardless of which transfer is taken, control will pass to statement 5 after X has been calculated. Any time this set of statements is executed, only one of the three possible calculations of X will be performed.

One further example will complete our discussion of the IF statement. The following statements will find the largest positive value of the ten variables, $\{X(1),X(2),X(3),X(4),X(5),X(6),X(7),X(8),X(9),X(10)\}$, and will then multiply this largest value by 2.0 and store the resulting product in Y.

.
.
.

```
        I=0
        XMAX=0.0
   11   I=I+1
        IF(X(I)−XMAX)13,13,12
   12   XMAX=X(I)
   13   IF(I−10)11,14,14
   14   Y=XMAX*2.0
```

.
.
.

The loop from statement 11 to statement 13 will be passed through ten times. The IF statement following statement 11 will transfer control to statement 12 only when the current $X(I) > XMAX$; thus the variable XMAX will contain the largest value of the $X(I)$'s when control reaches statement 14.

The usefulness of the branching statement should be stressed — it is the backbone of modern digital computer programming because it allows branching within the program according to conditions present at the time particular control statements are executed.

DO Statement. The DO statement is a special control statement which causes a program to make repeated passes through a loop called a DO loop. The general form of the DO statement is

$$DO\ n\ i=m1,m2,m3$$

where "n" is a statement number, "i" is a nonsubscripted integer variable, and "m1", "m2", and "m3" are either nonsubscripted integer variables or integer constants. The DO statement causes the execution of all statements beginning with the one immediately following the DO and ending with the statement numbered "n", a specified number of times. The number of times a loop will be cycled through is given by the formula $\dfrac{m2-m1}{m3} + 1$. The first time through the DO loop "i" is set equal to "m1"; the second time through the loop "i" is incremented by "m3"; this process continues until "i" is equal to the largest value that is not greater than "m2." Then control is transferred to the statement immediately following statement number "n." The *range* of the DO statement is the set of statements which are repeatedly executed. The value of the index variable "i" is incremented by "m3", and when this value

becomes greater than "m2", control will pass to the statement immediately following the last statement in the range. If this value is less than
or equal to "m2", the loop is executed again. Note that since this comparison is performed at the end of the loop, the statements in the range
of the loop will always be executed at least once.

An example of a DO statement is

$$DO\ 20\ L=1,10,1$$

This DO statement says that the statements following it, up to and including statement number 20, are to be executed ten times. On the first
time through the loop $L = 1$; on the second pass $L = 2$; and so on until
the tenth and final pass $L = 10$. Another DO statement is

$$DO\ 270\ KJR=1,N,2$$

This DO statement will cause the statements through statement 270 to be
executed repeatedly with KJR having the following values during successive passes through the loop: first pass, $KJR = 1$; second pass, $KJR = 3$;
third pass, $KJR = 5$; and so on until KJR, when incremented by 2, is
larger than N at which time control passes to the statement following
statement number 270.

The index of the DO statement, the integer variable "i", is available
for use in computations throughout the range of the DO statement.

.

.

.

```
        J=1
        DO 30 I=1,N,1
  30    J=J*I
```

.

.

.

The first time through the loop $J = 1$ and $I = 1$ and statement 30 calculates $J = 1$; the second time $J = 1$ and $I = 2$, so statement 30 calculates
$J = 2$; the third time $J = 2$ and $I = 3$, and statement 30 calculates $J = 6$.
The loop is repeated "N" times and the value of J after N times through
the loop is N factorial, N!.

The index of the DO statement can also be used within the DO loop
as a subscript. The following DO loop calculates the sum of the first 100
values of the real array X(I).

```
        XSUM=0.0
        DO 10 I=1,100
  10    XSUM=XSUM+X(I)
```

During each passage through the loop, the current value of the index I is used as a subscript. When the increment "m3" is not specified, it is assumed to be unity and the second comma of the DO statement must be omitted. However, "m1" and "m2" must always be specified.

Several rules must be observed in using DO statements:

1. The values of the DO parameters "i", "m1", "m2" and "m3" must not be changed within the range of the DO statement. That is, these variables must not appear on the left side of any arithmetic statements within the DO loop.

2. The final statement within the range of the DO statement (statement number "n") cannot be another control statement (except the CONTINUE statement), but it may be an arithmetic or I/O statement.

3. Control cannot be transferred to the interior of a loop from outside that loop, unless transfer has previously occurred out of the loop at the same point; and even then, transfer back is permitted only if the values of the index variable "i" and the indexing parameters "m1", "m2", and "m3" are the same as they were when control was transferred out.

4. DO loops can be placed within other DO loops yielding nested loops, but each interior DO statement's range must be entirely within the range of all exterior DO statements.

An example of two nested DO loops follows.

$$\begin{aligned}
&\text{DO 740 K=1,10,2} \\
&\text{L=K+1} \\
&\text{DO 730 J=1,10} \\
730 \quad &Y(J)=X(J,K)+X(J,L) \\
740 \quad &N=N+1
\end{aligned}$$

The interior DO loop, which begins with the statement DO 730 J=1,10 and ends with statement 730, is completely within the outer DO loop. This nesting procedure can be repeated several times, yielding loops within loops within loops, as long as the interior loops are completely within the exterior ones. The rules for the nesting of DO loops allow two or more nested loops to have the same final statement.

$$\begin{aligned}
&\text{XSUM=0.0} \\
&\text{DO 130 I=1,12} \\
&\text{DO 130 J=1,15} \\
130 \quad &\text{XSUM=XSUM+X(I,J)}
\end{aligned}$$

In execution the outer loop is initiated first, $I = 1$, and then the inner loop is performed all 15 times; then control returns to the outer loop, I is set to 2 and the inner loop is again performed 15 times, etc. These nested loops will compute the sum of all the numbers of a 12 by 15 array X(I,J).

The examples in this book all use multiples of ten as statement numbers for final statements of DO loops. This is a useful convention because a glance at a section of a program allows one to immediately discern which statements are the ends of DO loop ranges.

Other Control Statements.   Several additional control statements are commonly used in FORTRAN. The CONTINUE statement is a dummy statement which is most commonly employed as the last statement in a DO loop, as in the following example:

```
         KMAX=K(1)
         DO 60 L=2,30
         IF (KMAX−K(L))55,60,60
     55  KMAX=K(L)
     60  CONTINUE
```

This loop will test the values of K(L) against the current value of KMAX each time through the loop and will transfer to statement 55 if K(L) is greater than KMAX in order to save that larger value. A dummy statement is needed to carry the statement number 60 and a CONTINUE statement is used. When the loop is finished, the variable KMAX will contain the largest value of the thirty K(L) values.

The STOP statement is the last statement within a program to be executed. Normally it is the next-to-last statement in a program. It terminates the execution of the program.

The END statement is always physically the last statement of a FORTRAN program or subprogram. It is a nonexecutable statement and it defines the end of a source program.

Example 3.

The following program calculates the two real roots of a quadratic equation, $aX^2 + bX + c = 0$, $a \neq 0$, according to the standard formula

$$ROOTS = \frac{-b \pm \sqrt{b^2 - 4ac}}{2a}.$$

To do so, the program first computes the value under the radical, $b^2 - 4ac$. If this value is negative, indicating that this particular combination of a, b and c will lead to imaginary solutions, the program terminates. If this value is 0 or is positive, indicating real roots, the program continues.

$$\left. \begin{matrix} A= \\ B= \\ C= \end{matrix} \right\} \text{ supply the values to be used}$$

RAD=B**2−4.0*A*C
IF (RAD)1,2,2
2   ROOT1=(−B+RAD**0.5)/(2.0*A)
    ROOT2=(−B−RAD**0.5)/(2.0*A)
1   STOP
    END

Input and Output Statements

Input and output statements, with their necessary auxilliary statements, establish communication between the FORTRAN program and the computer's input and output devices at the time of execution. Input to FORTRAN programs most frequently is from cards, and output is printed on paper. Teletypewriters, magnetic disks, drums, and tapes are also extensively used. In reading and writing data with any of these devices the computer must be told explicitly and exactly the form the numbers or letters are in (in the case of input) or the form in which they should be written (in the case of output). These specific instructions are given via the FORMAT statement, which will be described later in this section.

The forms of input and output statements differ according to the generation of FORTRAN being used. This section will deal with FORTRAN IV statements; Appendix D gives the equivalent FORTRAN II statements.

Input Statements.   The input statement has the general form

$$\text{READ (i,n) list}$$

where "i" refers to the symbolic input device, "n" is the statement number of the pertinent FORMAT statement, and "list" refers to the sequence of variables whose values are to be input upon execution of this READ statement. A specific example of a READ statement is as follows:

$$\text{READ (5,9) A,B,C,D}$$

This READ statement will read values into the variables A,B,C, and D from a card, using the input device assigned the logical unit number 5 and FORMAT statement 9. Many IBM computers use logical unit 5 for the card reader, and this convention will be followed here. Another READ statement is

$$\text{READ (5,19) (X(I),I=1,10)}$$

This READ statement inputs values from a card according to FORMAT statement 19. This time the "list" is comprised of an implied DO loop. Implied DO loops that appear in input/output "lists" function according to the same set of rules as ordinary DO statements. This statement will read ten values off the card(s) according to FORMAT statement 19 and assign the first value to X(1), the second to X(2), and so on through the tenth value which is assigned to X(10).

The logical unit numbers to be used in composing specific READ statements depend on several factors, and one must know local conventions at each computation center because it is at the local center that the logical unit numbers are assigned to the available input/output devices. A typical set of conventions is as follows:

Logical Unit Number	Input Device
5	Card reader
1–4,8–12	Magnetic tape, disk

Thus, the READ statements above could perform input from magnetic tape or disk by merely changing the logical unit number from 5 to, say, 8.

Output Statements.   The general form of output statements is

$$\text{WRITE (i,n) list}$$

where "i" refers to the symbolic output device, "n" is the statement number of the pertinent FORMAT statement, and the "list" is comprised of the variables whose values are to be output. A typical set of symbolic output device numbers is as follows.

Logical Unit Number	Output Device
6	Printer
7	Card punch
1–4,8–12	Magnetic tape, disk

Thus, a WRITE statement of the form

$$\text{WRITE (6,109) FR,BQ}$$

will output the values of variables FR and BQ according to FORMAT 109 to the printer, and a WRITE statement of the form

$$\text{WRITE (7,119)X,Y}$$

will output the values of the variables X and Y according to FORMAT 119 to the card punch. A similar statement can be used to WRITE output on magnetic tape, although the symbolic output number to be used depends on computation center conventions. Of course, to attempt to write to the card reader or to read from the printer will result in an execution error.

Lists. "Lists" that are used with either input or output statements in FORTRAN are formed from ordered strings of subscripted and non-subscripted variables. "Lists" are formed according to several rules:

1. Items forming a "list" can be subscripted or nonsubscripted variables. Implied DO loops may be used.
2. The items within a "list" are separated by commas.
3. Constants can appear in "lists" only as the parameters of implied DO loops.
4. The ranges of implied DO loops are specified with parentheses.
5. Implied DO loops can be nested just as ordinary DO loops. The order of execution is from the innermost parentheses out, analogous to ordinary nested DO loops. A set of parentheses is required for each implied DO loop. Redundant parentheses are permitted.

Examples of "lists" are shown below.

$$\text{A,B,C}$$
$$\text{K(3),FR(I)}$$
$$\text{C(1),C(2),C(3),H,NC}$$
$$\text{(X(I),I=1,10)}$$
$$\text{F,M(I),(R(K),K=1,5)}$$
$$\text{(Y(J),Z(J),J=1,100)}$$

An implied DO loop is exactly equivalent to writing out the string of subscripted variables. Thus, the final example above could be written as $Y(1),Z(1),Y(2),Z(2),...,Y(100),Z(100)$. An example of a "list" employing nested implied DO's is

$$\text{((Y(I,J),I=1,10),J=1,10)}$$

which will input values in the sequence $X(1,1),X(2,1),X(3,1),...,$ $X(10,1),X(1,2),X(2,2),...,X(10,10)$.

Free Input and Output Statements under WATFIV

The significant difference between most FORTRAN IV compilers and the WATFIV compiler is that WATFIV allows using "free" input and output statements. These free forms are very much easier to use than ordinary READ and WRITE statements because they require no FORMAT statements.

The free-form output statement is

PRINT,list

where the "list" is formed as described above. The values of all the real variables appearing in the "list" will be single-spaced on the printer in the following exponential form,

$$\pm 0.0000000E \pm 00$$

The numbers will be printed with seven digits to the right of the decimal point and a two-digit, base ten exponent. Thus, the output statement

PRINT,X

could result in the following printed line of output

b0.1000000Eb00

The free input statement is

READ,list

where the "list" is formed as described above. This statement causes values to be read from the next data card. If we assume the list is composed of real variables, the value to be read will have been punched into the data card as a sequence of floating point numbers with decimal points, separated by commas. For example, the combination of the free input statement

READ,A,B,C

and the data card

5.372,0.06,1.0

causes the variables to have the following values: A = 5.372, B = 0.06, and C = 1.0.

These free input and output statements make the writing of simple programs much easier than they would be otherwise. Input and output statements in FORTRAN IV ordinarily require FORMAT statements. These are discussed in the next section.

FORMAT Statements. Each input or output statement requires reference to a FORMAT statement that describes the type of conversion to be used in transmission of the quantities. The general form of the FORMAT statement is

$$n \text{ FORMAT } (s1,s2,...,sm)$$

where "n" is the identifying statement number which links the FORMAT statement with the input or output statements that refer to it. FORMAT statements are not executable statements, and they may be physically placed almost anywhere in the FORTRAN program. Ordinarily, they are placed adjacent to the input or output statement they belong with or at either end of the program. The specifications, "s1","s2",...., following the word FORMAT are different for real or integer variables. Each variable in an I/O list is described by a specification in a FORMAT statement. If there are fewer specifications than variables in an I/O list, the FORMAT statement is automatically repeated, *but a new record is read or written* in completing the variable list. If there are more specifications than variables in a list, the extra specifications are ignored.

Type of Variable Transmitted	Specification Form
Integer	rIw
Real	rFw.d

For integer quantities the "I" specification is used. The "I" is followed by an integer, represented above by "w", which gives the number of spaces (decimal digits plus the sign) making up the quantity being transmitted. This is known as the width of the field, whence the "w." The "r" represents a repetition factor. Its presence means repeat the following format specification "r" times. If "r" is not coded, its absence implies a repetition factor of 1.

Several examples of READ statements for inputting the values of integer variables and their associated FORMAT statements now follow.

1. Input data for an integer variable from a card.

$$\text{READ}(5,9)K$$
$$9 \quad \text{FORMAT}(I5)$$

The first five columns of the card are read. If these five columns contained bbb20, the value 20 would be input for K.

2. Input the values for several integer variables.

READ(5,19)IR,JA,I2
19   FORMAT(I5,I4,I4)

or

19   FORMAT(I5,2I4)

The first five columns of the card are input and assigned to the variable IR; the next four columns to JA; the next four to I2. The data card might be

bbb201000bbb7
↑   ↑   ↑   ↑
card column   1   5   9   13

3. Input the values for a subscripted integer variable from a card using an implied DO loop.

READ (5,29)(K(I),I=1,3)
29   FORMAT(I8,I8,I8)

or

29   FORMAT(3I8)

The first eight columns of the card will be input for K(1), the next eight columns for K(2), the third eight columns for K(3).

These three READ statements are inputting data from cards, and accordingly, they each reference Logical Unit Number 5, which by our convention refers to the card reader. In each case where an example data card has been shown, note that each set of digits is right justified within its specification field. This is because FORTRAN numeric formats do not differentiate between blanks and zeros. Leading blanks (zeros) are of course ignored; however, trailing blanks (zeros) in a field form a part of the number, e.g. bbb20 = 20, but b20bb = 02000 = 2000. Embedded blanks, bb2b0, will be converted to zeros: bb2b0 = 00200 = 200. For FORMAT statements used with READ statements, the minimum width of the specifications needed is obtained directly from the maximum size of the numbers to be input.

In developing FORMAT statements for the output of integer variables, the maximum size of the number being output once again determines the minimum specification width. To output seven-digit integers requires a specification of "I8" or larger (one extra space for the sign). Upon being output the integer variable's value is automatically right-adjusted within the given specification width. Thus, the five digit number 54321 when output with an "I8" specification would appear as bbb54321, where the digits have been right-adjusted.

Transmission of the values of real variables uses the "F" conversion. Its form is rFw.d where "w" is an integer which specifies the total width of the field, and "d" is an integer specifying the number of spaces to the right of the decimal point, and "r" is the repetition factor. Correspondence between some "F" specifications and numbers for input and output follows.

INPUT

Specification	Quantity	Internal Representation
F10.4	27.56789	27.5678
F10.5	27.56789	27.56789
F10.6	27.56789	27.567890
F8.4	123456789	1234.5678

OUTPUT

Specification	Internal Representation	Printed Value
F10.5	234.56789	234.56789
F10.6	234.56789	234.567890
F10.6	−234.56789	**********
F10.0	0.123456	0.

For input if a decimal point is present in the input quantity, its position overrides that specified by the "d" portion of the field descriptor. If more digits are punched to the right of the decimal point than the "d" portion specifies, the rightmost digits are truncated. For output the "w" portion — in addition to room for the fractional part of the quantity — must allow for a decimal point, at least one digit to the left of the point, and generally one more position for a sign; although if the quantity will never be negative this extra place is not required. For output under "F" format then, the minimum field width is 2, and preferably 3. Should insufficient space be allocated on output, a row of asterisks of length "w" will be printed by many machines. (However, some compilers will ignore the error and print only the *least* significant digits.) The minimum "F" specification for output of F2.0 will allow only the printing of the values 0 through 9 followed by a decimal point automatically inserted by FORTRAN.

Some examples of READ statements for inputting the values of real variables and their associated FORMAT statements follow.

4.   Input the values for several real variables from a card.

$$READ\ (5,9)X,Y,Z$$
$$9\quad FORMAT\ (F10.3,F15.7,F10.3)$$

The first ten columns of the card will be input for the value of X; the next fifteen for Y; and the next ten for Z. The data card might be

bb1.02bbbb−20.32109bbbbbbb0.052bbbb

card column   1   11   26   35

Thus X will equal 1.02, Y will equal −20.32109, and Z will equal 0.052. Note that punching the decimal point permits the proper justification of each number. Had no decimal points been punched:

bb1b02bbbb−20b32109bbbbbbb0b052bbbb

card column   1   11   26   35

The resulting values would have been

$$X=10020.0$$
$$Y=-2003210.9$$
$$Z=520.0$$

Without decimal points on the data card, the FORMAT statement specifies an assumed point to the left of the rightmost 3 digits of the first variable field (X), an assumed point to the left of the rightmost 7 digits of the second variable field (Y), and an assumed point to the left of the rightmost 3 digits of the last variable field (Z). Again, embedded blanks and trailing blanks will be read as zeros.

5. Input the values of several real variables from a card using an implied DO loop.

$$READ\ (5,19)(X(I),I=1,3)$$
$$19\quad FORMAT\ (F10.3,F10.3,F10.3)$$

or

$$19\quad FORMAT\ (3F10.3)$$

The data card might be

bbb−0.302bbb1.520bbbbbbb2.170b

card column   10   20   30

Note that if a decimal point is punched, trailing blanks will not affect the value of the number read, and:

$$X(1)=-0.302$$
$$X(2)=1.520$$
$$X(3)=2.170$$

Integer and real specifications may be mixed only if the correct correspondence is maintained with the variables in the READ statement "list" or WRITE statement "list." Again, fields may be repeated with either integer or real conversions by using an integer "n" before the "I" or "F". Thus 3F10.3 is the same as F10.3,F10.3,F10.3; and 2I5 is the same as I5,I5. For example,

6.   Read integer and real variables from the same card.

READ (5,59)N1,N2,(X(I),I=1,6)
59   FORMAT (2I10,6F10.3)

The first ten columns of the card will be input for N1; the next ten will be input for N2; the remainder of the card will be input to the array X(I) in blocks of ten columns for each X according to the repeated F10.3 specification.

Through the use of parentheses, sets of specifications may be repeated: (2(F10.3,I5)) is equivalent to F10.3 ,I5 ,F10.3,I5. Many compilers will permit only one additional level of parentheses within the FORMAT statement, e.g.,

99   FORMAT (5(2(F5.0)))

would not be legal.

Blanks may be introduced into input or output by using the "X" specification. Its general form is nX where "n" is a decimal integer which specifies the number of spaces to be skipped in the case of reading, or the number of blanks to be output in the case of writing.

7.   Example of the use of the nX specification.

READ (5,19)N,X,Y
19   FORMAT (I5,10X,2F10.3)

The first five spaces on the data card will be input for N; the next ten spaces will be skipped, regardless of their content; the values for X and Y will be taken from the next two fields of width ten each. An example data card is

After input, N equals 10, X equals 1.032, and Y equals 5.320.

FORMAT statements used for output are identical to those for input with one exception. The first character (digit) written to the *printer* is used as a carriage control digit. It is not printed. It merely controls the operation of the carriage spacing. The four most generally used carriage control characters are shown below.

Symbol	Function
"b"	Skip to the next line before printing.
"0"	Skip to the line following the next line (double-space) before printing.
"1"	Skip to the top of the next page before printing.
"+"	Suppress any spacing for this print line; this permits overprinting on a line.

When writing a record (a line) to the printer, the carriage control character is evaluated and the action it specifies is taken *before* any printing occurs.

When writing information to the card punch, magnetic tape, or to disk, a carriage control character is not used and should not be coded. In preparing FORMAT statements for use with WRITE statements to the printer, it must be remembered that the printer has 120 (some printers have 132 or more) print positions—not counting the carriage control position. The card punch has only 80 positions. If these lengths are exceeded, an output error will occur. Magnetic tapes and disks generally permit much longer records.

The slash "/" is used to indicate the end of an input or an output record. If a slash is coded in the FORMAT statement associated with a READ statement, a new record is input when the slash is encountered during the execution of the READ. When the slash is encountered in the specification list during a WRITE, a new output record is begun. If this WRITE were to a printer, then a new line would be started, and the *next* character to be written would be assumed to be a carriage control character.

A most useful technique for outputting strings of alphanumeric information is the use of literals, or pairs of apostrophes, in the FORMAT specification "list." Information enclosed in single quotes is transmitted directly to the output device. This facility permits clear labelling of one's output. The following are specific examples of outputting data using apostrophes that allow the inclusion of any alphanumeric characters in the output.

1. Write values of several integer variables to the printer.

WRITE(6,109)N,M,JA
109   FORMAT('b',3I5)

This WRITE statement would result in the following line of output if
N = 100, M = 20, and JA = 8.

carriage control
(skip to next
line before printing)
not printed ——————————————————————————┐
                                      ↓
                          bbb100bbb20bbbb8
                          ↑   ↑   ↑   ↑
        output column   1   5   10   15

The same output could be punched into a card by changing the symbolic output device number from 6 to 7 and by leaving out the unneces-
sary printer carriage control character "b."

WRITE(7,119)N,M,JZ
119   FORMAT(3I5)

These statements yield the following punched card of output

                          bb100bbb20bbbb8
                          ↑   ↑   ↑   ↑
        card column   1   5   10   15

2. Write values of both integer variables and real variables to the printer
    with labels:

WRITE(6,109)L,(A(K),K=1,L)
109   FORMAT('b',5X,'L=b',I3,/,'bTHEbLbVALUESbOF',
1 'bAbARE',/,'0',10F8.3)

If L = 3 and A(L) = −1.10, A(2) = 0.32, and A(3) = 7.9, then the resulting output would be

carriage control ↓
(not printed)   bL=3
                   bTHE L VALUES OF A ARE

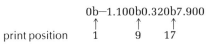

                   0b−1.100b0.320b7.900
                   ↑   ↑   ↑
    print position 1   9   17

The top line of output is straightforward. The slash causes the printer to
go to a new line, and there must now be another printer control character for the new line; the printer control character is combined with the
label to be printed on the second line. A third line is used to print the three
values of A(K), but the 0 causes a double-spacing before this line is
printed.

The examples in this book all use statement numbers ending in 9
for FORMAT's. Furthermore, FORMAT's are always placed at the ends
of our example programs. These conventions are useful because FOR-
MAT's are often a major source of trouble and need to be easily locatable. In addition, since FORMAT's are nonexecutable statements, some

confusion is avoided by not having them mixed among executable statements that are using statement numbers for control transfer.

Specification Statements

Specification statements give information about the allocation of storage for a program and about the constants and variables in the program. Specification statements include DIMENSION, COMMON, TYPE, EQUIVALENCE, and DATA statements. All except the DIMENSION statement will be discussed in Section 3 of this chapter.

DIMENSION Statement. The DIMENSION statement supplies the information necessary to allot sufficient storage for the subscripted variables used in the program. Its general form is as follows.

$$\text{DIMENSION a1(i1),a2(i2),}\ldots$$

Each "a" represents a subscripted variable name and the "i"'s represent a series of unsigned integer constants separated by commas that define the maximum size of the arrays. A single DIMENSION statement can allot memory space for many subscripted variables. A typical DIMENSION statement is

$$\text{DIMENSION A(10,10),K(50),NV(3)}$$

Here storage is allocated for 100 values of A, 50 values for K, and 3 values for NV. In FORTRAN programs the DIMENSION statement must precede the first appearance of any variable to which it refers, so the DIMENSION statement is usually the first statement in the program.

Subroutines and Subprograms

In writing FORTRAN programs it is often convenient to group together portions of calculations in order to retain clarity of the overall program. Several aspects of FORTRAN aid in this task.

Library Subprograms. Many algebraic, arithmetic, and trigonometric functions that are used repeatedly have been incorporated into computer systems as library subprograms and can be called on by the programmer. Each library subprogram has a unique keyword that is used to call it. To use a library subprogram, the subprogram's name is followed by the argument (or arguments) which is the dependent variable in the function to be evaluated. The library subprogram names can be used interchangeably with variables of the same type. Some examples of the use of library subprograms follow.

$$X=SIN(A)$$

The real variable *X* is set equal to the value of the trigonometric sine of the value of *A*.

$$Y=SQRT(BQ)$$

The square root of the value of the variable **BQ** is taken and stored in the variable **Y**. The argument of the library subprogram can be an arithmetic expression of the correct type.

$$Y=2.0*EXP(1.0-W(I))$$

The value of the expression in parentheses will be used as a power for *e* (the base of the Naperian logarithm), the result multiplied by 2.0 and the product stored in the variable **Y**.

Each library subprogram possesses a type, and it must have the correct number and type of arguments passed to it when it is invoked. A list of the basic subprograms commonly employed is given in Table 3–1. A complete list of the library subprograms available on any particular computer-compiler combination may be obtained from the relevant manufacturer and/or computation center manuals.

TABLE 3–1   Basic Library Subprograms

Name	Entry Name	Number of Arguments	Type
exponential	EXP	1	REAL
natural log	ALOG	1	REAL
log base ten	ALOG10	1	REAL
absolute value	ABS	1	REAL
absolute value	IABS	1	INTEGER
sine	SIN	1	REAL
cosine	COS	1	REAL
tangent	TAN	1	REAL
square root	SQRT	1	REAL

The library subprograms supplied by computer manufacturers are normally based on methods that effect a compromise between execution speed and memory locations required. For most applications, users are well advised to use the library subprograms. However, advanced computer users can develop their own programs which can calculate functional values, etc. faster than the library subprograms in certain cases.

Arithmetic Statement Functions. In writing a FORTRAN program it is sometimes necessary to evaluate repeatedly a function which is not one of the provided library subprograms. In this case the programmer can define a subprogram by using the arithmetic statement function feature of FORTRAN. The general form of this statement is

$$name(a1,a2,...,an)=(expression)$$

where "name" represents the name of the statement function, the symbols "a1", "a2",...,"an" represent dummy nonsubscripted variables, and an expression using these dummy variables or other *nonsubscripted* variables appears on the right-hand side. The name of the statement function is comprised of one through six (five for 1130 Systems) alphanumeric characters with the leading character a letter that governs the type of the statement function in the same way as with variable names. Arithmetic statement functions must appear at the beginning of the main program before any executable statements. An example of a specific statement function whose type is real is

$$QUAD(A,B,C)=B**2-4.0*A*C$$

This statement function calculates the value of the expression on its right-hand side whenever it is called by the following statement that appears somewhere in the FORTRAN program.

$$R=QUAD(X(I),Y(I),Z(I))$$

The combination of the two statements is completely equivalent to the composite statement

$$R=Y(I)**2-4.0*X(I)*Z(I)$$

The arithmetic statement function allows the expression on its right-hand side to be evaluated for any set of three real arguments and is thus a convenience to the programmer. Two more examples of arithmetic statement functions are:

$$SUMM(A1,A2,A3)=A1+A2+A3+X+Z$$
$$CONV(OZ)=OZ/16.0$$

The first of these statements calculates the sum of the dummy variables plus the existent values of X and Z when the statement is called. The second function changes weights from ounces to pounds when called, as

$$POUNDS=CONV(OZ)$$

FUNCTION Subprograms.   The FUNCTION subprogram is an extension of the arithmetic statement function. Its general form is

FUNCTION name(a1,a2,...,an)
.
.
.
.
RETURN
END

The FUNCTION subprogram is compiled separately from the FORTRAN main program and any other subprograms, so the variables it uses are known only to it. The parameter list "a1","a2",...,"an" is made up of dummy arguments. They may be unsubscripted variable names or array names. The dummy arguments must match in type and dimension the list of names used when the FUNCTION is invoked. The type of the FUNCTION itself is governed by its name, which may be from one to six (five for 1130 Systems) alphanumeric characters (excluding the special characters) beginning with a letter. This beginning letter determines the function's type; A–H or O–Z means real, I–N signifies integer. The following example of a FUNCTION subprogram returns the maximum value in an array of known length each time it is invoked. The type of the FUNCTION is real.

Calling Program		*Function Subprogram*
DIMENSION VEC(50)		FUNCTION XMXVEC(I,Z)
.		DIMENSION Z(50)
.		XMXVEC=Z(1)
.		DO 20 N=2,I
N=50		IF(XMXVEC−Z(N))15,20,20
XMAX=XMXVEC(N,VEC)	15	XMXVEC=Z(N)
.	20	CONTINUE
.		RETURN
END		END

In this example the variable N is used in both the calling program and in the FUNCTION. However, it is not the same variable. The array VEC is passed to the FUNCTION and used there under the name Z. When the loop in the FUNCTION is exhausted, the maximum value in the array Z is returned to XMAX in the calling program. The return is insured by the RETURN statement, which generally must be the last executable statement in a FUNCTION. Since the FUNCTION is a type of program in and of itself, it is compiled separately from the main program and the last card of the FUNCTION subprogram must be an END.

SUBROUTINE Subprograms. The use of SUBROUTINE subprograms is a convenience which allows the programmer to set aside parts of the program for one of several reasons.

1. A calculation that is to be performed many times by a program can be set aside in a subroutine and then called from several parts of the main program.
2. For clarity of programming, various portions of the overall computation can be placed in separate subroutines. For example, input can be done by one subroutine, output by another, and the main program can be reserved for the actual computational part of the calculations.
3. Splitting of the overall program into sub-units allows the programmer to substitute different calculation subroutines into the overall computation with the least possible disruption of his program. For example, different calculation subroutines could be used with the same input and output subroutines. Or a standard subroutine to calculate the average and standard deviation of a group of observations could be written and then included in any program where the programmer wanted to do that calculation.

SUBROUTINE subprograms are separate programs in their own right. They bear strong resemblance to FUNCTION subprograms in that both use the same rules for dummy arguments, naming conventions (except that subroutines do not have type), and both require a RETURN and an END statement. The primary difference is that a FUNCTION subprogram may return one and only one value to a calling program, while a SUBROUTINE subprogram is unrestricted as to the number of values it may return. SUBROUTINES have their own sets of variables, arithmetic statement functions, specification statements, etc. *They remain entirely separate from their calling programs until a linkage is established between the calling program and the subroutine with the following calling statement.*

CALL subr (a1,a2,...,an)

This CALL statement appearing in the calling program is matched to the leading statement of the SUBROUTINE itself,

SUBROUTINE subr (b1,b2,...,bn)

where "subr" represents the name of the subprogram and (a1,a2,...,an) represents a list of subscripted and/or nonsubscripted variables. These appear in the calling program and must correspond on a one-to-one basis in type and dimensionality with the list (b1,b2,...,bn) which represents a list of subscripted and/or nonsubscripted variables appearing in the subroutine. Variables that correspond between the two lists are actually assigned to the same memory location. Subscripted variables appearing in the CALL and the SUBROUTINE statement must be dimensioned in both programs. For most FORTRAN compilers, subscripted variables need be given only a dummy dimension (a dimension of one) in subroutines, if they appeared in the pass list and have already been dimensioned in the main program.

Calling Program	*SUBROUTINE Subprogram*
DIMENSION X(100),Y(50) . . CALL SUBRT(X,Y) . . END	SUBROUTINE SUBRT (S,T) DIMENSION S(1),T(1) . . RETURN END

Another example of a SUBROUTINE follows:

```
      SUBROUTINE INPUT (X,Y,N)
      DIMENSION X(1),Y(1)
      READ (5,9) (X(I),Y(I),I=1,N)
    9 FORMAT (8F10.3)
      RETURN
      END
```

This is a complete subroutine. It would be used to read values for the variables X(I) and Y(I) from cards. It could be called by the following statement appearing in a calling program,

CALL INPUT (X,Y,N)

where the variables X and Y are dimensioned in *the calling program* to a size sufficient to contain N values. The following statement could also call SUBROUTINE INPUT,

CALL INPUT (A,B,N)

where A and B are subscripted real variables which are dimensioned in the main program. In this case when the CALL statement is executed, control shifts to the SUBROUTINE; its statements are executed and when control is returned to the calling program at the statement immediately following the CALL, the values of X(I) and Y(I) are the variables A(I) and B(I).

SUBROUTINE subprograms can be called either by main programs or by other SUBROUTINE subprograms. They are extremely convenient to use in a wide variety of programming situations, and they will be extensively used in the programs discussed in Part II of this book.

The RETURN statement is generally used in either FUNCTION or SUBROUTINE subprograms and signals the finish of the execution of the subprogram's statements. RETURN causes control to return to the calling program or subprogram at the statement immediately following the one that invoked the subprogram.

III–3. Additional Capabilities of FORTRAN IV

The topics introduced in the first two sections are the necessary core of FORTRAN that allow the programmer to do almost any calculation of which FORTRAN is capable. In this section some additional capabilities of FORTRAN will be presented.

Constants, Variables, and Expressions

In addition to the two types of constants, variables, and expressions previously introduced, there are two others — complex and logical — which are available for use in more sophisticated FORTRAN compilers.

Complex Quantities. A complex constant consists of an ordered pair of real constants which are separated by a comma and enclosed in parentheses. Just as in algebraic notation, the two parts represent the real and imaginary parts of the complex number, respectively. Complex constants appear as follows:

Complex Constant	Value
(4.2, −1.3)	$4.2 - 1.3i$
(3.0E−03, 2.0)	$.003 + 2.0i$

Complex variables are named by using one to six (five for 1130 Systems) alphanumeric characters. They must appear in a TYPE statement (to be discussed in a few pages) which declares them to be complex. The TYPE statement also assigns either 8 (standard) or 16 (optional) bytes per variable. Complex variables are used in arithmetic expressions, etc., identically to other types of variables.

Logical Quantities.   Logical constants specify one of two logical values: .TRUE. or .FALSE. Logical variables are named with one to six (five for 1130 Systems) alphanumeric characters. They must appear in a TYPE statement which declares them to be logical and either 4 (standard) or 1 (optional) bytes (or characters) long. Logical variables may be assigned values as follows.

B1=.TRUE.
GN=.TRUE.
FRED=.FALSE.

Logical expressions have the values .TRUE. or .FALSE. and are formed using six relational operators.

Relational Operator	Definition
.GT.	Greater than
.GE.	Greater than or equal to
.LT.	Less than
.LE.	Less than or equal to
.EQ.	Equal to
.NE.	Not equal to

These relational operators are used in combination with arithmetic expressions to form logical expressions. Some examples are

I .NE. 3
1.02E−02 .LT. X
A(I) .GE. Z8

Each of these logical expressions will have the logical value of .TRUE. or .FALSE. depending on the values of the variables. There are also three logical operators:

Logical Operator	Use	Meaning
.NOT.	.NOT.A	If A is .TRUE., then .NOT.A is .FALSE.
		If A is .FALSE., then .NOT.A is .TRUE.
.AND.	A.AND.B	A.AND.B is .TRUE. if and only if both A and B are .TRUE.
.OR.	A.OR.B	A.OR.B is .FALSE. if and only if both A and B are .FALSE.

Logical operators can only be used with logical expressions, variables, or constants to form larger logical expressions. Some examples follow.

$$(I.EQ.7).AND.(N.GT.0)$$
$$(2.0E-02.LE.X).OR.(5.0E-03.LE.Y.)$$

As in other expressions, parentheses are used to resolve ambiguities.

Additional Control Statements

FORTRAN has three additional control statements—the computed GO TO statement, the assigned GO TO statement, and the logical IF statement.

Computed GO TO Statement. The computed GO TO statement allows branching to one of several points in one step. Its general form is

$$GO\ TO\ (m1,m2,...mn),i$$

where "m1","m2",...,"mn" are executable statement numbers and "i" is a nonsubscripted integer variable whose value is one of the numbers 1,2,...n. When this statement is executed, control will transfer to statement number "m1" if "i" equals 1; statement "m2" if "i" equals 2, and so on. If "i" is outside the range from 1 through n, then, for the more sophisticated FORTRAN compilers, the next statement is executed. For the simpler compilers the results are unpredictable. For example,

.
.
.

```
GO TO (121,43,78,81),KL
GO TO 99
```
.
.
.

When this statement is executed, control will go to statement 121 if KL equals 1, it will go to statement 43 if KL equals 2, and so on. Again, for many compilers if KL is outside the range of 1 to 4, the next statement will be executed, transferring control to statement number 99. However, for other less advanced compilers, the action resultant when KL is out of range is undefined.

Assigned GO TO Statement. The assigned GO TO statement also allows branching to more than one point in one step. The ASSIGN statement and the assigned GO TO statement are used in conjunction with each other. Their general forms are

ASSIGN i TO L

.

.

GO TO L,(m1,m2,...mn)

where "i" is one of the executable statement numbers "m1","m2",..., "mn" and L is a nonsubscripted integer variable of length 4 bytes — to which is assigned one of the statement numbers "m1","m2",...,"mn." These two statements might be used as follows.

.

.

ASSIGN 51 to KOL

.

.

27   GO TO KOL,(2,7,51,78)

.

.

51   X=Y**Z

.

.

When Statement 27 is executed, it will transfer control to Statement 51. The assigned GO TO feature is not present in all FORTRAN compilers.

Logical IF Statement. The logical IF statement tests the value of a logical expression and executes a statement if the value of the logical expression is .TRUE. The general form of the logical IF statement is

IF (a) s

where "a" represents a logical expression and "s" represents any executable statement (except a DO statement or another logical IF statement). When the logical IF statement is executed, it evaluates the logical expression within the parentheses. If the expression "a" is .TRUE., the statement "s" is executed; if the expression "a" is .FALSE., control passes to the next statement in sequence. An example of the use of a logical statement follows.

$$IF (2.0E-05.GT.XMIN) GO TO 51$$

or

$$IF (2.0*10**(-5).GT.XMIN) GO TO 51$$

When the statement is executed, control will go to statement 51 if $XMIN > 2.0 \times 10^{-5}$, otherwise control will transfer to the next statement after the logical IF statement. Another example of a logical IF statement is

$$IF(X.GT.0.0) Y=SQRT(X)$$

which will have performed the indicated calculation only when X is greater than zero. This would prevent an attempt to take the square root of a nonpositive number. Again, the logical IF is not present in all FOR-TRAN compilers.

Input and Output

There are several additional capabilities in FORTRAN for the transmission of data in various forms.

Input and Output Statements. Input and output using magnetic tape, or disk, may be performed in two ways. The method using FORMAT statements was introduced previously. It may also be done in a form known as "binary" without any FORMAT statements, by using READ and WRITE statements of the following general form,

$$READ (i) list$$
$$WRITE (i) list$$

where "i" refers to the symbolic input or output device numbers. The number to be used depends on local conventions at each computation center. The lists used are formed identically to those used with formatted input and output statements. Binary reading and writing is significantly faster and more compact than the formatted statements because the binary transmission need not go through the system routines that format data. When a choice can be made, binary input/output operations are always preferable.

FORMAT Statements. Four additional format codes that are available with some FORTRAN compilers are the "E"-Conversion, the "A"-Conversion, the "L"-Conversion, and the "T"-Format code. Their general forms are

Specification Form	Type of Variable Transmitted
Ew.d	Real
Lw	Logical
Aw	Alphanumeric
Tw	Position Specification

As with the "F"-Conversion previously described, the "E"-Conversion may be used to transmit real data. Its form is Ew.d, where "w" is a decimal integer specifying the width of the data field, and "d" is a decimal integer specifying the number of places to the right of the decimal point for this field. Input must be a real number having an exponent field immediately to the right of the number. This exponent field is of the form "Esxx", where "s" represents a sign (a blank will be read as a +) and "xx" represents the power of 10 to which the real number is raised. Output under "E" format consists of a sign position (blank again means positive), a decimal point, a number of significant digits specified by "d" and four additional places for the "E", the sign of the exponent, and the two-digit exponent. For "E"-Conversion "w" should be greater than or equal to "d"+7 in order to allow space for the exponential part of the number, the decimal point and the leading sign.

Some examples of READ statements for inputting the values of real variables and their associated FORMAT statements follow.

1. Input the values for several real variables from a card.

READ (5,9) X,Y,Z

9   FORMAT (E10.3,E15.7,E10.3)

The first ten columns of the card will be input for the value of X; the next fifteen for Y; the next ten for Z. The data card might be

b1.020Eb00 − 20.3210987E − 12b0.052Eb00

    ↑   ↑   ↑

    10   25   35

Thus, X will equal 1.02, Y will equal $-20.3210987 \times 10^{-12}$, and Z will equal 0.052.

2. Input the values of several real variables from a card using an implied DO loop.

> READ (5,19) (X(I),I=1,3)
> 19   FORMAT (E10.3,E10.3,E10.3)

or

> 19   FORMAT (3E10.3)

The data card might be

$$-0.302E-02b1.520Eb00b2.170E-01$$
$$\uparrow \qquad\qquad \uparrow \qquad\qquad \uparrow$$
$$10 \qquad\qquad 20 \qquad\qquad 30$$

Integer and real specifications may be mixed as long as the correct correspondence is maintained with the variables in the READ statement or WRITE statement list. For example, note the following.

3. Read integer and real variables from the same card.

> READ (5,59)N1,N2,(X(I),I=1,6)
> 59   FORMAT (2I10,6E10.3)

The first ten columns of the card will be input for N1, the next ten will be input for N2, the remainder of the card will be input to the X(I) in blocks of ten columns for each value of X according to an E10.3 specification.

With the aid of parentheses, a set of specifications may be repeated: (2(E10.3,I5)) is equivalent to E10.3, I5, E10.4, I5.

The "L"-Conversion is used to transmit logical variables of width "w." Output of logical variables using an "L" conversion will result in the printing of an F or T right-adjusted in the allotted "w" spaces. Reading under an "L" conversion causes the value of the variable to be set to .TRUE. or .FALSE. depending on whether a T or an F is encountered first in a left to right sweep of the "w" spaces. If the "w" characters do not contain a T or an F, or if they are all blank, a value of .FALSE. is assumed.

The "A"-Conversion is used in transmission of alphanumeric characters including the special characters. Examples will best explain its use.

> READ (5,9) A1,A2,A3
> 9   FORMAT (3A4)

The data card might be

> EXAMPLEb0001...

Then the variables A1,A2, and A3 would contain the following information.

A1   EXAM
A2   PLEb
A3   0001

This could be written on paper output as a label with the following statements.

WRITE (6,19)A1,A2,A3
19   FORMAT (' 1 ' ,3A4)

And this results in the label at the top of a new page.

EXAMPLE0001

The "Tw" Format Code is used to point to the "w"th position within an input record from which data are to be read, or the "w"th position within an output record to which data are to be written. Since the first position, T1, of a printer record is the carriage control character, T10 would point to the 9th print position within a printer record. The format statement

19   FORMAT (1X,T20,'EXAMPLE ' ,T17,' AN ')

would produce the following print line.

AN EXAMPLE
↑   ↑ ↑
10   17 20

A valid input format is that shown below.

19   FORMAT (2I4,T1,A4)

If this format were used with the following READ statement (IDATA is assumed to be dimensioned at least 2):

READ (5,19) (IDATA(I),I=1,2),ADATA

the first four columns of an input data record read from I/O Unit 5 would be converted to fixed-point form and stored in IDATA(1); the second four columns would be read, converted and stored in IDATA(2); and the T1 format code would result in the first four columns of the data record being read a second time and stored, according to the A4 speci- fication, into ADATA.

Specification Statements

Several additional specification statements may be used: TYPE state- ments, COMMON statements, EQUIVALENCE statements, and DATA statements.

TYPE Statements. Explicit type statements may be used to assign the type of variables or functions in the program. Variables are implicitly typed by the first letter of their names. (The leading letters "I" through "N" type a variable as an integer, any other initial letter types a variable as real.) An explicit type statement can override such implicit typing. Additionally, on some computer systems, the programmer can choose the number of significant digits with which integer and real variables are to be stored. The general form of type statements used with IBM 360 and 370 FORTRAN are

$$\text{INTEGER} *2 \quad a(i1),b(i2),...$$
$$\text{INTEGER} *4 \quad a(i1),b(i2),...$$
$$\text{REAL} *4 \quad a(i1),b(i2),...$$
$$\text{REAL} *8 \quad a(i1),b(i2),...$$

where "a","b",... are variable or function names and "i1","i2",... are subscripts of one or more integers separated by commas. The integers in parentheses serve the same allocation function as in the DIMENSION statement; they tell how many memory locations are to be reserved for the particular variable they follow. Generally variables which appear in explicit type statements must not appear in the DIMENSION statement of the program. The numbers after the asterisk indicate the number of bytes (one byte is eight bits) used for storage of each value of the variable. For the IBM 360 series of computers and their related FORTRAN compilers, the permissible lengths in bytes for each variable type is given below.

Variable Type	Permissible Length (Bytes)		
Integer	2	or	$\underline{4}$
Real	$\underline{4}$	or	8
Complex	$\underline{8}$	or	16
Logical	1	or	$\underline{4}$

Default precision (length) for IBM 360 Systems is shown by an underline. A typical FORTRAN program might begin with these statements.

$$\text{DIMENSION N(10),A(25)}$$
$$\text{INTEGER} *2 \text{ K(25)}$$
$$\text{REAL} *8 \text{ X(100)}$$

The variable X is explicitly typed as real with 8 bytes of storage per location and 100 such reserved locations; the variable K is explicitly typed as integer with 2 bytes of storage for each of its 25 locations; the variable N is implicitly typed as integer (because of its leading letter) with 4 bytes for each of its 10 reserved locations; and the variable A is implicitly typed as real with 4 bytes for each of its 25 locations.

The two type statements which must be used with complex and logical variables are as follows:

$$COMPLEX*8 \quad a(i1),b(i2),...$$
$$COMPLEX*16 \quad a(i1),b(i2),...$$
$$LOGICAL*4 \quad a(i1),b(i2),...$$
$$LOGICAL*1 \quad a(i1),b(i2),...$$

Where "a","b",... are variable or function names and "i1","i2",... are subscripts of one or more integers separated by commas.

COMMON Statement. Use of the COMMON statement allows conservation of the limited memory of the computer. Its general form is

$$COMMON \ a,b,c,...$$

where "a","b","c",... are variables which usually are dimensioned in either a DIMENSION statement or in a type statement. In a FORTRAN program that contains a subprogram, an identical COMMON statement can appear in both the main program and the subprogram. This causes the variables which appear in the COMMON statement to be stored in a section of memory common to both the main program and the subprogram, rather than separately for the main program and subprogram. Such a COMMON statement might be of the form

$$COMMON \ M,X$$

where M and X are the variables whose values will be stored in a common area. The use of the COMMON statement in programs that use subprograms can effect a substantial savings in memory usage because different variables may be stored in the same physical locations. Of course, the programmer must be careful to insure that unintended mixing of variable types does not occur when using COMMON statements.

EQUIVALENCE Statement. The EQUIVALENCE statement allows conservation of storage by the programmer through the use of the same storage locations for several variables in the program. Its general form is

$$EQUIVALENCE \ (a,b,...),(c,d,...)$$

where "a","b","c","d",... are variables which may be subscripted. Normally they have a single subscript referring to the storage location in the array. For example,

EQUIVALENCE (N(1),A(1))

would cause the arrays N(I) and A(I) to begin in the same storage location and overlay each other. Presumably this would only be used if the array N(I) were needed early in the program and the array A(I) were used later. Note that the arrays N and A are of different types. This is perfectly permissible provided one does not attempt to use both arrays at the same time. Real data are stored internally in a totally different format than integer data. The EQUIVALENCE statement can be a powerful tool to conserve storage, as long as the logic of one's program lends itself to segmented computation.

Another powerful use for the EQUIVALENCE statement is as an alias assigner. Array input/output is considerably faster than implied DO loop input/output, and more convenient than specifying a long list of variable names.

Array Input/Output	*Implied DO Loop Input/Output*
DIMENSION X(20)	DIMENSION X(20)
READ(5,19) X	READ(5,19) (X(I),I=1,20)
19 FORMAT(10F5.0)	19 FORMAT(10F5.0)
.	.
.	.
.	.
END	END

In the above example the program on the left automatically fills the array X to its dimensioned size; it will execute more rapidly than the program on the right. Note that two input records will be read by both programs. (Why?)

Dealing with variables in array form has its advantages, but often one forgets that X(2) is really sex and X(4) is age, etc. EQUIVALENCE statements can help in this case. Assume that the above vector X represents twenty questions answered by an individual. The following program demonstrates the usefulness of the EQUIVALENCE statement by assigning meaningful aliases to elements in the array. Assume the identification number is punched in columns 1–5 of each card, the respondent's sex, age and marital status are contained in 6–10, 11–15, and 16–20, respectively. And the answers to 16 attitude questions are contained in 5 column fields beginning with 21–25 and ending with 46–50. Assume all answers are right-justified in their respective fields.

```
   DIMENSION X(20)
   EQUIVALENCE (X(1),CASE),(X(2),SEX),(X(3),AGE),
 1   (X(4),STMART),(X(5),ATT1),(X(6),ATT2),(X(7),ATT3),
     .
     .
     .

 4   (X(17),ATT13),(X(18),ATT14),(X(19),ATT15),(X(20),ATT16)
   READ(5,19) X
19   FORMAT(20F5.0)
     .
     .
     .

   END
```

Now, when we use SEX in our program, we are referencing the data read into the storage location of $X(2)$, etc.

DATA Statement.   The DATA statement allows initialization of variables at the beginning of a program. Its general form is

$$\text{DATA v1/d1/,v2/d2/,...,vn/dn/}$$

where each "v" is a list of variables, subscripted variables, or names of arrays; and each "d" is a list of constants (of the correct type) which can be preceded by a multiplier of the form "i", where "i" is an integer constant specifying repetition. For example,

$$\text{DIMENSION A(100)}$$
$$\text{DATA A/100*0.0/}$$

would set all 100 values of the variable $A(I)$ to zero, and

$$\text{DATA KGO/100/,X(3)/-2.02/}$$

would set the variable KGO equal to 100 and the variable $X(3)$ equal to -2.02. The DATA statement initializations are performed during the compilation of the program. The initializations are done only *once* per program run, so the data statement cannot be used to re-initialize variables during execution.

PART 2

Programs from the Social Sciences

Program 1-A.   Salary Calculation

Program 1-A reads an annual salary figure and calculates an average monthly wage.

The first executable statement is a READ instruction. This READ inputs into the variable ANUAL a number from an input record read from Input Unit 5. The FORMAT 9 statement controls the READ and specifies that the value read into ANUAL will come from the first six columns of the input record. This value will be read as a floating point (real) number with no places to the right of the decimal point. A typical input record is

b7500.

card column: 1   6

where the "b" stands for a blank.

The second executable statement computes an average monthly salary by dividing the value stored in ANUAL by 12.0. The result of this division is stored in XMTLY. Note that the divisor is a real number, 12.0, not a fixed point (integer) number, 12; and the quotient is stored as a real number. Consequently, this statement does not necessitate that the FORTRAN being used permit mixed mode arithmetic.

The third executable statement writes the value stored in ANUAL and the value stored in XMTLY to Output Unit 6 under the control of FORMAT 19. Output Unit 6 is assumed to be a line printer. Remember from the discussion in Chapter 3 that the first character of a *printer* output record is always a carriage control character and as such it is never printed. This is a frequent source of error, even for experienced programmers. Again, there are four carriage control characters, the "1" which advances the printer paper to the top of the next page, the "b" (blank) which spaces the printer paper one line, the "0" (zero) which spaces the printer two lines, and the "+" which causes the printer *not* to space before printing, thereby permitting multiple printing on the same line. When a programmer forgets the rule of the first character and attempts to begin printing his data in position 1 of the print line, not only will the first data character not be printed, but the spacing action taken by the printer will be unpredictable.

We have chosen to use the literal convention to output character data. It is considerably easier than the Hollerith convention (the wH, where "w" is the length of the character string immediately following the

"H"), because the exact number of characters in the string need not be counted. The character string is enclosed in single quotes. FORMAT 19 intersperses three character strings between the two F format items. The first string has as its first character a 1. This 1 is the carriage control character and it causes the printer to skip to the top of the next page. The first character actually printed is a blank.

Following the first character string, the value of ANUAL is printed. The specification F6.0 permits a sign, four digits, and a decimal point to be printed; or in the case of a positive number, five digits and a decimal point. No places to the right of the point will be printed. The point will be printed and it takes one of the six spaces allocated by the F6.0 specification. Should the value of ANUAL happen to be equal to or greater than 100000. (or equal to or less than −10000.), and consequently require more than five digits to the left of the point, the specification of F6.0 would be insufficient to permit this printing. This error would be indicated on many machines by the output of a string of six asterisks (∗∗∗∗∗∗). The second character string, bWHICHbISb$, is printed immediately following the value for ANUAL. This string precedes the value for XMTLY. XMTLY is assumed to lie in the range 99999.99 to −9999.99. Should it exceed this range, a string of eight asterisks will be printed. Remember, a plus sign is assumed, but a minus sign will use one of the positions specified in the w of the Fw.d specification. The value of XMTLY is followed by the third character string, bAbMONTH, which completes the format specification.

The final executable statement is the STOP statement, which terminates the execution of the program. The END statement simply tells the FORTRAN compiler that there are no more statements to this program. The END statement has meaning only to the compiler.

SOURCE PROGRAM

```
C     PROGRAM 1-A
      READ(5,9) ANUAL
      XMTLY=ANUAL/12.0
      WRITE(6,19) ANUAL,XMTLY
      STOP
    9 FORMAT(F6.0)
   19 FORMAT('1 ANNUAL SALARY IS $',F6.0,' WHICH IS $',F8.2,' A MONTH')
      END
```

INPUT DATA

```
CARD COLUMNS:
         1          2          3          4          5          6          7
1234567890 1234567890 1234567890 1234567890 1234567890 1234567890 1234567890
         8
1234567890

7500.
```

OUTPUT DATA

```
ANNUAL SALARY IS $ 7500. WHICH IS $  625.00 A MONTH
```

Program 1–B.   Salary Calculation

Program 1–B is a more general version of 1–A. This program will process input records in a continual fashion, reading an annual salary, calculating a monthly figure, and outputting these two values along with the value of a counter that keeps track of the number of records read. This processing continues until an annual salary with a zero or negative value is read. Therefore a blank card will suffice as a signal of end-of-data, since blanks are read as though they were zeros under "F", "I", and "E" format specifications. (Only by reading data with the "A" specification may one differentiate between blanks and zeros.)

The first executable statement is a WRITE statement under the control of FORMAT 9, which refers to Output Unit 6, which is assumed to be a line printer. FORMAT 9 is composed of only a carriage control character, "1" resulting in the printer skipping to the top of a new page. The second executable statement sets the value of the variable used as the counter (ISAL) equal to zero. Instead of using this statement, we could have used

DATA ISAL/0/

The DATA statement, at compilation time rather than at execution time, would establish a storage location for ISAL and would set this location equal to zero. ISAL is an integer (fixed point) variable. Consequently, we do not use decimal points in setting its value.

Statement number 1, which follows, is a READ statement identical in operation to the READ statement in Program 1–A. FORMAT 19 (idenical to FORMAT 9 in Program 1–A) controls the reading of a floating-point value into ANUAL. This value, read from Input Unit 5, is assumed to be six columns wide with no digits to the right of the decimal point.

The fourth executable statement, an IF test, tests the value just read into ANUAL. If this value is negative or zero, control is transferred to statement number 3, a STOP statement, and the program execution is terminated. If ANUAL is positive, control transfers to statement number 2. Statement number 2 calculates the average monthly salary by dividing the annual salary value by 12.0. This value is stored in XMTLY. (**NOTE:** *All members of this statement are real, so mixed mode arithmetic is avoided.*) The sixth executable statement increments the value of ISAL by 1, with no decimal point. ISAL is an integer counter for the number of salaries read and calculated.

The seventh executable statement is a WRITE instruction. This instruction causes an output record to be transmitted to Output Unit 6 under the control of FORMAT 29. Again, Output Unit 6 is assumed to be a line printer. FORMAT 29 is only slightly more complex than FOR–MAT 19 of Program 1–A. The carriage control character is a blank, generated by the 1X format item. We could have used in place of the 1X the character string "b" (where the b represents a blank). Either would produce a single spacing on the printer *before* printing. The remainder of the format list is made up of three character strings interspersed among the format specifications for ISAL, ANUAL, and XMTLY.

The character strings, surrounded by single quotes, are reproduced exactly. The first character of the first string, an F, will appear in the first *printing* position on the line printer. Following the first character string, the format item I2 is matched with the variable ISAL (format items match one-to-one from left to right with variables in the WRITE list). Since ISAL is an integer (fixed-point) variable, we use the I format item to print its value. Should the value of ISAL exceed two digits, either greater than 99 or less than −9, an error will result and two asterisks will be printed. The F6.0 will allow five digits and a decimal point to be printed (or a minus sign, four digits, and a point). Should ANUAL exceed these bounds, six asterisks will be printed. Note that we had to continue FORMAT 29 to a second card. This continuation is signaled by punching a nonzero character in column six of the continuation card.

The third character string follows the format item F6.0. The format list ends with the item F7.2, which matches with the variable XMTLY. This item permits printing a maximum value of 9999.99 or a minimum value of −999.99. Again, should these bounds be exceeded, a string of seven asterisks will be printed.

FORMAT 29 will produce a line 86 characters long (plus the carriage control character, which is not printed).

The eighth executable statement is an unconditional GO TO. When it is executed, control is immediately returned to statement number one, where another value for ANUAL is read. All the statements in this loop from statement number 1 through the eighth executable statement (the unconditional GO TO) are executed repeatedly until a value less than or equal to zero is read into ANUAL. When this value is tested by the IF statement (the fourth executable statement), control is transferred to statement number 3, the STOP statement, and program execution ceases.

The END statement signals the FORTRAN compiler that there are no more FORTRAN source statements to compile.

SOURCE PROGRAM

```
C        PROGRAM 1-B
         WRITE(6,9)
         ISAL=0
   1     READ(5,19) ANUAL
         IF(ANUAL) 3,3,2
   2     XMTLY=ANUAL/12.0
         ISAL=ISAL+1
         WRITE(6,29) ISAL,ANUAL,XMTLY
         GO TO 1
   3     STOP
   9     FORMAT('1')
  19     FORMAT(F6.0)
  29     FORMAT(1X,'FOR INDIVIDUAL NUMBER ',I2,' WHOSE ANNUAL SALARY IS $',
        1 F6.0,' HIS MONTHLY SALARY IS $',F7.2)
         END
```

INPUT DATA

```
CARD COLUMNS:
         1         2         3         4         5         6         7         8
1234567890123456789012345678901234567890123456789012345678901234567890123456789 0

 7500.
10000.
 4950.
              A BLANK CARD
```

OUTPUT DATA

```
FOR INDIVIDUAL NUMBER  1 WHOSE ANNUAL SALARY IS $ 7500. HIS MONTHLY SALARY IS $ 625.00
FOR INDIVIDUAL NUMBER  2 WHOSE ANNUAL SALARY IS $10000. HIS MONTHLY SALARY IS $ 833.33
FOR INDIVIDUAL NUMBER  3 WHOSE ANNUAL SALARY IS $ 4950. HIS MONTHLY SALARY IS $ 412.50
```

Program 1–C.   Salary Calculation

Program 1–C continues the salary problem. In its executable logic it is actually simpler than 1–B, i.e., there is no loop. It is used here to demonstrate what can happen in a series of calculations due to "roundoff error."

The first executable statement is a READ from Input Unit 5 under the control of FORMAT 9. This READ inputs a value for ANUAL. The program divides the value in ANUAL by 12.0 and stores the quotient in XMTLY. It then divides the value in XMTLY by 4.33 (the average number of weeks in a month) and stores this quotient in WEKLY. The value stored in WEKLY is divided by 40.0 to obtain an hourly wage.

The fifth executable statement multiplies the hourly wage, HORLY, by 40.0*52.0 and stores the product in Y. Y is subtracted from ANUAL, and the difference between these two values is stored in DIF. The next executable statement is a WRITE to Output Unit 6 under control of FORMAT 19 of the values stored in ANUAL, XMTLY, WEKLY, HORLY and DIF. Again, Output Unit 6 is assumed to be a line printer. The last executable statement is the STOP.

FORMAT 19 is really not as complex as it appears at first glance. It contains several character strings, surrounded by single quotes and interspersed among the format items that are matched with the five variables in the list of the WRITE statement. The first character of the first character string is a "1" which causes the printer to skip to the top of a new page. A new FORMAT character, the slash, is introduced in FORMAT 19. The slash signals the end of an output record, in this case the end of a print line. The next character to be written will be taken as a carriage control character. Following each slash in FORMAT 19 is a character string, the first character of which is a blank which causes a skip to the next print line

The value of DIF is due to the inaccurate representation of $4\frac{1}{3}$ by 4.33. Computational accuracy could be increased by carrying 4.33 to more decimal places, but values for ANUAL could never be recalculated exactly.

A good exercise would be to punch this sample program using different approximations of 4–1/3, starting with 4, and see how closely the original value for ANUAL is computed.

SOURCE PROGRAM

```
C     PROGRAM 1-C
      READ(5,9) ANUAL
      XMTLY=ANUAL/12.0
      WEKLY=XMTLY/4.33
      HORLY=WEKLY/40.0
      Y=HORLY*40.0*52.0
      DIF=ANUAL-Y
      WRITE(6,19) ANUAL,XMTLY,WEKLY,HORLY,DIF
      STOP
    9 FORMAT(F6.0)
   19 FORMAT('1 ANNUAL SALARY IS $',F6.0,' WHICH IS $',F7.2,' A MONTH'/
     1'  OR $',F7.2,' A WEEK OR $',F5.2,' AN HOUR.'/'  MULTIPLYING THE H
     2OURLY RATE TIMES 40 HOURS TIMES 52 WEEKS'/'  AND SUBTRACTING THE P
     3RODUCT FROM THE TRUE ANNUAL RATE'/'  GIVES A DIFFERENCE OF $',F6.2
     4/'  THIS DIFFERENCE DEMONSTRATES ROUNDING ERRORS WHICH MAY'/'  DEV
     5ELOP DURING PROGRAM EXECUTION.')
      END
```

INPUT DATA

```
CARD COLUMNS:
         1         2         3         4         5         6         7         8
1234567890123456789012345678901234567890123456789012345678901234567890123456789 0

7500.
```

OUTPUT DATA

```
ANNUAL SALARY IS $ 7500. WHICH IS $ 625.00 A MONTH
OR $ 144.34 A WEEK OR $ 3.61 AN HOUR.
MULTIPLYING THE HOURLY RATE TIMES 40 HOURS TIMES 52 WEEKS
AND SUBTRACTING THE PRODUCT FROM THE TRUE ANNUAL RATE
GIVES A DIFFERENCE OF $ -5.77
THIS DIFFERENCE DEMONSTRATES ROUNDING ERRORS WHICH MAY
DEVELOP DURING PROGRAM EXECUTION.
```

Program 1–D.   Salary Calculation

Continuing the salary problem, we note that Program 1–D introduces the use of the non-executable DIMENSION statement, two DO loops, and the library function, FLOAT, in calculating monthly salaries.

The first statement of Program 1–D is a DIMENSION. This statement sets aside 100 storage locations for the singly dimensioned array,

ANUAL. The first executable statement, the READ, inputs a value for a counter variable from Input Unit 5 and stores this value in NUMBR. FORMAT 9 specifies that this value is to be an integer, punched in columns 1 through 4 of the first input record. The next executable statement, the WRITE, outputs this value to Output Unit 6, assumed to be a line printer, according to FORMAT 19. The first item of FORMAT 19 is a character string. The first character of this string is a 1, causing the printer to skip to a new page before printing: the remainder of the character string, the value for NUMBR, and the second character string. NUMBR contains the number of annual salaries to be read in and used in later calculations. The third executable statement sets the value of the variable XAVE (a floating-point scalar) equal to zero.

The first DO loop, the fourth and fifth executable statements, causes NUMBR values to be read from Input Unit 5, one value per input record, and to be stored in ANUAL(1) through ANUAL(NUMBR). The first time the loop is executed, I is set equal to 1. An input record is read under control of FORMAT 29, which specifies that one real (floating-point) value be read from columns 1 through 6 of the input record. This value is stored in the first storage location of the array ANUAL, in ANUAL(1). I is then incremented by 1, becoming 2, and this new value is compared to the value stored in NUMBR. If this new value is less than or equal to NUMBR, statement number 10, the READ, is executed again. A new data record is read from Input Unit 5, and the value taken from columns 1 through 6 of this record is stored in ANUAL(2). I is again incremented by 1, and this new value is compared to the value stored in NUMBR. When I exceeds NUMBR, control drops to the first executable statement following statement number 10. (Note that since the third index value of the DO statement is 1, which tells the DO to increment the index variable I by 1, coding the 1 is not necessary.) The following statement is identical in function to the fourth executable statement.

DO 10 I=1,NUMBR

The sixth through ninth executable statements form the second DO loop in the program. I is again used as the index variable for the loop. It is first set equal to 1. The first executable statement within this loop accumulates the values stored in ANUAL(1) through ANUAL(NUMBR). Each time it is executed, this statement takes the value stored in XAVE, adds to it the value stored in ANUAL(I), and stores this sum back in XAVE. The second executable statement in the loop divides ANUAL(I) by 12.0 and stores the quotient in XMTLY. The last executable statement, statement number 20, sends to Output Unit 6 (under control of FORMAT 39) the present value of I, ANUAL(I), and the value of XMTLY just calculated. I is then incremented by 1, and its new value is compared to NUMBR; if this new value is less than or equal to NUMBR, control continues through the loop. When I exceeds NUMBR, control drops to the statement immediately following statement number 20. Again

DO 20 I=1,NUMBR

is identical in function to

DO 20 I=1,NUMBR,1

The tenth executable statement, the statement immediately following statement number 20, introduces the use of the library function FLOAT. This function, provided by most FORTRAN compilers, converts the fixed-point expression in parentheses to a floating-point number. Some FORTRAN compilers permit mixed mode expressions and would allow the statement

XAVE=XAVE/NUMBR

as well as

XAVE=XAVE/FLOAT(NUMBR)

We could also have used the two statements below

X=NUMBR
XAVE=XAVE/X

and obtained the same results. Because some compilers do *not* permit mixed mode expressions, we will avoid their use in our example programs. In general, even if the compiler you use permits mixing modes in expressions, if you avoid such mixing your programs will usually execute somewhat more rapidly.

The eleventh executable statement writes the values for NUMBR and XAVE to Output Unit 6, under the control of FORMAT 49. The last executable statement is the STOP, which terminates program execution.

FORMAT 9, FORMAT 19, and FORMAT 29 are straightforward. FORMAT 39 uses the 1X format item to generate a blank as a carriage control character. FORMAT 49 introduces the zero as a carriage control character. The zero causes the printer to *double space* before printing. The following three forms for FORMAT 49 would result in identical action being taken by the printer (double spacing).

```
49   FORMAT ( ' 0 ', ' FOR THE ',I4, etc.
49   FORMAT (1H0, ' FOR THE ',I4, etc.
49   FORMAT ( ' 0 FOR THE ',I4, etc.
```

SOURCE PROGRAM

```
C       PROGRAM 1-D
        DIMENSION ANUAL(100)
        READ(5,9) NUMBR
        WRITE(6,19) NUMBR
        XAVE=0.0
        DO 10 I=1,NUMBR,1
     10 READ(5,29) ANUAL(I)
        DO 20 I=1,NUMBR,1
        XAVE=XAVE+ANUAL(I)
        XMTLY=ANUAL(I)/12.0
     20 WRITE(6,39) I,ANUAL(I),XMTLY
        XAVE=XAVE/FLOAT(NUMBR)
        WRITE(6,49) NUMBR,XAVE
        STOP
      9 FORMAT(I4)
     19 FORMAT('1 SALARY ANALYSIS FOR ',I4,' INDIVIDUALS.')
     29 FORMAT(F6.0)
     39 FORMAT(1X,'FOR INDIVIDUAL NUMBER ',I4,' WHOSE ANNUAL SALARY IS $',
        1 F6.0,' HIS MONTHLY SALARY IS $',F7.2)
     49 FORMAT('0',' FOR THE ',I4,' INDIVIDUALS IN THIS ANALYSIS, THE AVER
        1AGE SALARY IS $',F9.2)
        END
```

INPUT DATA

```
CARD COLUMNS:
        1         2         3         4         5         6         7         8
1234567890123456789012345678901234567890123456789012345678901234567890123456789012345678901234567890

  10
7500.
12200.
14500.
15600.
29000.
14000.
 8750.
 9208.
 5693.
13500.
```

OUTPUT DATA

```
   SALARY ANALYSIS FOR   10 INDIVIDUALS.
   FOR INDIVIDUAL NUMBER    1 WHOSE ANNUAL SALARY IS $ 7500. HIS MONTHLY SALARY IS $ 625.00
   FOR INDIVIDUAL NUMBER    2 WHOSE ANNUAL SALARY IS $12200. HIS MONTHLY SALARY IS $1016.67
   FOR INDIVIDUAL NUMBER    3 WHOSE ANNUAL SALARY IS $14500. HIS MONTHLY SALARY IS $1208.33
   FOR INDIVIDUAL NUMBER    4 WHOSE ANNUAL SALARY IS $15600. HIS MONTHLY SALARY IS $1300.00
   FOR INDIVIDUAL NUMBER    5 WHOSE ANNUAL SALARY IS $29000. HIS MONTHLY SALARY IS $2416.67
   FOR INDIVIDUAL NUMBER    6 WHOSE ANNUAL SALARY IS $14000. HIS MONTHLY SALARY IS $1166.67
   FOR INDIVIDUAL NUMBER    7 WHOSE ANNUAL SALARY IS $ 8750. HIS MONTHLY SALARY IS $ 729.17
   FOR INDIVIDUAL NUMBER    8 WHOSE ANNUAL SALARY IS $ 9208. HIS MONTHLY SALARY IS $ 767.33
   FOR INDIVIDUAL NUMBER    9 WHOSE ANNUAL SALARY IS $ 5693. HIS MONTHLY SALARY IS $ 474.42
   FOR INDIVIDUAL NUMBER   10 WHOSE ANNUAL SALARY IS $13500. HIS MONTHLY SALARY IS $1125.00

   FOR THE   10 INDIVIDUALS IN THIS ANALYSIS, THE AVERAGE SALARY IS $ 12995.10
```

Program 1–E.   Salary Calculation

We will belabor the salary example only once more. This program introduces the non-executable DATA statement and a more complex use of IF statements to determine maximum and minimum values from a set of numbers. This program does not use the DIMENSION statement as did Program 1–D (and consequently it requires less storage), but it will do the same job and more. (Program 1–D did not really need to dimension an array. See if you can rewrite it so that it will produce the same output without defining ANUAL as an array.)

The first statement of Program 1–E is the non-executable DATA statement. The DATA statement sets initial values for XAVE, XMIN and XMAX equal to 0.0, 999999.0, and 0.0, respectively. Consider why XMIN is set to a large number, and XMAX to a small number, as you explore this program.

The first READ and the first WRITE are identical to those in Program 1–D, as are FORMAT 9 and FORMAT 19. There is only one DO loop in this program, but it is a long one. Again, I is used as the index variable. The initial value for I is 1, and it will be increased by 1 (we have coded no third index value) after control reaches statement number 20, until its incremented value *exceeds* that stored in NUMBR. The second READ, the first executable statement in the loop, inputs the I-th value of ANUAL under the control of FORMAT 29. Each execution of this READ will cause a new record to be read from Input Unit 5. From this card the first six columns will be stored in ANUAL. The next executable statement simply accumulates the sum of these values and stores this sum in XAVE. Again the monthly salary is computed and stored in XMTLY. The seventh through the eleventh executable statements (the third through the seventh statements in the loop) determine whether the present value in ANUAL is greater than all others that have been read, less than all others, or neither.

The seventh executable statement tests the expression (XMAX − ANUAL). If ANUAL is greater than XMAX, the maximum value read to this point, control is transferred to statement number 11. At statement number 11, the value in ANUAL replaces the value currently stored in XMAX. Control then unconditionally transfers to statement number 20. (A maximum cannot simultaneously be a minimum, except in the trivial case where all values tested are identical.) If ANUAL equals XMAX, no replacement is necessary; nor is a minimum test needed, so control transfers directly to statement number 20. If ANUAL is not equal to or greater than the current maximum value, then perhaps it is the minimum value. To test for this, if ANUAL is less than XMAX, control is transferred to statement number 12.

Statement number 12, the second IF test, evaluates the expression (XMIN−ANUAL). If ANUAL is greater than or equal to the current value of XMIN, control is transferred to statement number 20. If ANUAL is less than the current value of XMIN, then the expression (XMIN−ANUAL) will be positive and control will be transferred to statement number 13. At statement number 13, the current value for XMIN is replaced by the value stored in ANUAL. Statement number 20 causes the current value of I, ANUAL and XMTLY to be written to Output Unit 6 under the control of FORMAT 39 in a fashion identical to Program 1–D. The current value for I is increased by 1. This new value is compared to the value stored at NUMBR. As long as I is less than, or equal to NUMBR, the statements within the loop continue to be executed.

When the loop has been executed NUMBR times, when I is incremented to a value that exceeds NUMBR, control drops to the first executable statement after the end of the loop. This statement calculates the average annual salary (XAVE) for the NUMBR annual salaries read. The next executable statement writes to Output Unit 6 the minimum annual salary read, XMIN; the maximum annual salary, XMAX; and the average of all the salaries read, XAVE. FORMAT 49 controls this output. The last executable statement, STOP, terminates the program.

SOURCE PROGRAM

```
C      PROGRAM 1-E
       DATA XAVE,XMIN,XMAX/0.0,999999.0,0.0/
       READ(5,9)  NUMBR
       WRITE(6,19) NUMBR
       DO 20 I=1,NUMBR
       READ(5,29) ANUAL
       XAVE=XAVE+ANUAL
       XMTLY=ANUAL/12.0
       IF(XMAX-ANUAL) 11,20,12
    11 XMAX=ANUAL
       GO TO 20
    12 IF(XMIN-ANUAL) 20,20,13
    13 XMIN=ANUAL
    20 WRITE(6,39) I,ANUAL,XMTLY
       XAVE=XAVE/FLOAT(NUMBR)
       WRITE(6,49) XMAX,XMIN,XAVE
       STOP
     9 FORMAT(I4)
    19 FORMAT('1 SALARY ANALYSIS FOR ',I4,' INDIVIDUALS.')
    29 FORMAT(F6.0)
    39 FORMAT(1X,'FOR INDIVIDUAL NUMBER ',I4,' WHOSE ANNUAL SALARY IS $',
      1 F6.0,' HIS MONTHLY SALARY IS $',F7.2)
    49 FORMAT('0',' THE MAXIMUM SALARY IN THE GROUP IS $',F6.0/
      1' THE MINIMUM SALARY IN THE GROUP IS $',F6.0/
      2' THE AVERAGE SALARY IN THE GROUP IS $',F9.2)
       END
```

INPUT DATA

```
CARD COLUMNS:
        1         2         3         4         5         6         7         8
1234567890123456789012345678901234567890123456789012345678901234567890123456789 0

   10
 7500.
12200.
14500.
15600.
29000.
14000.
 8750.
 9208.
 5693.
13500.
```

OUTPUT DATA

```
SALARY ANALYSIS FOR   10 INDIVIDUALS.
FOR INDIVIDUAL NUMBER     1 WHOSE ANNUAL SALARY IS $ 7500. HIS MONTHLY SALARY IS $ 625.00
FOR INDIVIDUAL NUMBER     2 WHOSE ANNUAL SALARY IS $12200. HIS MONTHLY SALARY IS $1016.67
FOR INDIVIDUAL NUMBER     3 WHOSE ANNUAL SALARY IS $14500. HIS MONTHLY SALARY IS $1208.33
FOR INDIVIDUAL NUMBER     4 WHOSE ANNUAL SALARY IS $15600. HIS MONTHLY SALARY IS $1300.00
FOR INDIVIDUAL NUMBER     5 WHOSE ANNUAL SALARY IS $29000. HIS MONTHLY SALARY IS $2416.67
FOR INDIVIDUAL NUMBER     6 WHOSE ANNUAL SALARY IS $14000. HIS MONTHLY SALARY IS $1166.67
FOR INDIVIDUAL NUMBER     7 WHOSE ANNUAL SALARY IS $ 8750. HIS MONTHLY SALARY IS $ 729.17
FOR INDIVIDUAL NUMBER     8 WHOSE ANNUAL SALARY IS $ 9208. HIS MONTHLY SALARY IS $ 767.33
FOR INDIVIDUAL NUMBER     9 WHOSE ANNUAL SALARY IS $ 5693. HIS MONTHLY SALARY IS $ 474.42
FOR INDIVIDUAL NUMBER    10 WHOSE ANNUAL SALARY IS $13500. HIS MONTHLY SALARY IS $1125.00

THE MAXIMUM SALARY IN THE GROUP IS $29000.
THE MINIMUM SALARY IN THE GROUP IS $ 5693.
THE AVERAGE SALARY IN THE GROUP IS $ 12995.10
```

Program 2–A.   Mean of a Set of Data

Program 2–A calculates the mean or average of a set of data. The end of the input data set is signaled by the reading of a blank card. The non-executable REAL statement is introduced.

Assume we've recorded the ages for all members of a small, intimate undergraduate-graduate seminar of 50 students. Each age is punched in columns 4 and 5 of a card.

The first statement of the program is a non-executable REAL. Remember, normally all variables whose names begin with I through N are fixed-point variables. The REAL statement causes the program to treat NUMBR as a floating-point variable. The second statement is also non-executable, a DATA statement which assigns NUMBR and SUM the initial value of zero.

The first executable statement reads in a value for AGE from Input Unit 5 controlled by FORMAT 9. This value is tested in the second executable statement. If it is equal to zero or is negative (keypunchers sometimes make mistakes), control is transferred to statement number 100. If it is positive, control is transferred to statement number 2. Statement number 2 accumulates the sum of the ages read:

$$S = \sum_{i=1}^{n} AGE_i \text{ for } n \text{ ages.}$$

The next executable statement accumulates the actual number of data records read in. The fifth executable statement is an unconditional transfer of control back to statement number 1, the READ.

When a card is read that is blank in columns 4 and 5, has zeros in 4 and 5, or has a negative value in 4 through 5, control is transferred to statement number 100. (Remember, in FORTRAN under all but the A format specification, blanks are read as zeros.) At statement number 100, an IF test is executed to be sure the number of cases is correct for our example class. If we have input the correct number of cases, the average age is calculated by statement number 101 and stored in AVERG. The number of cases read, and the average age is written to Output Unit 6 under control of FORMAT 19. The program execution is then terminated.

If, however, too many or too few cases were read, control transfers to statement number 102. This is a WRITE statement that outputs the actual number of cases read. The program execution terminates following this WRITE. Any number of STOP statements are permitted in a program.

Note that FORMAT 9 will read only two columns of data. This does not permit a decimal point to be punched (unless no one is older than nine).

SOURCE PROGRAM

```
C      PROGRAM 2-A
       REAL NUMBR
       DATA NUMBR,SUM/2*0.0/
    1  READ(5,9) AGE
       IF (AGE) 100,100,2
    2  SUM=SUM+AGE
       NUMBR=NUMBR+1.0
       GO TO 1
  100  IF(50.0-NUMBR) 102,101,102
```

SOURCE PROGRAM (continued)

```
101 AVERG=SUM/50.0
    WRITE(6,19) NUMBR,AVERG
    STOP
102 WRITE(6,29) NUMBR
    STOP
  9 FORMAT(3X,F2.0)
 19 FORMAT('1',' FOR ',F4.0,' STUDENTS, THEIR AVERAGE AGE IS ',F6.2)
 29 FORMAT('1',' A NO NO.  WE EXPECTED 50, BUT WE READ ',F4.0)
    END
```

INPUT DATA

```
CARD COLUMNS:
          1         2         3         4         5         6         7         8
1234567890123456789012345678901234567890123456789012345678901234567890123456789012345678901234567890
    19
    20
    24
    21
    20
    20
    18
    19
    28
    27
    29
    24
    20
    21
    21
    22
    23
    21
    20
    20
    19
    19
    18
    17
    20
    34
    20
    21
    22
    23
    23
    28
    26
    26
    24
    25
    26
    22
    21
    19
    20
    28
    23
    23
    23
    25
    34
    31
    30
    32
              A BLANK CARD
```

OUTPUT DATA

FOR 50. STUDENTS, THEIR AVERAGE AGE IS 23.18

Program 2-B.   Mean of a Set of Data

Program 2–B is a more general approach to determining the mean of a set of data. The code used here allows calculation of the mean when the number of observations to be read is unknown.

COUNT and SUM are initialized to zero by the DATA statement. Statement number 1 reads a value into the variable DATA. FORTRAN compilers can differentiate between "DATA" used as a variable and "DATA" used as a non-executable statement. If the value read into DATA is greater than zero, control is transferred to statement number 2. Otherwise control transfers to statement number 100.

Statement number 2 accumulates the values read into DATA, storing this sum in SUM. COUNT is incremented by 1.0, and control is transferred back to statement number 1.

Statement number 100 calculates the average value by dividing SUM by the number of data items read, COUNT. The next statement makes use of the library subprogram statement function IFIX. IFIX converts the real expression in parentheses to a fixed value.

The WRITE statement is by now quite familiar as is the STOP statement.

SOURCE PROGRAM

```
C      PROGRAM 2-B
       DATA COUNT,SUM/2*0.0/
    1  READ(5,9) DATA
       IF(DATA) 100,100,2
    2  SUM=SUM+DATA
       COUNT=COUNT+1.0
       GO TO 1
  100  AVERG=SUM/COUNT
       NUMBR=IFIX(COUNT)
       WRITE(6,19) NUMBR,AVERG
       STOP
    9  FORMAT(3X,F2.0)
   19  FORMAT('1',' FOR ',I4,' UNITS: MEAN=',F6.2)
       END
```

INPUT DATA

```
CARD COLUMNS:
         1         2         3         4         5         6         7         8
1234567890123456789012345678901234567890123456789012345678901234567890123456789012345678901234567890
    20
    47
    16
    20
    19
    20
    20
    20
    24
    26
    30
    32
    33
    43
    42
    19
    18
    20
    22
    23
    21
    24
              A BLANK CARD
```

OUTPUT DATA

```
FOR    22 UNITS: MEAN= 25.41
```

Program 2–C.   Mean of a Set of Data

This program adds two capabilities to Programs 2–A and 2–B. First, we read up to 100 values for a variable and store these values in the array X. The exact number of values we will read is given to the program by the first READ statement. A fixed-point value is read into NUMBR from columns 1 through 3 of the first data card. Then, NUMBR values are read, one per data card from columns 1 through 5 of succeeding cards under the control of FORMAT 19.

The second capability is the calculation of the standard deviation of the data array, in addition to the calculation of the mean. The standard deviation of an array is a measure of the dispersion of the values of that array around the array's mean. One formula for calculating the standard deviation is [1]

$$S = \sqrt{\frac{\sum_{i=1}^{N} (X_i - \overline{X})^2}{N}},$$

in which $\overline{X}$ is the mean and each X_i is a value. But this formula requires two calculation passes (iterations) through the array.

A frequently used computing formula for the standard deviation is [2]

$$S = \sqrt{\frac{\sum_{i=1}^{N} X_i^2}{N} - \overline{X}}.$$

This formula requires only one pass through the data array. In this pass, we can calculate ΣX_i^2 and ΣX_i, the sum of the squared values of each member of the array and the sum of the values of each member, respectively. By dividing ΣX_i by N, we obtain $\overline{X}$. The seventh, eighth, ninth and eleventh statements of Program 2–C perform these operations.

The tenth statement floats the value of NUMBR and stores this value in XNUM. The eleventh statement calculates the mean as done in earlier programs. The twelfth statement calculates the standard deviation of the array and stores this value in STD. Note that some compilers provide a library subprogram statement function for calculating the square root of an expression. This function is used in the same fashion as FLOAT. The statement

$$\text{STD=SQRT((SUM/XNUM)–XBAR**2)}$$

is identical in the answer it produces to the twelfth statement of Program 2–C. (Provided, of course, that the compiler in use has the SQRT function.)

The WRITE and STOP statements are by now quite familiar in their function.

SOURCE PORGRAM

```
C      PROGRAM 2-C
       DIMENSION X(100)
       READ(5,9) NUMBR
       DO 10 I=1,NUMBR
```

[1] Blalock, Hubert M.: *Social Statistics*, McGraw-Hill, Inc., New York, N.Y., 1960, pp. 68–69.
[2] *Ibid.*

SOURCE PROGRAM (continued)

```
10 READ (5,19) X(I)
   SUM=0.0
   SUMSQ=0.0
   DO 20 I=1,NUMBR
   SUM=SUM+X(I)
20 SUMSQ=SUMSQ+X(I)**2
   XNUM=NUMBR
   XBAR=SUM/XNUM
   STD=((SUMSQ/XNUM)-XBAR**2)**0.5
   WRITE (6,29) NUMBR,XBAR,STD
   STOP
 9 FORMAT(I3)
19 FORMAT(F5.0)
29 FORMAT('1FOR ',I3,' OBSERVATIONS  MEAN=',F6.2,'  STANDARD DEVIATIO
  1N=',F6.2)
   END
```

INPUT DATA

```
CARD COLUMNS:
         1         2         3         4         5         6         7         8
1234567890 1234567890 1234567890 1234567890 1234567890 1234567890 1234567890 1234567890

 27
    97
    95
    20
    43
    12
    56
    55
    23
    24
    20
    16
    50
    23
    24
    50
    45
    22
    33
    31
    42
    62
    20
    30
    13
    31
    20
    45
```

OUTPUT DATA

```
FOR  27 OBSERVATIONS  MEAN= 37.11  STANDARD DEVIATION= 21.68
```

Program 2–D.   Mean of a Set of Data

Program 2–C may be segmented into two distinct parts. Data must be input and output, and answers must be calculated. Program 2–D demonstrates this segmentation through the use of a subroutine to perform the required calculations. The main program inputs data, calls the subroutine, and outputs results.

The calculation of the mean and standard deviation of an array of data is a chore frequently encountered in social science research. By writing a subroutine to find the mean and standard deviation of an array, we will have it available for use in a later program.

The major rule for writing subroutines as discussed in Chapter 3 is that arguments in the subroutine list,

SUBROUTINE ANYNAME (argument list)

must match arguments in the call list,

CALL ANYNAME (argument list)

in number, order and type. If five variable names (say X, Y, Z, N, M) are passed to a subroutine, then the subroutine argument list must have five variable names. If, in the above, X and Z are arrays, then the first and third members of the subroutine list must also be arrays. The first three variables in the call list are real and the last two are fixed-point, so the first three variables in the subroutine list must be real and the last two, fixed-point. Constants may be passed from the calling program to the subroutine; e.g.,

CALL TEST (X,Y,2,3.0)
.
.
.

SUBROUTINE TEXT (U,V,I,A)

When TEST is called, I will be set equal to 2, and A will contain the value 3.0. Since a constant is a single value, it must be matched with a scalar variable. The type requirement must be followed. Constants may be passed through the argument list from a subroutine to its calling program, but there is little use for this since each time the subroutine is called, it will return the same value in that position of its argument list.

Subroutines are completely separate from each other and from their calling program (which may be another subroutine). Consequently, the variables and statement numbers used in a subroutine are unique to it and in no way conflict with similar variables or statement numbers used in other subroutines or in the main program. This, of course, is not true of the variables passed through the argument list, or of variables that may be passed through the use of the COMMON statement.

In the example that follows, the subroutine DESC is passed a scalar, NUMBR, and an array, X, from the calling program. DESC returns to the calling program values for two scalar variables, XBAR and STD. Both the main program and DESC use the variable I and the statement number 10, but these are separate unique I's and separate unique statement number 10's. The calling program and a subroutine share storage *only* through their argument list (or through the use of COMMON).

The main program, then, sets aside 100 storage locations for the floating-point array X. It next reads from Input Unit 5 via FORMAT 9 the number of values it is to input into X. The second and third executable statements form a loop which is executed NUMBR times and which fills NUMBR positions of X. The fourth executable statement is the CALL to the subroutine. The argument list of the CALL statement contains four variable names. The first is a fixed-point scalar, NUMBR; the second a floating-point array, X; and the third and fourth are floating-point scalars. The subroutine will return in these last two variables the mean and standard deviation of the array X. The last two executable statements of our main program are the WRITE, by FORMAT 29, and the STOP statement.

The subroutine DESC has four variable names in its argument list. The names are different from those in the CALL list, but *they are of the same number, order and type*. N is a fixed-point scalar, it is matched to NUMBR. Y is a floating-point array, it is matched with X. Z1 and Z2 are floating-point scalars matched with XBAR and STD, respectively. Y is known by the subroutine to be an array because Y is dimensioned as such in the subroutine. (Some FORTRAN compilers require only a dimension of 1 be given in a subroutine to denote an array, but for general compatibility we will use the full dimension.)

S and SS are accumulators to be used for developing ΣY and ΣY^2 and are first set equal to zero. The subroutine loop accumulates these sums. Note that S and SS and statement number 10 are known only within the subroutine.

Z1 is the mean. The standard deviation, Z2, is calculated as it was in Program 2–C. The last executable statement of the subroutine, the RETURN, causes control to return to the calling program at the statement immediately following the CALL DESC (...) statement.

After executing the CALL statement — after the subroutine has returned control to the calling program, XBAR and STD contain the mean and standard deviation of the NUMBR values of X. Before the CALL, however, XBAR and STD are undefined.

The WRITE statement outputs the values of NUMBR, XBAR and STD to Output Unit 6 under control of FORMAT 29 as in Program 2-C. The final executable statement is the STOP.

SOURCE PROGRAM

```
C       PROGRAM 2-D
        DIMENSION X(100)
        READ(5,9)  NUMBR
        DO 10 I=1,NUMBR
    10  READ(5,19)  X(I)
        CALL  DESC(NUMBR,X,XBAR,STD)
        WRITE(6,29)  NUMBR,XBAR,STD
        STOP
     9  FORMAT(I3)
    19  FORMAT(F5.0)
    29  FORMAT('1FOR ',I3,' OBSERVATIONS  MEAN=',F6.2,'  STANDARD DEVIATIO
       1N=',F6.2)
        END
```

SOURCE DESCRIPTION

```
C       SUBROUTINE DESC
        SUBROUTINE DESC(N,Y,Z1,Z2)
        DIMENSION Y(100)
        XN=N
        S=0.0
        SS=0.0
        DO 10 I=1,N
        S=S+Y(I)
    10  SS=SS+Y(I)**2
        Z1=S/XN
        Z2=((SS/XN)-Z1**2)**0.5
        RETURN
        END
```

INPUT DATA

```
CARD COLUMNS:
         1         2         3         4         5         6         7         8
12345678901234567890123456789012345678901234567890123456789012345678901234567890

13
 97
 84
 26
 50
 32
 40
 50
 13
 20
 40
 42
 38
 35
```

OUTPUT DATA

FOR 13 OBSERVATIONS MEAN= 43.62 STANDARD DEVIATION= 22.60

Program 3. Frequency Distribution

Program 3 inputs an unordered vector of up to 100 values, counts the occurrence of each unique value in the input vector, orders the unique values, and outputs the ordered vector of unique values and the count of their occurrence.

The DIMENSION statement sets aside storage for 100 values for the vector DATA, and storage for a 2-column by 100-row matrix, FREQ. The first column of FREQ will be used to contain the unique values of DATA. Each row in the second column of FREQ will contain the count of the number of occurrences of the unique value contained in the same row of column one of FREQ. The DATA statement sets all 200 locations of FREQ to 0.0. Note that there is no conflict in the use of "DATA" as a variable name.

The first READ statement inputs the number of data values to be read into DATA by the second READ statement. FREQ (1,1), the first row of the first column of FREQ, is set equal to the first value of DATA. A counter, K, which will contain the number of unique values of the vector DATA, is set equal to 1. Two loops, one within the other, are then executed. The outer loop, using I as its index variable, loops across all statements up to and including statement number 30, NUMBR−1 times (the initial value of I is 2). The inner loop, using J as its index variable, loops to statement 20, K times. If the J-th row of column 1 of the matrix FREQ contains the same value as DATA(1), the program branches to statement number 25 where the value in the J-th row of column 2 of FREQ is incremented by 1.0; i.e., the number of occurrences of this value is incremented by 1. I is then incremented by 1 and the J loop is begun again. If FREQ(J,1) is not equal to DATA(I), J is incremented by 1; its value tested against K; and if it is less than or equal to K, the J loop continues. If the J loop is exhausted before a match to DATA(I) is found, then the DATA(I) value is unique. K, the counter of unique values, is incremented by 1; FREQ(K,1) is set equal to DATA(I), and control is transferred to statement number 30. I is incremented by 1 and tested against NUMBR. This process continues for all values read into the vector, DATA.

Upon completion of the I loop, FREQ(1,1) through FREQ(K,1) contain the K unique values of DATA(1) through DATA(NUMBR). K, of course, can never be greater than NUMBR. FREQ(1,2) through FREQ(K,2) contain the frequency of occurrence of the values in FREQ(1,1) through FREQ(K,1), respectively.

The next section of the program, from the statement L=K−1 through statement number 40, sorts the unique values into ascending order. The second column of the matrix FREQ is reordered along with the sort on the first column. The sort is accomplished through the use of two or more DO loops, both terminating with statement number 40. L is set to one less than the number of unique values, K. The outer loop, using I as its index variable, is executed L times. M is set to 1 greater than I for each cycle through the outer loop. The inner loop, whose index variable is J, loops from M to K (the number of unique values). J, then, is always greater than I.

The one IF statement within the loops tests the value of FREQ(I,1) against the values of FREQ(I+1,1) through FREQ(K,1). Each time a value from the list FREQ(I+1,1) to FREQ(K,1) is found to be less than FREQ(I,1) control is transferred to statement number 35. TEMP1 and TEMP2 are used in the exchange of the smaller and larger values and their associated frequencies (the second column of the matrix FREQ).

Upon completion of the I loop, both columns of FREQ have been sorted into ascending order. The WRITE statement outputs to a line printer (Output Unit 6) under the control of FORMAT 29 each unique value and its associated frequency. FORMAT 29 specifies a skip to a new page, a line skip, and a print of title information, − up to 100 values and frequencies, one value and its frequency per line.

The last executable statement of the program is the STOP.

SOURCE PROGRAM

```
C      PRCGRAM 3     FREQUENCY DISTRIBUTION
       DIMENSION DATA(100),FREQ(100,2)
       DATA FREQ/100*0.0,100*1.0/
       READ(5,9) NUMBR
       READ(5,19) (DATA(I),I=1,NUMBR)
       FREQ(1,1)=DATA(1)
       K=1
       DO 30 I=2,NUMBR
       DO 20 J=1,K
       IF(DATA(I)-FREQ(J,1)) 20,25,20
    20 CONTINUE
       K=K+1
       FREQ(K,1)=DATA(I)
       GO TO 30
    25 FREQ(J,2)=FREQ(J,2)+1.0
```

SOURCE PROGRAM (continued)

```
30 CONTINUE
   L=K-1
   DO 40 I=1,L
   M=I+1
   DO 40 J=M,K
   IF(FREQ(J,1)-FREQ(I,1)) 35,40,40
35 TEMP1=FREQ(I,1)
   TEMP2=FREQ(I,2)
   FREQ(I,1)=FREQ(J,1)
   FREQ(I,2)=FREQ(J,2)
   FREQ(J,1)=TEMP1
   FREQ(J,2)=TEMP2
40 CONTINUE
   WRITE(6,29) ((FREQ(I,J),J=1,2),I=1,K)
   STOP
 9 FORMAT(I4)
19 FORMAT(10F8.0)
29 FORMAT('1'/'      VALUE   FREQUENCY'/100(1X,F9.0,5X,F4.0/))
   END
```

INPUT DATA

```
CARD COLUMNS:
         1         2         3         4         5         6         7         8
1234567890123456789012345678901234567890123456789012345678901234567890123456789 0

  60
      -123     -456     -987     -453    -4567    -1497    -9997    -1245     -012  -97654
      1234      555     1753     7994      224     4567     4225     1025     9741    0024
      1234      555     1753     7994      224     4567     4225     1025     9741    0024
      1234      555     1753     7994      224     4567     4225     1025     9741    0024
      1234      555     1753     7994      224     4567     4225     1025     9741    0024
      5785     2456    97534     5420      954     4237     -234     5432    -5423    2456
```

OUTPUT DATA

```
VALUE      FREQUENCY
-97654.       1.
 -9997.       1.
 -5423.       1.
 -4567.       1.
 -1497.       1.
 -1245.       1.
  -987.       1.
  -456.       1.
  -453.       1.
  -234.       1.
  -123.       1.
   -12.       1.
    24.       4.
   224.       4.
   555.       4.
   954.       1.
  1025.       4.
  1234.       4.
```

OUTPUT DATA (continued)

```
1753.        4.
2456.        2.
4225.        4.
4237.        1.
4567.        4.
5420.        1.
5432.        1.
5785.        1.
7994.        4.
9741.        4.
97534.       1.
```

Program 4.   Bar Graph

Program 4 contains a very simple main program and a somewhat more complex subroutine. The program was structured in this fashion to permit the use of this subroutine in later examples.

The main program sets aside 100 storage locations for a vector, Y. The DATA statement assigns the character "*" to the variable ALPHA. The READ statement inputs from Input Unit 5, 100 values for Y under the control of FORMAT 9. Ten values from each input record are read. The subroutine, BRGRF is then called.

The subroutine is passed four arguments. The first is the number of values to be graphed (this is the number of units along the horizontal "X" axis to be used). The second argument is the number of units to be assigned to the vertical, or "Y", axis. The third is the data vector and the fourth, the symbol to be used in printing the bars. When control returns from BRGRF, the program is terminated by the STOP statement.

The subroutine's argument list matches NVX with the number of units along the "X" axis, NVY with the number of units along the "Y" axis, FOFX with the data vector, and SYMBL with the character to be used in printing the bars. FOFX is dimensioned 100. POINT and VEC are two vectors used by and known only to the subroutine. They are dimensioned 102 and 100, respectively. POINT is filled with periods by the DATA statement. Another variable, BLANK—again known only to the subroutine—is set equal to the character blank.

The first executable statement in the subroutine sets YMAX equal to 0.0. The first DO loop, looping over the instruction up to and including statement number 10, finds the maximum positive value in the vector FOFX. This value is stored in YMAX.

The next executable statement calculates the value of one unit along the "Y", or vertical, axis of the bar graph by dividing YMAX by the number of "Y" units. K is set equal to the number of "X" units plus 2. The first WRITE statement, under control of FORMAT 9, outputs to Output Unit 6 (assumed to be a line printer) K periods by writing K members of the vector POINT. FORMAT 9 specifies a skip to a new page, a skip of 10 print positions, and a print of up to 102 characters.

The final computational section of the subroutine is composed of two DO loops. The outer loop uses I as its index variable and loops to statement number 40 from 1 to NVY, the number of values of FOFX. The inner loop loops to statement number 30, using J as its index variable, NVX. The IF test determines the appropriate position within the vector VEC in which to store a bar graph character (SYMBL). Each time the inner, or J, loop is exhausted, control passes to statement number 40 where VEC(1) through VEC(NVX) is printed, preceded and followed by the printing of a period—POINT(1). The values of VEC are either a blank or the character stored in SYMBL. Each completion of the inner loop results in the filling of VEC. Each completion of the outer loop results in the printing of one row of the bar graph, beginning at the top of the graph and working down to the base.

When the outer loop is exhausted, control passes to the last two WRITE statements in the subroutine. The first, under control of FOR-MAT 29, writes the base of the box of periods surrounding the bar graph. The "+" carriage control character in FORMAT 29 causes the line of periods to be printed across the bottom of each column of the graph. In other words, no line skip is performed following the last execution of the WRITE at statement number 40. The final WRITE outputs the value of YUNIT according to the specifications of FORMAT 39. The last executable statement in the subroutine is the RETURN, causing control to be returned to the main program at the statement immediately following the call to the subroutine.

Note that this subroutine will produce proper results only for non-negative data values. Generalizing the subroutine to handle both positive and negative values for FOFX would make an excellent exercise. (*Hint:* Find the minimum value of FOFX as well as the maximum, and proceed from there.)

SOURCE PROGRAM

```
C      PROGRAM 4   BARGRAPH PROGRAM
       DIMENSION Y(100)
       DATA ALPHA/'*'/
       READ(5,9)  (Y(I),I=1,100)
       CALL BRGRF(100,50,Y,ALPHA)
       STOP
    9  FORMAT(10F8.0)
       END
```

SUBROUTINE BRGRF

```
C      BARGRAPH SUBROUTINE
       SUBROUTINE BRGRF(NVX,NVY,FOFX,SYMBL)
       DIMENSION FOFX(100),POINT(102),VEC(100)
       DATA POINT/102*'.'/,BLANK/' '/
       YMAX=0.0
       DO 10 I=1,NVX
       VEC(I)=BLANK
       IF(FOFX(I)-YMAX) 10,10,5
    5  YMAX=FOFX(I)
   10  CONTINUE
       YUNIT=YMAX/FLOAT(NVY)
       K=NVX+2
       WRITE(6,9)  (POINT(I),I=1,K)
       DO 40 I=1,NVY
       DO 30 J=1,NVX
       IF(FOFX(J)-FLOAT(NVY+1-I)*YUNIT) 30,30,25
   25  VEC(J)=SYMBL
   30  CONTINUE
   40  WRITE(6,19) POINT(1),(VEC(J),J=1,NVX),POINT(1)
       WRITE(6,29) (POINT(I),I=1,K)
       WRITE(6,39) YUNIT
       RETURN
    9  FORMAT('1',10X,102A1)
   19  FORMAT(11X,102A1)
   29  FORMAT('+',10X,102A1)
   39  FORMAT(//'  EACH UNIT ON THE Y-AXIS REPRESENTS ',F15.4)
       END
```

INPUT DATA

```
CARD COLUMNS:
            1         2         3         4         5         6         7         8
  1234567890123456789012345678901234567890123456789012345678901234567890123456789 0

   984.    532.    107.    426.    542.    984.    321.    027.    865.    143.
   465.    432.    104.    698.    742.    102.    443.    210.    045.    955.
   042.    447.    761.    320.    654.    794.    221.    002.    667.    875.
   214.    632.    133.    646.    643.    224.    775.    644.    213.    465.
   763.    322.    321.    465.    621.    326.    667.    579.    954.    213.
   446.    543.    215.    754.    321.    464.    543.    217.    654.    673.
   243.    214.    653.    346.    656.    347.    702.    301.    232.    475.
   542.    424.    024.    357.    657.    651.    467.    621.    324.    667.
   213.    475.    432.    340.    324.    765.    130.    464.    676.    562.
   034.    654.    651.    046.    465.    116.    465.    132.    132.    732.
```

OUTPUT DATA

EACH UNIT ON THE Y-AXIS REPRESENTS 19.6800

Program 5.   Median and Mode for Ungrouped Data

The median value of a set of data is the value at the midpoint of the set. There are exactly the same number of values greater than the median as there are values less than it. If there are 99 items in a data set, the median is the 50th item when the data set is in order (either ascending or descending). If the data set has 100 items, then following an ordering the median would be one half of the sum of the 50th and 51st values. The mode is simply the most frequently occurring value.

Program 5 makes use of two subroutines in finding the median and mode of a vector of data. The first subroutine, FREQD, is a rewriting of Program 3, altering it to a subroutine form. The major differences between FREQD as a main program and as a subroutine are:

1.   The use of two vectors, Y and Z, in place of the matrix FREQ.
2.   The zeroing of Y and Z in the subroutine.
3.   The omission of the READ and WRITE statements in the subroutine.

The logic remains essentially unchanged from that employed in Program 3. The second subroutine, DESC1, calculates the median and the mode from the ordered vectors of unique values and frequency of occurrence produced by FREQD.

The main program sets aside storage for the three vectors: DATA, ORDER, and COUNT. The first executable statement reads from Input Unit 5 the number of values to be read into DATA. The second READ fills DATA with NUMBR values under the control of FORMAT 19. The third executable statement calls the subroutine FREQD. There are five variables in the argument list of the call to FREQD. NUMBR is the number of data values, DATA is the vector of NUMBR values. Upon the return from FREQD, ORDER will contain the unique values of DATA in ascending sequence, COUNT will contain the frequence of occurrence of these values, and NEWN will contain the number of unique values found among the NUMBR values of DATA. ORDER, COUNT, and NEWN are all undefined until control returns from FREQD.

After return from FREQD, the next executable statement in the main program outputs to Unit 6 the NEWN values of ORDER and COUNT under control of FORMAT 29. FORMAT 29 causes a skip to a new page, a line skip, the printing of a header line, and the printing of up to 100 values of ORDER and COUNT, one pair of values to a print line.

Following this WRITE is the CALL to subroutine DESC1. DESC1 is passed NUMBR, NEWN, ORDER, and COUNT. It returns the median in XMED and the mode in XMODE. Until the return from DESC1, XMED and XMODE are undefined. The last WRITE statement in the main program outputs to Output Unit 6 XMED and XMODE under control of FORMAT 39. The final executable statement in the main program is the STOP.

The subroutine DESC1 receives the number of original values of DATA in N, the number of unique values of DATA (the number of values in ORDER and COUNT) in NCAT. ORDER is known to the subroutine as the vector X, and COUNT as the vector C.

Both X and C are dimensioned 100. The first executable statement in DESC1 divides N by 2 and stores the *truncated* result in MID. ISUM is set to zero. The first DO loop sums the frequency of the ordered unique values of DATA until this sum is equal to or greater than MID. Should this sum (ISUM) *exactly* equal MID, control passes to statement number 15 at which point the median is calculated by dividing the sum of the two unique values X(I) and X(I+1) by 2.0. Control then transfers to statement number 21. If ISUM exceeds MID, control transfers to statement number 20 where the median, XMD, is set equal to the unique value X(I).

At statement number 21, XMAX is set to zero in preparation to finding the unique value with the largest frequency of occurrence, the mode. The last loop in DESC1 performs this search. When the loop is exhausted, J contains the position of the largest value within the vector C. (This is not strictly true, J will then be the position of the *first* maximum value within C should there be more than one; consequently, this subroutine will find only the first mode should there be more than one.) The last executable statement in DESC1 before the RETURN stores the modal value, X(J), in XMO.

SOURCE PROGRAM

```
C      PROGRAM 5  CALCULATE MEDIAN AND MODE FOR UNGROUPED DATA
       DIMENSION DATA(100),ORDER(100),COUNT(100)
       READ(5,9) NUMBR
       READ(5,19) (DATA(I),I=1,NUMBR)
       CALL FREQD(NUMBR,DATA,ORDER,COUNT,NEWN)
       WRITE(6,29) (ORDER(I),COUNT(I),I=1,NEWN)
       CALL DESC1(NUMBR,NEWN,ORDER,COUNT,XMED,XMODE)
       WRITE(6,39) XMED,XMODE
       STOP
    9  FORMAT(I4)
   19  FORMAT(10F8.0)
   29  FORMAT('1'/'      VALUE       FREQUENCY'/100(1X,F9.0,5X,F4.0/))
   39  FORMAT(///' THE MEDIAN IS ',F9.0,5X,'THE MODE IS ',F9.0)
       END
```

SUBROUTINE FREQD

```
C      SUBROUTINE FREQD
       SUBROUTINE FREQD(N,X,Y,Z,K)
       DIMENSION X(100),Y(100),Z(100)
       DO 10 I=1,N
       Y(I)=0.0
    10 Z(I)=1.0
       Y(1)=X(1)
       K=1
       DO 30 I=2,N
       DO 20 J=1,K
       IF(X(I)-Y(J)) 20,25,20
    20 CONTINUE
       K=K+1
       Y(K)=X(I)
       GO TO 30
    25 Z(J)=Z(J)+1.0
    30 CONTINUE
       L=K-1
       DO 40 I=1,L
       M=I+1
       DO 40 J=M,K
       IF(Y(J)-Y(I)) 35,40,40
    35 TEMP1=Y(I)
       TEMP2=Z(I)
       Y(I)=Y(J)
       Z(I)=Z(J)
       Y(J)=TEMP1
       Z(J)=TEMP2
    40 CONTINUE
       RETURN
       END
```

SUBROUTINE DESC1

```
C      SUBROUTINE DESC1
       SUBROUTINE DESC1(N,NCAT,X,C,XMD,XMO)
       DIMENSION X(100),C(100)
       MID=N/2
       ISUM=0
       DO 10 I=1,NCAT
       ISUM=ISUM+IFIX(C(I))
       IF(ISUM-MID) 10,15,20
    10 CONTINUE
    15 XMD=(X(I+1)+X(I))/2.0
       GO TO 21
    20 XMD=X(I)
    21 XMAX=0.0
       DO 25 I=1,NCAT
       IF(XMAX-C(I)) 22,25,25
    22 XMAX=C(I)
       J=I
    25 CONTINUE
       XMO=X(J)
       RETURN
       END
```

INPUT DATA

```
CARD COLUMNS:
        1          2          3          4          5          6          7          8
1234567890 1234567890 1234567890 1234567890 1234567890 1234567890 1234567890 1234567890
100  67       14      22       30     38     46      57      62      70
     32.      46.      13.      82.    86.    66.     65.     50.     69.     10.
     48.      27.      45.      30.    57.    54.     25.     39.     49.     68.
     61.      30.      57.      66.    53.    40.     63.     74.     43.     51.
     38.      63.      54.      71.    71.    32.     52.     57.     73.     42.
     64.      58.      37.      14.    46.    33.     66.     48.     50.     73.
     59.      55.      71.      78.    24.    59.     82.     59.     51.     77.
     51.      58.      20.      71.    60.    57.     44.     50.     15.     55.
     76.      64.      53.      59.    52.    94.     55.     37.     48.     82.
     46.      71.      55.      47.    31.    36.     58.     53.     25.     36.
     53.      11.      38.      36.    63.    25.     57.     45.     74.     42.
```

OUTPUT DATA

VALUE	FREQUENCY
10.	1.
11.	1.
13.	1.
14.	1.
15.	1.
20.	1.
24.	1.
25.	3.
27.	1.
30.	2.
31.	1.
32.	2.
33.	1.
36.	3.
37.	2.
38.	2.
39.	1.
40.	1.
42.	2.
43.	1.
44.	1.
45.	2.
46.	3.
47.	1.
48.	3.
49.	1.
50.	3.
51.	3.
52.	2.
53.	4.
54.	2.
55.	4.
57.	5.
58.	3.
59.	4.
60.	1.
61.	1.
63.	3.
64.	2.
65.	1.
66.	3.
68.	1.

OUTPUT DATA (continued)

```
69.      1.
71.      5.
73.      2.
74.      2.
76.      1.
77.      1.
78.      1.
82.      3.
86.      1.
94.      1.
```

THE MEDIAN IS   53.   THE MODE IS   57.

Program 6.   Skewness and Kurtosis

Program 6 is an expansion and rewriting of the subroutine DESC discussed in Program 2–D. This new subroutine, DESC2, calculates the skewness and the kurtosis of a vector of data, in addition to calculating the vector's mean and standard deviation.

The main program sets aside 100 storage locations for the input vector, DATA. The first READ statement reads from Input Unit 5 the number of items to be read into DATA. The second READ statement inputs NUMBR values into DATA according to FORMAT 19. The next executable statement is a CALL to DESC2 which has six variables in the argument list of the CALL. NUMBR is the number of data values; DATA is the vector of the data values; and XBAR, STD, SKEW, and XKURT are floating-point scalars that will contain, upon return from DESC2, the mean, standard deviation, skewness, and kurtosis, respectively, of the vector DATA. The WRITE statement outputs to Unit 6 these four values, along with the number of values of DATA, according to FORMAT 29. The T-format specification is used here for the first time. The T acts as a tab, or pointer, command. "Tw" specifies that the items following the T code will be output beginning in position "w" of the output record. The first character in a record sent to the printer is the carriage control. Therefore, the specification T20 will result in the printing of the items that follow the T, beginning in the 19th *print* position. The final executable instruction in the main program is the STOP statement.

If we define M1, M2, M3 and M4 as follows: [1]

$$M1 = \frac{1}{N}\sum_{i=1}^{N} X_i \qquad\qquad M3 = \frac{1}{N}\sum_{i=1}^{N} X_i^3$$

$$M2 = \frac{1}{N}\sum_{i=1}^{N} X_i^2 \qquad\qquad M4 = \frac{1}{N}\sum_{i=1}^{N} X_i^4,$$

where X is a vector of length N, then we may take advantage of a set of equations for the calculation of the mean, standard deviation, skewness, and kurtosis that will execute rapidly. The mean is simply equal to M1. The standard deviation is given by the formula

$$S = (M2 - M1^2)^{1/2},$$

also

$$Skewness = \frac{M3 - 3(M1M2) + 2M1^3}{S^3}$$

and

$$Kurtosis = \frac{M4 - 4(M1M3) + 6(M1^2M2) - 3M1^4}{S^4}.$$

Note that for computation purposes

$$S^3 = (M2 - M1^2)^{3/2}$$

and

$$S^4 = (M2 - M1^2)^2.$$

The subroutine DESC2 uses these formulae in its calculations. The argument list of the SUBROUTINE statement match N to NUMBR (the number of data values), and X to DATA (the data vector). S1, S2, S3 and S4 will contain — upon completion of DESC2 and the return to the main program — the mean, standard deviation, skewness and kurtosis, respectively, of the data vector.

The first executable statement of the subroutine is a test of the value of N. If N is less than or equal to 0, an error condition exists and control is transferred to statement number 20. An error message is printed according to FORMAT 9 and the program terminates. This demonstrates the use of a STOP statement in a subroutine. If N is greater than 0, control passes to statement number 1 and execution continues.

At statement 1, the value for N is floated and stored in SN for subse-

[1] See Chapter 3 in *Psychological Statistics*, 3rd Edition, Quinn McNemar, John Wiley and Sons, Inc. 1962. Acknowledgement is due Professor Lewis F. Carter, University of California, Riverside, who first suggested to us the calculation algorithm used in DESC2.

quent use in calculations. Note that we did not explicitly call the function FLOAT. Most FORTRAN compilers now in use will automatically provide floating (and fixing) operations as required. S1 through S4 are then set to zero. The only loop in the subroutine accumulates the sum of X, the sum of X^2, the sum of X^3, and the sum of X^4. These sums are stored in S1 through S4, respectively.

The next four statements divide S1 through S4 by SN, storing the results back in S1 through S4. S1 at this point is the mean of the data vector. S1 through S4 are identically M1 through M4. The numerators for skewness and kurtosis are next calculated and stored in S3 and S4, respectively. The square of S1 is subtracted from S2 and the result stored in S2. S2 is now the variance, the standard deviation squared.

An IF test is next performed on the value of S2. If S2 is less than or equal to zero, an error condition exists and control is transferred to statement number 20. It is possible for S2, the variance, to equal zero if all the values of the data vector are the same. If the variance is greater than zero, control passes to statement number 15.

At statement number 15, the S4 term that was the numerator of the kurtosis formula is divided by S2 squared. Since S2 is equal to $(M2 - M1^2)^2$, $S2^2$ equals $(M2 - M1^2)^4$. A normal distribution will have a kurtosis of $3 \pm$ insignificant variation. It is usual to subtract 3 from the kurtosis value to "standardize" kurtosis to zero. The resulting kurtosis measure will be positive for a leptokurtic distribution (a distribution more pointed than normal) and negative for a platykurtic distribution (flatter than normal).

S3 is next divided by $S2^{3/2}$, which is $(M2 - M1^2)^3$. The result is stored back into S3. A negative value means the distribution of the values of the data vector are skewed to the right of the mean of the vector, a positive value means a skew to the left of the mean. A normal curve has a skew of $0 \pm$ insignificant variation. Finally, the square root of S2 is obtained and stored back into S2. The square root of the variance, $(M2 - M1^2)$, is the standard deviation.

The RETURN statement follows the calculation of the standard deviation and returns control to the main program at the statement immediately following the CALL DESC2 (argument list).

SOURCE PROGRAM

```
C      PROBLEM 6    ADDITION OF SKEWNESS AND KURTOSIS CALCULATIONS TO
C              DESC SUBROUTINE
C
       DIMENSION DATA(100)
       READ(5,9) NUMBR
       READ(5,19)(DATA(I),I=1,NUMBR)
       CALL DESC2(NUMBR,DATA,XBAR,STD,SKEW,XKURT)
       WRITE(6,29) NUMBR,XBAR,STD,SKEW,XKURT
       STOP
     9 FORMAT(I4)
    19 FORMAT(10F8.0)
    29 FORMAT('1 FOR THE DATA ARRAY CONTAINING ',I4,' MEMBERS:'//
      1'   MEAN=',T20,F8.2/'   STANDARD DEVIATION=',T20,F8.2/
      2'   SKEWNESS=',T20,F8.2/'   KURTOSIS=',T20,F8.2)
       END
```

SUBROUTINE DESC2

```
C      SUBROUTINE DESC2
       SUBROUTINE DESC2(N,X,S1,S2,S3,S4)
       DIMENSION X(100)
       IF(N) 20,20,1
     1 SN=N
       S1=0.0
       S2=0.0
       S3=0.0
       S4=0.0
       DO 10 I=1,N
       S1=S1+X(I)
       S2=S2+X(I)**2
       S3=S3+X(I)**3
    10 S4=S4+X(I)**4
       S1=S1/SN
       S2=S2/SN
       S3=S3/SN
       S4=S4/SN
       S4=S4-(4.0*S1*S3)+(6.0*S2*S1**2)-(3.0*S1**4)
       S3=S3-(3.0*S1*S2)+(2.0*S1**3)
       S2=S2-(S1**2)
       IF(S2) 20,20,15
    15 S4=(S4/S2**2)  - 3.0
       S3= S3/S2**1.5
       S2=SQRT(S2)
       RETURN
    20 WRITE(6,9)
     9 FORMAT(' ***** ERROR IN INPUT DATA *****'/
      1 ' N<=0 OR THE STANDARD DEVIATION <=0'/' CHECK INPUT DATA BEFORE P
      2ROCEEDING FURTHER')
       STOP
       END
```

INPUT DATA

```
CARD COLUMNS:
        1          2          3          4          5          6          7          8
1234567890 1234567890 1234567890 1234567890 1234567890 1234567890 1234567890 1234567890

100
    32.        46.        13.        82.        86.        66.        65.        50.        69.        10.
    48.        27.        45.        30.        57.        54.        25.        39.        49.        68.
    61.        30.        57.        66.        53.        40.        63.        74.        43.        51.
    38.        63.        54.        71.        71.        32.        52.        57.        73.        42.
    64.        58.        37.        14.        46.        33.        66.        48.        50.        73.
```

INPUT DATA (continued)

59.	55.	71.	78.	24.	59.	82.	59.	51.	77.
51.	58.	20.	71.	60.	57.	44.	50.	15.	55.
76.	64.	53.	59.	52.	94.	55.	37.	48.	82.
46.	71.	55.	47.	31.	36.	58.	53.	25.	36.
53.	11.	38.	36.	63.	25.	57.	45.	74.	42.

OUTPUT DATA

FOR THE DATA ARRAY CONTAINING 100 MEMBERS:

```
MEAN=                51.59
STANDARD DEVIATIO    17.68
SKEWNESS=            -0.25
KURTOSIS=            -0.22
```

Program 7. Difference of Means Test

Program 7 makes use of the subroutine DESC2 in calculating the difference between the means of two data vectors. The test statistic, Student's t, is computed according to the formula

$$t = \frac{(\overline{X}_1 - \overline{X}_2) - (\mu_1 - \mu_2)}{\hat{\sigma}(\overline{X}_1 - \overline{X}_2)},$$

where $\sigma(\overline{X}_1 - \overline{X}_2)$ is the estimate of the standard error of the difference between the two sample means. It is assumed that the two samples were drawn from two populations with equal means. Therefore, the second parenthesized term in the formula is dropped in the program. The formula used for computing the estimate of the standard error of the difference between two means is

$$\hat{\sigma}(\overline{X}_1 - \overline{X}_2) = \left(\frac{S_1^2}{N_1 - 1} + \frac{S_2^2}{N_2 - 1} \right)^{1/2},$$

where S_1 and S_2 are the standard deviations, and N_1 and N_2, the number of cases in data vector one and data vector two, respectively.

The first statement of the program sets aside 100 storage locations for the two arrays, X and Y. The first READ inputs the number of values to be read into X. This number is then floated and stored in XN. (Note that the floating is performed implicitly by simply setting XN equal to

NUMX.) The second READ inputs NUMX values of the first data vector and then stores in X(1) through X(NUMX). The next three statements perform the same task for the second data vector. Both arrays are filled according to FORMAT 19, which specifies that the data be input ten values per card (Input Unit 5 is assumed to be a card reader), each value punched in an 8 column field with no places to the right of the decimal point.

Two calls to DESC2 are then executed. The first returns the mean, standard deviation, skewness, and kurtosis of the X array. The second call returns the same information for the Y array. Neither the skewness nor the kurtosis values are used in further computations. They are output in the summary table.

Value T is calculated in a straightforward fashion. The program next computes the degrees of freedom for determining the significance of the t value under the assumption that the standard deviations of the two populations from which the samples were drawn are *not* equal. (It is left to the reader to generalize the calculation of T for the case when the means of the two populations are unequal, and these means are known.)

The formula used in this program for determining the degrees of freedom under the assumption of unequal population variances is given in Yeomans [1] as follows.

$$
\text{Degrees of Freedom} = \frac{\left(\dfrac{S_1^{\,2}}{N_1} + \dfrac{S_2^{\,2}}{N_2}\right)^2}{\dfrac{\left(\dfrac{S_1}{N_1}\right)^2}{N_1 + 1} + \dfrac{\left(\dfrac{S_2}{N_2}\right)^2}{N_2 + 1}} - 2
$$

rounded to the nearest whole number. Under the condition that the variances of the two populations are equal, the degrees of freedom calculation reduces to $N_1 + N_2 - 2$. In such a case, the formula used in this program will provide a value for *DF* that is somewhat less statistically efficient than the reduced equation.

The computation of DF is done in two steps. The first calculation is the complex half of the formula, the second statement subtracts the 2 from the previous result. The rounding to the nearest whole number is performed by the last computational statement in the program: 0.5 is added to the floating-point value stored in DF, and this sum is then fixed (truncated) and stored in IDF.

The WRITE statement outputs the means, standard deviations, skewnesses and kurtoses of the data vectors, the t value, and the value for

[1] Yeomans, K. A., *Applied Statistics for the Social Scientist: Volume Two*, Penguin Books Ltd., Middlesex, England, 1968, p. 105.

degrees of freedom, all under the control of FORMAT 29. Again, Output Unit 6 is assumed to be a line printer. FORMAT 29 makes liberal use of the T-format code, but it is essentially straightforward.

The last executable statement of the program is the STOP.

SOURCE PROGRAM

```
C     PROGRAM 7      A DIFFERENCE CF MEANS TEST
C     WITH A CORRECTION FOR DEGREES OF FREEDOM BASED CN
C     THE ASSUMPTION THAT THE TWO SAMPLE STANDARD DEVIATIONS ARE NOT EQUAL
      DIMENSION X(100),Y(100)
      READ(5,9) NUMX
      XN=NUMX
      READ(5,19)(X(I),I=1,NUMX)
      READ(5,9) NUMY
      YN=NUMY
      READ(5,19)(Y(I),I=1,NUMY)
      CALL DESC2(NUMX,X,XMEAN,XSTD,XSKEW,XKURT)
      CALL DESC2(NUMY,Y,YMEAN,YSTD,YSKEW,YKURT)
      T=(XMEAN-YMEAN)/SQRT((XSTD**2/(XN-1.0))+(YSTD**2/(YN-1.0)))
      DF=( (XSTD**2/XN + YSTD**2/YN)**2) /
     1 ( (XSTD**2/XN)**2/(XN+1.0) + (YSTD**2/YN)**2/(YN+1.0) )
      DF=DF-2.0
      IDF=IFIX(DF+0.5)
      WRITE(6,29) NUMX,NUMY,XMEAN,YMEAN,XSTD,YSTD,XSKEW,YSKEW,
     1 XKURT,YKURT,T,IDF
      STOP
    9 FORMAT(I4)
   19 FORMAT(10F8.0)
   29 FCRMAT('1',T40,'SUMMARY ANALYSIS OF TWO ARRAYS'//T43,'ARRAY 1',
     1 T54,'ARRAY 2'/T21,'NUMBER=',T41,I6,6X,I6/T21,'MEAN=',T41,F8.2,
     2 4X,F8.2/T21,'STANDARD DEVIATION=',T41,F8.2,4X,F8.2/T21,
     3 'SKEWNESS=',T41,F8.2,4X,F8.2/T21,'KURTOSIS=',T41,F8.2,4X,F8.2/
     4 T31,'T=',F8.3,T47,'DEGREES OF FREEDOM=',I5)
      END
```

INPUT DATA

```
CARD COLUMNS:
      1                 2         3         4         5         6         7         8
1234567890123456789012345678901234567890123456789012345678901234567890123456789012345678901234567890

100
      32.     46.     13.     82.     86.     66.     65.     50.     69.     10.
      48.     27.     45.     30.     57.     54.     25.     39.     49.     68.
      61.     30.     57.     66.     53.     40.     63.     74.     43.     51.
      38.     63.     54.     71.     71.     32.     52.     57.     73.     42.
      64.     58.     37.     14.     46.     33.     66.     48.     50.     73.
      59.     55.     71.     78.     24.     59.     82.     59.     51.     77.
      51.     58.     20.     71.     60.     57.     44.     50.     15.     55.
      76.     64.     53.     59.     52.     94.     55.     37.     48.     82.
      46.     71.     55.     47.     31.     36.     58.     53.     25.     36.
      53.     11.     38.     36.     63.     25.     57.     45.     74.     42.
```

INPUT DATA (continued)

```
100
  26.     75.     75.     35.     54.     26.     48.     47.     68.     30.
  20.     64.     81.      8.     71.     37.     25.     23.     37.     38.
  24.     26.     43.     45.     38.     55.     53.     42.     33.     23.
  51.     35.     46.     61.     45.     49.     54.     40.     47.     69.
  56.     56.     59.     47.     71.     55.     35.     27.     24.     58.
  37.     57.     47.     41.     32.     56.     42.     51.     41.     16.
  49.     41.     42.     51.     64.     68.     15.     63.     40.     30.
  50.     59.     15.     44.     53.     19.     35.     33.     42.     59.
  18.     28.     16.     38.     51.     44.     20.     65.     63.     37.
  49.     58.     35.     70.     21.     55.     56.     56.     44.     50.
```

OUTPUT DATA

```
                      SUMMARY ANALYSIS OF TWO ARRAYS

                         ARRAY 1      ARRAY 2
NUMBER=                    100          100
MEAN=                     51.59        44.21
STANDARD DEVIATION=       17.68        15.87
SKEWNESS=                 -0.25        -0.05
KURTOSIS=                 -0.22        -0.60
             T=    3.091     DEGREES OF FREEDOM=   198
```

Program 8.   Simple One-Way Analysis of Variance

Program 8 is a program for the calculation of a simple one-way analysis of variance test on up to 10 groups of data, each group containing up to 100 data values—or observations. Unequal group N's are permitted. (For the theory underlying the computations, see any good social or psychological statistics text.[1]) Essentially, one-way analysis of variance simply performs a difference-of-means test for more than two sample means. The assumption is that all samples (data groups) have been drawn from the same population. Therefore the means and the standard deviations of the samples should be equal within sampling fluctuation. The test statistic used, the F ratio, is computed along with the necessary degrees of freedom to determine if this F is significant (if the sample

---

[1] e.g., Blalock, H. M., *Social Statistics,* McGraw-Hill Book Co., New York, 1960.

e.g., Huntsberger, D. V., *Elements of Statistical Inference,* 2nd Ed., Allyn and Bacon, Inc., Boston, 1972.

e.g., Schoeninger, D. W. and Insko, C. A., *Introductory Statistics for the Behavioral Sciences,* Allyn and Bacon, Inc., Boston, 1971.

means differ by more than would be expected due to chance). A summary table is printed including the F and the degrees of freedom.

Storage is set aside for the data arrays, 10 groups of up to 100 values each, in the matrix DATA (10,100). Ten locations are allocated to each of the variables: SUM, SUMSQ, NUMS and XMEAN. The scalars GSUM, GSSUM, NTOT, and SGRP and the vectors SUM and SUMSQ are set to zero by the DATA statement. Note that NTOT is set to a fixed-point zero, while the rest are set to a floating-point zero. The first READ statement inputs into NGRPS the number of groups (samples) that will be read. A test is performed on NGRPS to insure that it is greater than 1. If it is not, control transfers to statement number 31 where an error message is output and program execution stops. If NGRPS is greater than or equal to 2, control proceeds to statement number 1.

Statement number 1 is the beginning of the DO loop which controls the inputting of the sample data. The loop is executed NGRPS times. The first READ statement inputs NUM, the number of values for the I-th group. This number is stored in NUMS(I), and it is added to NTOT. The last READ in the loop, at statement number 10, inputs the NUM values of the group I into DATA(1,I) through DATA(NUM,I).

At the completion of the first DO loop, the vector NUMS(1) through NUMS(NGRPS) contains the number of values in each data group, and NTOT contains the total number of all observation.

The second DO loop again loops NGRPS times. Upon completion of this loop, GSUM will contain the sum of all observations, GSSUM will contain the sum of the squares of all observations, SUM(1) through SUM(NGRPS) will contain the sum of the observations in group 1 through group NGRPS, respectively.

Next, the total sums of squares, TSS, and the total degrees of freedom, ITDF, are calculated. The third, and last, DO loop in the program also loops NGRPS times. Upon its completion, XMEAN(1) through XMEAN(NGRPS) contain the mean of each group of observations; and SGRP contains the sum of the observations in each group quantity squared and divided by the number in each group. SGRP is used in the computations of the between and within sums of squares.

Following the third loop are the calculations of the various output statistics. WSS is the within-groups sum of squares. BSS is the between-groups sum of squares. IDFB and IDFW are the degrees of freedom associated with the between and within sums of squares, respectively. F is the ratio of the between-groups variance to the within-groups variance.

The first four WRITE statements output a title, the number of each group, (1 through NGRPS), the number in each group, the group means, and the summary information contained in the analysis of variance table.

Note the repetition factor that is used in conjunction with the underline character contained in single quotes (literals) to produce a tabular design. Again, the T-format code is frequently used.

Following the four WRITE's is an IF test on the number of groups. If NGRPS equals 2, then control transfers to statement number 40 where a t value is computed. The t is printed and the program stops. In the case of exactly two groups, the F ratio simply equals t^2.

Should NGRPS be greater than 2, control transfers to statement number 50, the F value is printed, and the program terminates.

SOURCE PROGRAM

```
C       PROGRAM 8    SIMPLE ONE-WAY ANALYSIS OF VARIANCE   UNEQUAL GROUP N'S ALLOWED
        DIMENSION DATA(100,10),SUM(10),SUMSQ(10),NUMS(10),XMEAN(10)
        DATA GSUM,GSSUM,NTOT,SGRP,SUM,SUMSQ/0.0,0.0,0,0.0,10*0.0,10*0.0/
        READ(5,9) NGRPS
        IF(NGRPS-2) 31,1,1
  1     DO 10 I=1,NGRPS
        READ(5,9) NUM
        NUMS(I)=NUM
        NTOT=NTOT+NUM
  10    READ(5,19) (DATA(K,I),K=1,NUM)
        DO 20 I=1,NGRPS
        K=NUMS(I)
        DO 20 J=1,K
        GSUM=GSUM+DATA(J,I)
        GSSUM=GSSUM+DATA(J,I)**2
        SUM(I)=SUM(I)+DATA(J,I)
  20    SUMSQ(I)=SUMSQ(I)+DATA(J,I)**2
        TSS=GSSUM-GSUM**2/FLOAT(NTOT)
        ITDF=NTOT-1
        DO 30 I=1,NGRPS
        XMEAN(I)=SUM(I)/FLOAT(NUMS(I))
  30    SGRP=SGRP+SUM(I)**2/FLOAT(NUMS(I))
        WSS=GSSUM-SGRP
        BSS=SGRP-GSUM**2/FLOAT(NTOT)
        IDFB=NGRPS-1
        IDFW=NTOT-NGRPS
        VEB=BSS/FLOAT(IDFB)
        VEW=WSS/FLOAT(IDFW)
        F=VEB/VEW
        WRITE(6,29) (I,I=1,NGRPS)
        WRITE(6,39) (NUMS(I),I=1,NGRPS)
        WRITE(6,49) (XMEAN(I),I=1,NGRPS)
        WRITE(6,59) BSS,IDFB,VEB,WSS,IDFW,VEW,TSS,ITDF
        IF(NGRPS-2) 31,40,50
  31    WRITE(6,69)
        STOP
  40    T=SQRT(F)
        WRITE(6,79) T
        STOP
  50    WRITE(6,89) F
        STOP
  9     FORMAT(I3)
  19    FORMAT(10F8.0)
  29    FORMAT('1S I M P L E    O N E - W A Y   A N A L Y S I S   O F   V A
       1 R I A N C E'///1X,'GROUP',T10,10(3X,I3,4X))
  39    FORMAT(1X,'NUMBER',T10,10(3X,I3,4X))
  49    FORMAT(1X,'GRP MEAN',T10,10(F8.2,2X))
  59    FORMAT(///T10,'SOURCE',T20,'SUMS OF SQUARES',T37,'DF',
       1 T43,'VARIANCE ESTIMATE'/'+',T10,51('_')//T10,'BETWEEN',T22,F12.1,
       2 T36,I3,T46,F12.1/T10,'WITHIN',T22,F12.1,T36,I3,T46,F12.1/T10,
       3 51('_')//T15,'TOTAL',T21,F13.1,T36,I3)
```

SOURCE PROGRAM (continued)

```
 69 FORMAT(1X,20('*'),1X,' ERROR. NUMBER OF GROUPS LESS THAN 2')
 79 FORMAT(//T30,'VALUE FOR T=',F10.3)
 89 FORMAT(//T30,'VALUE FOR F=',F10.3)
    END
```

INPUT DATA

```
CARD COLUMNS:
          1          2          3          4          5          6          7          8
1234567890123456789012345678901234567890123456789012345678901234567890123456789012345678901234567890

 3
30
   3245.     6542.     6246.     6243.     7654.     7624.     7621.     4536.     0545.     5623.
   0223.     3214.     3210.     6546.     3432.     6432.     3213.     4324.     6516.     6546.
   6227.     2104.     3214.     4624.      632.     6544.     6547.     6204.     6516.     6513.
20
   3241.     3244.     9813.     7321.     7546.     9513.     9721.     4321.     3214.     3214.
   2143.     8432.     6510.     2324.     9523.     0213.     4621.     6210.     -326.     3214.
40
   3216.     6216.     3026.     6515.     6112.     6519.     4321.     4679.     3214.     6543.
   3216.     3205.     6219.     3210.     6465.     6513.     7998.     4321.     6543.     6217.
   6242.     3210.     7654.     3213.     4324.     7657.     6513.     7689.     6210.     4321.
   3216.     7621.     7621.     4321.     5024.     0215.     9210.     2431.     4321.     4321.
```

OUTPUT DATA

```
S I M P L E   O N E - W A Y   A N A L Y S I S   O F   V A R I A N C E


GROUP          1          2          3
NUMBER        30         20         40
GRP MEAN  4955.33    5200.60    5240.05


    SOURCE____SUMS_OF_SQUARES__DF.____VARIANCE_ESTIMATE_

    BETWEEN        1495552.0      2           747776.0
    WITHIN       479665408.0     87          5513395.0
    -------------------------------------------------------

       TOTAL     481160960.0     89


              VALUE FOR F=      0.136
```

Program 9.   Contingency Table Analysis

The contingency table is a frequently used tool for the analysis of bivariate nominal or ordinal relationships. Program 9 is a simple routine for table building. It permits up to 10 values for both the row and the column variable. These values need not be contiguous; e.g., 1,2,4,6 is as permissible as 1,2,3,4. They need not even be ordered; however, since the columns (and rows) will be headed and output according to the order in which the legitimate values are entered on the second input card it is suggested they be in ascending order for clarity. They must be positive integer values, zero is a permissible value. The concern of this program is simply to read in a set of data containing two variables, determine if the values of these two variables are "legitimate", and produce a contingency table. An expansion of this program that includes various statistics is undertaken in Program 10.

Storage is allocated for the table, ITAB(10,10), and for several vectors. IRTOT, ICTOT, NRV and NCV are "data containers." PAD, LABEL and DASH are used to output editing symbols. The use of these variables will be explained later.

The initial values for ITAB, IRTOT, and ICTOT are set to zeros and for PAD, to blanks. LABEL is set equal to the character string ROWbTOTALS, where "b" represents a blank, and DASH is set equal to three underline characters.

The first READ inputs the number of rows, NR, and the number of columns, NC—of which the table will be composed, and NCASE, the total number of cases to be read. NR is the number of permissible row variable values; NC, the number of permissible column values. The second READ inputs the values to be considered legitimate for the row variable into the vector NCV. Note that the first two READ's used the same format statement. The first WRITE outputs a header, along with the value in NCASE.

The first DO loop, iterating from 1 to NCASE, is begun. The third READ inputs a value for the row variable and for the column variable according to FORMAT 19. (This READ could have used FORMAT 9.) The second DO loop, nested within the first, tests the row value just read against the values stored in the vector NRV. If a match is not found, if the value is not "legitimate", control transfers to statement number 100 where an error message is printed and execution stops. If a match is found, control transfers to statement 3 where the third DO loop, also nested within the first, performs a similar check on the column variable value. If it is not "legitimate", control branches to statement 101, an error message is printed, and the program terminates. If it, too, is a legitimate value, a match is found within the vector NCV, control transfers to statement number 4.

At this point, statement number 4, J contains the *position* within the vector of row values, and K, the *position* within the vector of column values, of the two data values read in the third READ. Statement 4, then, increments ITAB(J,K) by 1. The J-th position within IRTOT is incremented by 1, as is the K-th position within ICTOT. The outer loop terminated on the CONTINUE statement, statement number 5. The outer loop is executed NCASE times, or until a data error is encountered.

Upon completion of the outer loop, ITAB contains the proper cell values; IRTOT, the totals for each row in the table; and ICTOT, the totals for each table column. It remains only to output these values. L is set equal to 6 times the number of columns in the table. The first WRITE outputs L blanks followed by the character string stored in LABEL. Since the number of columns may vary from run to run, this dynamic positioning of the character string is required. There is no straightforward way to alter constants in FORMAT statements during program execution.

The next WRITE outputs the permissible column values (vector NCV) according to FORMAT 49. The last WRITE before the final DO loop underlines the column values just written. FORMAT 79 uses the "+" carriage control character so as not to skip to a new line; DASH(1), DASH(2) and DASH(3) are written NC times.

The final DO loop in the program outputs the IKT-th permissible row value, a row from ITAB: ITAB(IKT,1) ... ITAB(IKT,NC), and the IKT-th value of IRTOT, which is the total of the frequencies in the row. Statement number 6, the last statement of the DO, underlines the permissible row value, again through the use of the "+" carriage control character to supress a line skip.

The final WRITE of the program outputs under each column of the table the total frequency for that column, ICTOT(1) ... ICTOT(NC). This WRITE is followed by a STOP.

There are two points within this program that might seem a bit mystifying. The first is the use of the two inner loops to determine the proper position within ITAB(J,K), to increment for each observation. The second is the dynamic spacing of the character string, ROWb TOTALS. Consider the logic carefully for it demonstrates useful programming techniques.

SOURCE PROGRAM

```
C     PROGRAM 9   CONTINGENCY TABLE ANALYSIS
      DIMENSION ITAB(10,10),IRTOT(10),ICTOT(10),NRV(10),NCV(10),
     1 PAD(60),LABEL(10),DASH(3)
      DATA ITAB,IRTOT,ICTOT,PAD,LABEL,DASH/120*0,60*' ','R','O','W',' ',
     1 'T','O','T','A','L','S',3*'_'/
      READ(5,9) NR,NC,NCASE
      READ(5,9) (NRV(I),I=1,NR),(NCV(I),I=1,NC)
      WRITE(6,29) NCASE
      DO 5 I=1,NCASE
      READ(5,19) IROW,ICOL
      DO 1 J=1,NR
      IF(IROW-NRV(J)) 1,2,1
    1 CONTINUE
      GC TO 100
    2 DO 3 K=1,NC
      IF(ICOL-NCV(K)) 3,4,3
    3 CONTINUE
      GO TO 101
    4 ITAB(J,K)=ITAB(J,K)+1
      IRTOT(J)=IRTOT(J)+1
      ICTOT(K)=ICTOT(K)+1
    5 CONTINUE
      L=6*NC
      WRITE(6,39) (PAD(I),I=1,L),LABEL
      WRITE(6,49) (NCV(I),I=1,NC)
      WRITE(6,59) ((DASH(I),I=1,3),J=1,NC)
      DO 6 IKT=1,NR
      WRITE(6,69) NRV(IKT),(ITAB(IKT,I),I=1,NC),IRTOT(IKT)
    6 WRITE(6,79) (DASH(I),I=1,3)
      WRITE(6,89) (ICTOT(I),I=1,NC)
      STOP
  100 WRITE(6,109) IROW,(NRV(I),I=1,NR)
      STOP
  101 WRITE(6,119) ICOL,(NCV(I),I=1,NC)
      STOP
    9 FORMAT(20I4)
   19 FORMAT(2I4)
   29 FORMAT('1',T30,'C O N T I N G E N C Y   T A B L E   A N A L Y S I
     1S'///' FOR',I6,' CASES.')
   39 FORMAT(///T29,70A1)
   49 FORMAT(T27,10(3X,I3))
   59 FCRMAT('+',T27,10(3X,3A1))
   69 FORMAT(//T25,I2,11I6)
   79 FORMAT('+',T24,3A1)
   89 FORMAT(//T8,'COLUMN TOTALS',T27,10I6)
  109 FCRMAT(' ILLEGAL ROW VALUE. VALUE=',I4,' LEGAL VALUES=',10I5)
  119 FORMAT(' ILLEGAL COLUMN VALUE. VALUE=',I4,'  LEGAL VALUES=',10I5)
      END
```

INPUT DATA

```
CARD COLUMNS:
        1         2         3         4         5         6         7         8
1234567890123456789012345678901234567890123456789012345678901234567890123456789012345678901234567890

   3    5  20
   0    1    2    1    2    3    4    6
   0    1
   1    2
   2    3
   0    4
```

INPUT DATA (continued)

```
1    6
2    6
0    6
1    4
2    3
0    2
1    1
2    1
0    1
1    2
2    3
0    2
1    3
2    2
0    6
0    6
```

OUTPUT DATA

C O N T I N G E N C Y   T A B L E   A N A L Y S I S

FOR   20 CASES.

	__1	__2	__3	__4	__6	ROW TOTALS
__0	2	2	0	1	3	8
__1	1	2	1	1	1	6
__2	1	1	3	0	1	6
COLUMN TOTALS	4	5	4	2	5	

Program 10. Contingency Table Analysis and Associated Statistics

A contingency table alone is of little use. Program 10 is an expansion of Program 9, adding the calculation and output of several summary statistics and altering the input logic slightly—which permits execution to continue when illegal (missing) input values for the row and/or column variable are encountered.

The DIMENSION and DATA statements are identical to those in the

previous program. A switch, ISWCH, is set to zero before the first parameter card is read. The first parameter card contains the number of rows,
the number of columns and the number of cases to be read. NCASE is
floated and stored in XN for use in floating-point calculations. The
second parameter card containing the legitimate values for the row and
column variables is read into NRV and NCV, respectively. Note the
shift in jargon: The first two cards contain limits to be used in processing
the input data set; therefore, they are known as parameter cards.

The first WRITE is identical to that in Program 9. The input DO loop,
with the two nested loops which test the legitimacy of the row and
column values, is essentially the same as that of Program 9; with the
exception that whenever a non-legal value for the row or column variable is encountered control is transferred to statement number 1000. At
statement number 1000, XN is decremented by 1.0 and control transfers to statement number 5, the end of the outer loop. When a non-legal
value is found, the program reduces the actual number of cases to be
further processed by 1.0, and reads another case.

The 26 statements following the completion of the outer loop, the
data input loop, are new. The first and second statements test the number
of row and column values. Should either be equal to 1, control passes
directly to the output segment of the program beginning at statement
number 24. The summary statistics are meaningless for a *1-by-N* or an
N-by-1 table. Should both be equal to 2, control transfers to statement 13,
where chi-square is calculated according to the simple formula

$$\chi^2 = N \frac{(ad - bc)^2}{(a + b)(c + d)(a + c)(b + d)}$$

for the 2-by-2 table:

a	b
c	d

where $N = a + b + c + d$. Note that the components making up the de-
nominator in the statement calculating chi-square could have been replaced with the floated values of IRTOT(1) , IRTOT(2) , ICTOT(1) , and
ICTOT(2), respectively.

For a 2-by-2 table, the exact probability of obtaining the previously calculated chi-square *by chance* is given by Fisher's exact text. For the above table

$$P = \frac{(a+b)!\,(c+d)!\,(a+c)!\,(b+d)!}{N!\,a!\,b!\,c!\,d!},$$

P is computed through the use of the FUNCTION subprogram FACTR. FACTR is called and passed two floating-point arguments. It returns the factorial of the *sum* of these two arguments. To obtain the factorial of just one value, the second argument is coded as 0.

The first executable statement of FACTR fixes the sum of the two arguments and stores this sum in N. Z is set equal to 1.0. The DO loop — using I as its index variable — loops from 2 to N, computing the product of Z times the floated value of I, and storing this product back into Z. Upon completion of the "I" loop, FACTR is set equal to Z. The last executable statement of the function is the RETURN. Care is advised in using this function. The maximum factorial computable on an IBM 360 series computer is 56!. Any larger factorial will result in exponent over-flow: a number greater than 16^{63} (approximately 10^{75}).

After the computation of P, control transfers to statement 22.

If NR and NC are not both equal to 2, control transfers to statement 20. The next eight statements, including the two DO loops, compute Chi Square by the standard formula

$$\chi^2 = \sum \frac{(Fe - Fo)^2}{Fe}$$

where Fe is the expected cell frequency and Fo is the observed frequency in that cell. IDF is set equal to NR (the number of rows) minus 1 times NC (the number of columns) minus 1. Control transfers to statement number 22.

At statement number 22, the contingency coefficient, C, is computed. Next Phi is calculated and, preparatory to output, the actual number of cases used in the computation is fixed and stored in NN. Control branches to statement number 24.

Statement number 23 is reached if and only if the number of rows or the number of columns equal 1. If this condition occurs, ISWCH is set to 1 before the output segment of the program is executed.

The output segment begins with statement number 24 where L is set equal to 6 times the number of columns, as in Program 9. The next seven statements are identical to the output statements section of Program 9. They function to output the contingency table along with row and column totals.

The last seven executable statements of Program 10 serve to output the number of cases included in the table and the summary statistics appropriate for the table. First the total number of cases used is printed according to FORMAT 99. Then ISWCH is tested. If it is equal to or less than zero, execution of the output segment continues. If ISWCH is equal to 1, control transfers to statement 33, which is a STOP.

At statement number 31, the product of NC and NR is tested. If NC and NR both equal to 2, then Fisher's exact probability has been calculated and control transfers to statement 35 where the values for chi-square, P, the contingency coefficient, and Phi are printed and the program terminates.

If NC times NR is greater than 4, control transfers to statement number 32 where chi-square, the degrees of freedom associated with it, the contingency coefficient, and Phi are printed. Program execution then terminates at statement number 33.

Two sets of data are used with this example program. The first demonstrates the generation of a 2-by-2 table and its associated output. Both the row and column variables are permitted only the values 1 and 2.

The second data set generates a 3-row-by-4-column table. The permitted values for the row variable are 1, 2 and 3; for the column variable they are 1, 2, 3 and 4.

A worthwhile exercise would be the generalization of Program 10 to include the capability of calculating and outputing cell percentages by row total, column total, and table total. Once the actual cell frequencies have been generated and stored in ITAB, this is a relatively easy task.

SOURCE PROGRAM

```
C     PROGRAM 10  CONTINGENCY TABLE ANALYSIS WITH ASSOCIATED STATISTICS
      DIMENSION ITAB(10,10),IRTOT(10),ICTOT(10),NRV(10),NCV(10),
     1 PAD(60),LABEL(10),DASH(3)
      DATA ITAB,IRTOT,ICTOT,PAD,LABEL,DASH/120*0,60*' ','R','O','W',' ',
     1 'T','O','T','A','L','S',3*'_'/
      ISWCH=0
      READ(5,9) NR,NC,NCASE
      XN=FLOAT(NCASE)
      READ(5,9) (NRV(I),I=1,NR),(NCV(I),I=1,NC)
      WRITE(6,29) NCASE
      DO 5 I=1,NCASE
      READ(5,19) IROW,ICOL
      DO 1 J=1,NR
      IF(IROW-NRV(J)) 1,2,1
    1 CONTINUE
      GO TO 1000
    2 DO 3 K=1,NC
      IF(ICOL-NCV(K)) 3,4,3
    3 CONTINUE
 1000 XN=XN-1.0
      GO TO 5
    4 ITAB(J,K)=ITAB(J,K)+1
      IRTOT(J)=IRTOT(J)+1
```

SOURCE PROGRAM (continued)

```
      ICTOT(K)=ICTOT(K)+1
    5 CONTINUE
      IF(NR-1)  23,23,11
   11 IF(NC-1)  23,23,12
   12 IF(NR*NC-4)  23,13,20
   13 C1=ITAB(1,1)
      C1=FLOAT(ITAB(1,1))
      C2=FLOAT(ITAB(1,2))
      C3=FLOAT(ITAB(2,1))
      C4=FLOAT(ITAB(2,2))
      CHI=(XN*((C1*C4-C2*C3)**2))/ ((C1+C2)*(C3+C4)*(C1+C3)*(C2+C4))
      P=(FACTR(C1,C2)*FACTR(C3,C4)*FACTR(C1,C3)*FACTR(C2,C4)) /
     1(FACTR(XN,0.)*FACTR(C1,0.)*FACTR(C2,0.)*FACTR(C3,0.)*FACTR(C4,0.))
      GO TO 22
   20 SSODE=0.0
      SUMEX=0.0
      DO 21 I=1,NR
      DO 21 J=1,NC
      OBEXP=FLOAT(ICTOT(J)*IRTOT(I))/XN
      SUMEX=SUMEX+OBEXP
   21 SSODE=SSODE+FLOAT(ITAB(I,J)**2)/OBEXP
      CHI=SSODE-SUMEX
      IDF=(NR-1)*(NC-1)
   22 C=SQRT(CHI/(CHI+XN))
      PHI=CHI/XN
      NN=IFIX(XN)
      GO TO 24
   23 ISWCH=1
   24 L=6*NC
      WRITE(6,39) (PAD(I),I=1,L),LABEL
      WRITE(6,49) (NCV(I),I=1,NC)
      WRITE(6,59) ((DASH(I),I=1,3),J=1,NC)
      DO 6 IKT=1,NR
      WRITE(6,69) NRV(IKT),(ITAB(IKT,I),I=1,NC),IRTOT(IKT)
    6 WRITE(6,79) (DASH(I),I=1,3)
      WRITE(6,89) (ICTOT(I),I=1,NC)
      WRITE(6,99) NN
      IF(ISWCH) 31,31,33
   31 IF(NC*NR-4) 32,35,32
   32 WRITE(6,109) CHI,IDF,C,PHI
   33 STOP
   35 WRITE(6,119) CHI,P,C,PHI
      STOP
    9 FORMAT(20I4)
   19 FORMAT(2I4)
   29 FORMAT('1',T30,'C O N T I N G E N C Y    T A B L E    A N A L Y S I
     1S'///' FOR',I6,' CASES.')
   39 FORMAT(///T29,70A1)
   49 FORMAT(T27,10(3X,I3))
   59 FORMAT('+',T27,10(3X,3A1))
   69 FORMAT(//T25,I2,11I6)
   79 FORMAT('+',T24,3A1)
   89 FORMAT(//T8,'COLUMN TOTALS',T27,10I6)
   99 FORMAT(//T30,'TABLE TOTAL=',I6)
  109 FORMAT(/T35,'CHI SQUARE=',T50,F10.2/T30,'DEGREES OF FREEDOM=',T60,
     1 I7/T30,'CONTINGENCY COEFFICIENT=',T60,F10.2/T30,'PHI SQUARED=',
     2 T60,F10.2)
  119 FORMAT(/T35,'CHI SQUARE=',T50,F10.2/T30,'FISHER''S EXACT TEST=',
     1    T60,F10.4/T30,'CONTINGENCY COEFFICIENT=',T60,F10.2/T30,
     2 'PHI SQUARED=',T60,F10.2)
      END
```

FUNCTION FACTR

```
   FUNCTION FACTR(X,Y)
   N=IFIX(X+Y)
   Z=1.0
   DO 10 I=2,N
10 Z=Z*FLOAT(I)
   FACTR=Z
   RETURN
   END
```

INPUT DATA SET ONE

```
CARD COLUMNS:
         1         2         3         4         5         6         7         8
1234567890123456789012345678901234567890123456789012345678901234567890123456789 0

    2    2  50
    1    2   1    2
    1    3
    1    2
    1    0
    2    3
    2    4
    3    2
    2    1
    2    0
    0    4
    1    2
    1    3
    2    3
    3    3
    3    1
    3    2
    3    2
    3    3
    2    2
    2    1
    1    2
    2    2
    1    1
    1    3
    4    2
    2    4
    3    4
    1    4
    1    4
    1    2
    3    2
    2    1
    1    0
    2    1
    2    2
    4    3
    3    4
    3    4
    3    3
    2    2
    1    1
    1    4
    1    2
    1    3
    2    4
    2    1
    2    3
    3    4
    3    4
    2    1
    2    4
```

INPUT DATA SET TWO

```
CARD COLUMNS:
            1         2         3         4         5         6         7         8
1234567890 1234567890 1234567890 1234567890 1234567890 1234567890 1234567890 1234567890

    3    4   50
    1    2    3    1    2    3    4
    1    3
    1    2
    1    0
    2    3
    2    4
    3    2
    2    1
    2    0
    0    4
    1    2
    1    3
    2    3
    3    3
    3    1
    3    2
    3    2
    3    3
    2    2
    2    1
    1    2
    2    2
    1    1
    1    3
    4    2
    2    4
    3    4
    1    4
    1    4
    1    2
    3    2
    2    1
    1    0
    2    1
    2    2
    4    3
    3    4
    3    4
    3    3
    2    2
    1    1
    1    4
    1    2
    1    3
    2    4
    2    1
    2    3
    3    4
    3    4
    2    1
    2    4
```

OUTPUT DATA SET ONE

CONTINGENCY TABLE ANALYSIS

FOR   50 CASES.

ROW TOTALS

	_ _1	_ _2	ROW TOTALS
_ _1	2	5	7
_ _2	6	4	10
COLUMN TOTALS	8	9	

TABLE TOTAL=   17

CHI SQUARE=	1.63
FISHER'S EXACT TEST=	0.1814
CONTINGENCY COEFFICIENT=	0.30
PHI SQUARED=	0.10

OUTPUT DATA SET TWO

CONTINGENCY TABLE ANALYSIS

FOR   50 CASES.

	_ _1	_ _2	_ _3	_ _4	ROW TOTALS
_ _1	2	5	4	3	14
_ _2	6	4	3	4	17
_ _3	1	4	3	5	13
COLUMN TOTALS	9	13	10	12	

TABLE TOTAL=   44

CHI SQUARE=	4.78
DEGREES OF FREEDOM=	6
CONTINGENCY COEFFICIENT=	0.31
PHI SQUARED=	0.11

Program 11. Correlation and Regression

This program calculates and outputs the means and standard deviations for a pair of data vectors of any length, the Pearson Product Moment Correlation Coefficient for the two vectors, the F value for determining the significance of the correlation, the degrees of freedom associated with the F, the shared variation between the two vectors, and, assuming the first vector to be the independent variable, the slope and intercept of the regression equation.

The DATA statement assigns the value zero to SUMX, SUMY, SUMXS, SUMYS and SUMXY. The first READ inputs a parameter card that contains the number of cases to be read. This value is floated and stored in XN. INSRT is set equal to the number of cases minus 2.

The only DO loop in the programs controls the inputting of NUMBR pairs of data points according to FORMAT 19. These values, X and Y, are summed and stored in SUMX and SUMY, respectively. The sum of the crossproduct, X times Y, is stored in SUMXY. The sums of the squares of X and Y are stored in SUMXS and SUMYS, respectively.

When the loop is completed, the means and standard deviations of the X and Y values read are computed. The slope of the regression equation b, is computed by

$$b = \frac{N(\Sigma\ XY) - (\Sigma\ X)(\Sigma\ Y)}{N\ \Sigma\ X^2 - (\Sigma\ X)^2}\ ,$$

and the intercept, a, by

$$a = \frac{(\Sigma\ Y - b\ \Sigma\ X)}{N}.$$

These give the values for the least squares equation

$$y = a + bx.$$

The correlation coefficient is computed according to

$$r = \frac{N\ \Sigma\ XY - (\Sigma\ X)(\Sigma\ Y)}{\{(N\ \Sigma\ X^2 - \{\Sigma\ X\}^2)(N\ \Sigma\ Y^2 - \{\Sigma\ Y\}^2)\}^{1/2}}$$

and the shared variation is simply r^2.

The F ratio is computed according to the formula

$$F = \frac{r^2}{1 - r^2}\ (N - 2).$$

The only WRITE statement of the program outputs the previously computed statistics according to FORMAT 29. This specification makes liberal use of repetition factors on the underline character, and the T-format code in preparing a summary table.

The last executable statement of the program is the STOP.

Note that if the two data vectors are perfectly correlated, an r of ± 1.0, execution errors will occur in the calculation of the F value due to division by zero. A simple expansion of this program to include a test on the value of RSQ before the calculation of F, with a branch around this computation when RSQ = 1.0, will correct this potential problem.

SOURCE PROGRAM

```
      PROGRAM 11 CORRELATICN AND REGRESSION
      DATA SUMX,SUMY,SUMXS,SUMYS,SUMXY/5*0.0/
      READ(5,9) NUMBR
      XN=FLOAT(NUMBR)
      INSRT=NUMBR-2
      DO 10 I=1,NUMBR
      READ(5,19) X,Y
      SUMX=SUMX+X
      SUMY=SUMY+Y
      SUMXY=SUMXY+X*Y
      SUMXS=SUMXS+X**2
   10 SUMYS=SUMYS+Y**2
      XMEAN=SUMX/XN
      YMEAN=SUMY/XN
      STDX=(1.0/XN)*SQRT(XN*SUMXS-SUMX**2)
      STDY=(1.0/XN)*SQRT(XN*SUMYS-SUMY**2)
      B=(XN*SUMXY-SUMX*SUMY)/(XN*SUMXS-SUMX**2)
      A=(SUMY-B*SUMX)/XN
      R=(XN*SUMXY-SUMX*SUMY)/SQRT((XN*SUMXS-SUMX**2)*(XN*SUMYS-SUMY**2))
      RSQ=R**2
      F=(RSQ/(1.0-RSQ))*(XN-2.0)
      WRITE(6,29) NUMBR,XMEAN,YMEAN,STDX,STDY,R,INSRT,F,RSQ,B,A
      STOP
    9 FORMAT(I3)
   19 FORMAT(2F10.2)
   29 FORMAT('1',T20,'C O R R E L A T I O N   A N D   R E G R E S S I O
     1N'///T20,'SAMPLE SIZE=',I4//T30,'INDEPENDENT (X)',T50,'DEPENDENT (
     2Y)'/'+',T30,15('_'),T50,13('_')//T26,'MEAN=',T35,F9.2,T53,F9.2/
     3 T12,'STANDARD DEVIATION=',T35,F9.2,T53,F9.2//T20,'CORRELATION (R)
     4    =',F7.4,4X,'F(1,',I3,')=',F7.2/T15,'SHARED VARIATION (R**2) ='
     5 ,F7.4//T30,'SLOPE (B)=',2X,F9.4/T26,'INTERCEPT (A)=',2X,F9.2)
      END
```

INPUT DATA

```
CARD COLUMNS:
     1          2          3          4          5          6          7          8
1234567890 1234567890 1234567890 1234567890 1234567890 1234567890 1234567890 1234567890

13
     2.13      809.
     2.52      763.
    11.86      612.
     2.55      492.
     2.87      679.
     4.23      635.
     4.62      859.
     5.19      228.
     6.43      897.
     6.70      867.
     1.53      513.
     1.87      335.
    10.38      868.
```

OUTPUT DATA

```
       C O R R E L A T I O N    A N D    R E G R E S S I O N

       SAMPLE SIZE=   13

                       INDEPENDENT (X)      DEPENDENT (Y)

                MEAN=        4.84               658.23
   STANDARD DEVIATION=       3.14               207.55

       CORRELATION (R)    = 0.3015    F(1, 11) =   1.10
  SHARED VARIATION (R**2) = 0.0909

                  SLOPE (B) =    19.9311
              INTERCEPT (A) =     561.83
```

Program 12.   Correlation and Regression with Scatter Plot

Program 12 is an expansion of Program 11 to include a scatter plot of the input data points and a printing of the calculated least squares regression line as given by the equation $Y = A + BX$. The actual plotting is accomplished through the use of a subroutine, PLOT, and a function, ZMAX. Four statements are added to Program 11, the DIMENSION, to reserve space for up to 999 pairs of points (pairs of X and Y values), the two statements needed to save the input values of X and Y: XX(I)=X and

YY(I)=Y, and the call to PLOT. With these exceptions the main program is identical in operation and output to Program 11.

PLOT is passed the vector of X values and the vector of Y values, the computed intercept, A, the computed slope, B, and the total number of observations, NUMBR. The DIMENSION statement reserves space for up to 999 values for X and Y. Ten locations are set aside for VEC, and storage for a matrix, MTRX, with 50 rows and 90 columns is allocated. MTRX will contain the scatter plot and will be printed one row at a time.

Through the use of a DATA statement IPT, ISTAR, IO, and IBLNK are set equal to ".", "*", "0", and "b", respectively. MTRX is also set to blanks. The first and second executable statements call the function ZMAX, passing to it a vector and the length of the vector. ZMAX returns the maximum positive value in the vector. The logic of the function is straightforward. It makes use of a logical IF, however, instead of an arithmetic IF. Note that the code

$$\text{IF(ZM}-\text{Z(I)) 9,9,10}$$
$$\text{9 \quad ZM}=\text{Z(I)}$$
$$\text{10 \quad CONTINUE}$$

is identical in function to

$$\text{IF(ZM.GT.Z(I)) GO TO 10}$$
$$\text{ZM}=\text{Z(I)}$$
$$\text{10 \quad CONTINUE}$$

XUNIT is set equal to 1.05 times XMAX, the maximum value in the X vector, divided by 90, the number of X-axis units in the scatter plot. XUNIT is the width, in units of X, of one column along the X-axis. Similarly YUNIT will be the width, in units of Y, of one row along the Y-axis. Using the 1.05 multiplier assures some blank space along the top and the right side of the plot.

The next segment of the subroutine is a rather complicated DO loop, using I as its index variable and looping N times, once for each case, or pair of data points. Its purpose is to determine the appropriate cell within MTRX associated with a pair of points (X(I),Y(I)) and to place in that cell the proper symbol, a "."(IPT) if the cell contains a blank, or a "*" if the cell already has a ".".

XLEVL is set to zero. The first inner loop using K from 1 to 91 determines the column whose associated value is just greater than X(I). This column is stored in IX. YLEVL is set to zero and a similar operation using J from 1 to 51 finds the appropriate row whose associated value is just greater than Y(I). The row is stored in IY. MTRX(IY,IX) is tested. The appropriate symbol is stored. If MTRX(IY,IX) already contains a "*", no restoring is done. When the "I" loop is exhausted MTRX contains blanks where no data pairs fell, "."'s where one pair fell, and "*"'s where more than one pair fell.

K and YLEVL are next set to zero. The fourth loop in the program, using I from 1 to 90, calculates the appropriate position of the regression line through the use of the constants A and B. The Y value for the I-th column is computed and stored in YV. YV is tested against YLEVL. If YLEVE is less than YV, a new value for YLEVL is computed (the row count is increased by 1 and multiplied by UNIT). The test is performed again. This procedure continues until a value for YLEVL just exceeds YV. At this point, control transfers to statement number 36. K now is the appropriate row for the I-th column of the regression line. In the location MTRX(K,I) the letter "O" is stored. YLEVL and K are reset to zero and the "I" loop continues. Upon completion of the "I" loop, MTRX contains blanks, "."'s, "*"'s, and "O"'s. The "O"'s will replace any "."'s or "*"'s that might have already been stored in the cells through which the regression line passes.

The final segment of the subroutine is involved with outputting MTRX and UNIT and YUNIT. The first WRITE produces a header line and column headers at both sides of the scatter plot. The fifth loop, I from 1 to 50, produces the actual scatter plot one row at a time on Output Unit 6. K is set equal to 51–I. YV for this row is calculated (the 50th row is printed first, of course). A new library subprogram library function, MOD, is employed for the first time. MOD is passed two arguments, a number and a base. It returns the remainder of the division of the number by the base. This remainder is tested by the IF statement. If the particular value of I is exactly divisible by 5, if the remainder is zero, control transfers to statement number 46; otherwise, control branches to statement number 45. At statement number 45, one row of MTRX is printed according to FORMAT 19. Control then is transferred to the end of the loop. At statement number 46 the previously calculated value of YV is printed before and after the row of MTRX, under control of FORMAT 29. Note that it would be more efficient to calculate YV only for rows divisible by 5, and not for every row as is done in this example.

When MTRX has been completely printed, it remains only to print the base axis, the X-axis values for every 10th column, the values for XUNIT and YUNIT, and the legend for the scatter plot symbols. The appropriate X values are computed in the sixth and last DO loop, and stored in VEC. The final WRITE outputs the base of the scatter plot, VEC(1) ... VEC(10), the values for XUNIT and YUNIT, and the legend. Note that VEC is written without an explicit DO loop. This is perfectly permissible, provided the complete array is to be output.

The last executable statement of the subroutine is the RETURN to the main program.

SOURCE PROGRAM

```
C     PROGRAM 12    CORRELATION AND REGRESSION WITH SCATTER PLOT
      DIMENSION XX(999),YY(999)
      DATA SUMX,SUMY,SUMXS,SUMYS,SUMXY/5*0.0/
      READ(5,9) NUMBR
      XN=FLOAT(NUMBR)
      INSRT=NUMBR-2
      DO 10 I=1,NUMBR
      READ(5,19) X,Y
      XX(I)=X
      YY(I)=Y
      SUMX=SUMX+X
      SUMY=SUMY+Y
      SUMXY=SUMXY+X*Y
      SUMXS=SUMXS+X**2
   10 SUMYS=SUMYS+Y**2
      XMEAN=SUMX/XN
      YMEAN=SUMY/XN
      STDX=(1.0/XN)*SQRT(XN*SUMXS-SUMX**2)
      STDY=(1.0/XN)*SQRT(XN*SUMYS-SUMY**2)
      B=(XN*SUMXY-SUMX*SUMY)/(XN*SUMXS-SUMX**2)
      A=(SUMY-B*SUMX)/XN
      R=(XN*SUMXY-SUMX*SUMY)/SQRT((XN*SUMXS-SUMX**2)*(XN*SUMYS-SUMY**2))
      RSQ=R**2
      F=(RSQ/(1.0-RSQ))*(XN-2.0)
      WRITE(6,29) NUMBR,XMEAN,YMEAN,STDX,STDY,R,INSRT,F,RSQ,B,A
      CALL PLOT(XX,YY,A,B,NUMBR)
      STOP
    9 FORMAT(I3)
   19 FORMAT(2F10.2)
   29 FORMAT('1',T20,'C O R R E L A T I O N    A N D    R E G R E S S I O
     1N'///T20,'SAMPLE SIZE=',I4//T30,'INDEPENDENT (X)',T50,'DEPENDENT (
     2Y)'/'+',T30,15('_'),T50,13('_')//T26,'MEAN=',T35,F9.2,T53,F9.2/
     3 T12,'STANDARD DEVIATION=',T35,F9.2,T53,F9.2//T20,'CORRELATION (R)
     4    =',F7.4,4X,'F(1,',I3,') =',F7.2/T15,'SHARED VARIATION (R**2) ='
     5 ,F7.4//T30,'SLOPE (B) =',2X,F9.4/T26,'INTERCEPT (A) =',2X,F9.2)
      END
```

SUBROUTINE PLOT

```
      SUBROUTINE PLOT(X,Y,A,B,N)
      DIMENSION X(999),Y(999),MTRX(50,90),VEC(10)
      DATA IPT,ISTAR,IO,IBLNK,MTRX/'.','*','O',' ',4500*' '/
      XMAX=ZMAX(X,N)
      YMAX=ZMAX(Y,N)
      XUNIT=(1.05*XMAX)/90.0
      YUNIT=(1.05*YMAX)/50.0
      DO 30 I=1,N
      XLEVL=0.0
      DO 10 K=1,91
      XLEVL=XUNIT*FLOAT(K)
      IF(X(I).LE.XLEVL) GO TO 15
   10 CONTINUE
   15 IX=K
      YLEVL=0.0
      DO 20 J=1,51
      YLEVL=YUNIT*FLOAT(J)
      IF(Y(I).LE.YLEVL) GO TO 25
   20 CONTINUE
   25 IY=J
      IF(MTRX(IY,IX).EQ.IPT) MTRX(IY,IX)=ISTAR
      IF(MTRX(IY,IX).EQ.IBLNK) MTRX(IY,IX)=IPT
   30 CONTINUE
      K=0
      YLEVL=0.0
      DO 40 I=1,90
      YV=A+B*(XUNIT*FLOAT(I))
   35 IF(YV.LE.YLEVL) GO TO 36
      K=K+1
```

SUBROUTINE PLOT (continued)

```
      YLEVL=YUNIT*FLOAT(K)
      GO TO 35
36    MTRX(K,I)=IO
      YLEVL=0.0
      K=0
40    CONTINUE
      WRITE(6,9)
      DO 50 I=1,50
      K=51-I
      YV=(50.0-FLOAT(I))*YUNIT
      IF(MOD(I,5)) 45,46,45
45    WRITE(6,19) (MTRX(K,J),J=1,90)
      GO TO 50
46    WRITE(6,29) YV,(MTRX(K,J),J=1,90),YV
50    CONTINUE
      VEC(1)=0.0
      DO 60 I=2,10
60    VEC(I)=FLOAT((I-1)*10)*XUNIT
      WRITE(6,39) VEC,XUNIT,YUNIT,IPT,ISTAR,IO
      RETURN
 9    FORMAT('1',T45,'S C A T T E R   P L O T'///T2,'Y-VALUE',T106,
     1 'Y-VALUE'/'+',T2,7('_'),T106,7('_'))
19    FORMAT(T13,'I',90A1,'I')
29    FORMAT(3X,F8.0,'-I',90A1,'I-',F8.0)
39    FORMAT('+',T13,92('_')/T13,9('I',9X),'I'/T7,10(F8.1,2X)//T20,
     1 'X UNIT=',F7.2/T20,'Y UNIT=',F7.2/T10,'A POINT, (',A1,'), REPRESE
     2NTS ONE DATA VALUE.'/T10,'A STAR, (',A1,'), REPRESENTS MORE THAN O
     3NE DATA VALUE.'/T10,'THE ',A1,' CHARACTERS REPRESENT THE ACTUAL RE
     4GRESSION LINE.')
      END

      FUNCTION ZMAX(Z,N)
      DIMENSION Z(999)
      DATA ZM/-99999.9/
      DO 10 I=1,N
      IF(ZM.GT.Z(I)) GO TO 10
      ZM=Z(I)
10    CONTINUE
      ZMAX=ZM
      RETURN
      END
```

INPUT DATA

```
CARD COLUMNS:
        1         2         3         4         5         6         7         8
1234567890123456789012345678901234567890123456789012345678901234567890123456789 0

13
       2.13      809.
       2.52      763.
      11.86      612.
       2.55      492.
       2.87      679.
       4.23      635.
       4.62      859.
       5.19      228.
       6.43      897.
       6.70      867.
       1.53      513.
       1.87      335.
      10.38      868.
```

Page 1 of OUTPUT DATA

```
      C O R R E L A T I O N     A N D     R E G R E S S I O N


      SAMPLE SIZE=   13

                    INDEPENDENT (X)      DEPENDENT (Y)

              MEAN =          4.84             658.23
 STANDARD DEVIATION=          3.14             207.55

        CORRELATION  (R)     = 0.3015    F(1, 11) =   1.10
  SHARED VARIATION  (R**2)   = 0.0909

                    SLOPE  (B) =    19.9311
                 INTERCEPT (A) =   561.83
```

Page 2 of OUTPUT DATA

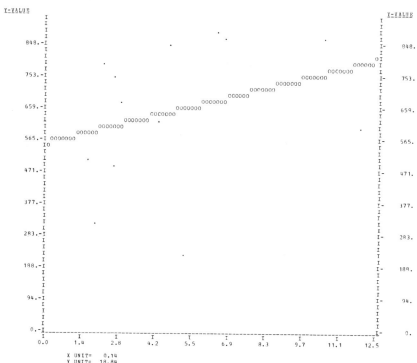

```
                            S C A T T E R   P L O T

Y-VALUE                                                                      Y-VALUE
        I                                                          I
        I                                                          I
        I                                .     .                   I
        I                                                      .   I
 848.-I                          .                                 I-   848.
        I                                                          I
        I                                                        0 I
        I              .                                000000   I
 753.-I              .                            000000 0000000   I-   753.
        I                                      0000000              I
        I                                00000000                   I
        I                           000000                          I
        I               .       0000000                             I
 659.-I                    0000000                                  I-   659.
        I           000000 0000000                                  I
        I      0000000  .                                           I
        I   000000                                              .   I
 565.-I 0000000                                                    I-   565.
        I0                                                          I
        I      .       .                                            I
        I                                                          I
 471.-I                                                            I-   471.
        I                                                          I
        I                                                          I
        I                                                          I
 377.-I                                                            I-   377.
        I                                                          I
        I       .                                                  I
        I                                                          I
 283.-I                                                            I-   283.
        I                                                          I
        I                  .                                       I
        I                                                          I
 188.-I                                                            I-   188.
        I                                                          I
        I                                                          I
        I                                                          I
  94.-I                                                            I-   94.
        I                                                          I
        I                                                          I
        I                                                          I
   0.-I----------------------------------------------------------I-   0.
        I       I       I       I       I       I       I       I       I       I
       0.0     1.4     2.8     4.2     5.5     6.9     8.3     9.7    11.1    12.5

              X UNIT=   0.14
              Y UNIT=  18.84
  A POINT, (.), REPRESENTS ONE DATA VALUE.
  A STAR, (*), REPRESENTS MORE THAN ONE DATA VALUE.
  THE O CHARACTERS REPRESENT THE ACTUAL REGRESSION LINE.
```

Program 13.   Execution Time FORMAT Specification

Most FORTRAN compilers permit the use of FORMAT specifications defined during the execution of a program. This is a relatively simple facility to use, and it greatly increases the flexibility of frequently used programs. To be able to specify the format of one's data set at the time of execution permits one to use a program, stored as a load module, on data sets of quite different form. Not to have to compile and link-edit a program each time it is used frequently provides a substantial savings in computer time.

This facility is used by declaring an array to hold the FORMAT statement. Into this array is input under A specification the complete FORMAT statement—excluding a statement number and the word "FORMAT", but including both the left parenthesis and the right parenthesis. The array's name is used in place of a statement number when reading or writing under the control of this FORMAT statement.

In the example program, two arrays are defined, FMTIN and FMTOT, and both are dimensioned 20. Into FMTIN under the format specification 20A4 is read

$$(2F5.0,10X,8F2.0)$$

into FMTOT also under format specification 20A4 is read

$$(1X,10F10.0)$$

Both FMTIN and FMTOT contain images of FORMAT statements, without statement numbers or the word "FORMAT."

The second READ statement in the example program inputs ten values into the array X using the image stored in FMTIN for its FORMAT specifications. The fourth WRITE statement similarly uses the image stored in FMTOT for its output FORMAT specifications.

SOURCE PROGRAM

```
C      PROGRAM 13    EXECUTION TIME FORMAT SPECIFICATION
       DIMENSION FMTIN(20),FMTOT(20),X(10)
       READ(5,9) (FMTIN(I),I=1,20),(FMTOT(I),I=1,20)
       READ(5,FMTIN)  (X(I),I=1,10)
       WRITE(6,19)  (FMTIN(I),I=1,20)
       WRITE(6,29)  (FMTOT(I),I=1,20)
       WRITE(6,39)
       WRITE(6,FMTOT)  (X(I),I=1,10)
    9  FORMAT(20A4)
   19  FORMAT('  INPUT FORMAT IS ->',20A4)
   29  FORMAT(' OUTPUT FORMAT IS ->',20A4)
   39  FORMAT('   DATA WRITTEN OUT UNDER CONTROL OF THE OUTPUT FORMAT:')
       STOP
       END
```

INPUT DATA

```
CARD COLUMNS:
        1         2         3         4         5         6         7         8
1234567890123456789012345678901234567890123456789012345678901234567890123456789 0

(2F5.0,10X,8F2.0)
(1X,10F10.0)
1234.5678.          1.2.3.4.5.6.7.8.
```

OUTPUT DATA

```
INPUT FORMAT IS -> (2F5.0,10X,8F2.0)
OUTPUT FORMAT IS ->(1X,10F10.0)
  DATA WRITTEN OUT UNDER CONTROL OF THE OUTPUT FORMAT:
    1234.    5678.       1.       2.       3.       4.       5.       6.       7.       8.
```

Program 14.   Coin Tossing

One of the classical problems that is considered in the study of statistics and the application of statistics to social science problems is the repeated tossing of an unbiased coin. The probability of obtaining a head or a tail on any toss of an unbiased coin is exactly one half. However, the tossing of a coin N times will only lead to exactly N/2 heads (or tails) in the limit as N becomes infinitely large. This problem uses a random number generator to simulate the tossing of such an unbiased coin N times.

The program consists of a main program and a subroutine named RANDU. RANDU is explicitly coded in this program, but it is commonly available to users of IBM computers which have the Scientific Subroutine Package implemented on their machines. RANDU uses the power residual method for calculating uniformly distributed random real numbers between 0.0 and 1.0.[1] It requires three parameters. IX is the starting value for the computation of the random number. The first value for IX must be furnished the subroutine and must be an odd integer of no more than nine digits. IY is returned by the subroutine. IY is a random integer that is used as the starting value for the next call to RANDU. X is the random real value. The coding presented for RANDU is specific for use on a 32 bit oriented machine such as the IBM 360 and 370 Series com-

---

[1] *SYSTEM/360 Scientific Subroutine Package, Programmers Manual*, H20–0205. IBM. *Random Number Generation and Testing*, GC20–8011. IBM.

puters. This code will not produce correct results on IBM 1130 Computers. However, any subroutine that returns a uniformly distributed random number will allow this program to function properly.

The main program begins by reading the total number of tests to be run and the starting value for IX. The next 24 statements comprise the major computational loop, using KK as the index variable, looping KKN times. The second READ statement inputs two integer variables. N is the number of calls to RANDU, the number of "coin flips," to be performed for this test; IWRIT is the frequency with which the output statistics will be written.

The first WRITE statement outputs the test number, the number of "coin flips" for this test, the frequency with which output statistics will be written during this test, and the starting value of IX for the first call to RANDU during this test. Four integer accumulators are set to zero. The second loop is begun, using I as the index variable, looping N times (the number of "coin flips").

The subroutine RANDU is called and IX is set equal to the returned value of IY. X, the random real value, is tested against 0.5. If X is less than or equal to 0.5, control passes to statement number 1 where the total number of heads during this test, IHEAD, is incremented by 1; the number of heads in this trial, ITRL, is incremented by 1, and control transfers to statement number 3. If X is greater than 0.5, control passes to statement number 2, where the accumulator of the number of tails, ITAIL, is incremented by 1.

At statement number 3, a test is performed to determine if summary output should be produced at this value of I. If the value of I is perfectly divisible by IWRIT, that is the remainder of I/IWRIT is zero, control passes to statement number 4. Otherwise control transfers to the end of the "I" loop.

At statement number 4, summary statistics are developed. PCT is set equal to the percentage of heads accumulated since this test began. DEV is computed as the deviation of PCT from 50%. DEV1 is the percentage of heads since *the last output* of the summary statistics. DEV2 is the deviation of DEV1 from 50%. The second WRITE statement outputs these statistics. ITRL is set back to zero, and the "I" loop continues.

SOURCE PROGRAM

```
C     PROGRAM 14 COIN TOSSING
      READ(5,9) KKN,IX
      DO 20 KK=1,KKN
      READ(5,39) N,IWRIT
      WRITE(6,19) KK,N,IWRIT,IX
      ITOT=0
      ITAIL=0
      IHEAD=0
      ITRL=0
      DO 10 I=1,N
      CALL RANDU(IX,IY,X)
      IX=IY
      IF(X-0.5) 1,1,2
    1 IHEAD=IHEAD+1
      ITRL=ITRL+1
      GO TO 3
    2 ITAIL=ITAIL+1
    3 IF(MOD(I,IWRIT)) 10,4,10
    4 PCT=(FLOAT(IHEAD)/FLOAT(I))*100.0
      DEV=50.0-PCT
      DEV1=(FLOAT(ITRL)/FLOAT(IWRIT))*100.0
      DEV2=50.0-DEV1
      WRITE(6,29) I,IHEAD,ITAIL,PCT,DEV,DEV1,DEV2
      ITRL=0
   10 CONTINUE
   20 CONTINUE
      STOP
    9 FORMAT(I5,I10)
   19 FORMAT('1TEST NUMBER ',I3/T20,'NUMBER OF TRIALS ',I5/T20,'PRINT ST
     1ATISTICS EVERY ',I5,' TRIALS'/T20,'RANDOM STARTER IS',I10//
     2 T5,'TRIAL',T15,'HEADS',T25,'TAILS',T35,'PERCENT',T45,'PERCENT',
     3 T55,'PERCENT HEADS',T70,'PERCENT DEVIATION'/T35,'HEADS',T45,
     4 'DEVIATION',T57,'THIS SET',T70,'THIS SET OF TRIALS'/T44,
     5'(CUMULATIVE)',T57,'OF TRIALS'/)
   29 FORMAT(T5,I5,T15,I5,T25,I5,T33,F10.2,T43,F10.2,T55,F10.2,T74,F8.4)
   39 FORMAT(2I5)
      END
```

INPUT DATA

```
CARD COLUMNS:
         1         2         3         4         5         6         7         8
12345678901234567890123456789012345678901234567890123456789012345678901234567890

    2     99773
 2000   100
20000  1000
```

Page 1 of OUTPUT DATA

TEST NUMBER   1

```
                NUMBER OF TRIALS  2000
                PRINT STATISTICS EVERY    100 TRIALS
                RANDOM STARTER IS    99773
```

TRIAL	HEADS	TAILS	PERCENT HEADS	PERCENT DEVIATION (CUMULATIVE)	PERCENT HEADS THIS SET OF TRIALS	PERCENT DEVIATION THIS SET OF TRIALS
100	52	48	52.00	-2.00	52.00	-2.0000
200	104	96	52.00	-2.00	52.00	-2.0000
300	159	141	53.00	-3.00	55.00	-5.0000
400	209	191	52.25	-2.25	50.00	0.0
500	254	246	50.80	-0.80	45.00	5.0000
600	296	304	49.33	0.67	42.00	8.0000
700	339	361	48.43	1.57	43.00	7.0000
800	388	412	48.50	1.50	49.00	1.0000
900	437	463	48.56	1.44	49.00	1.0000
1000	483	517	48.30	1.70	46.00	4.0000
1100	528	572	48.00	2.00	45.00	5.0000
1200	578	622	48.17	1.83	50.00	0.0
1300	632	668	48.62	1.38	54.00	-4.0000
1400	692	708	49.43	0.57	60.00	-10.0000
1500	741	759	49.40	0.60	49.00	1.0000
1600	788	812	49.25	0.75	47.00	3.0000
1700	839	861	49.35	0.65	51.00	-1.0000
1800	891	909	49.50	0.50	52.00	-2.0000
1900	937	963	49.32	0.68	46.00	4.0000
2000	988	1012	49.40	0.60	51.00	-1.0000

Page 2 of OUTPUT DATA

TEST NUMBER   2

```
                NUMBER OF TRIALS 20000
                PRINT STATISTICS EVERY   1000 TRIALS
                RANDOM STARTER IS 2024736509
```

TRIAL	HEADS	TAILS	PERCENT HEADS	PERCENT DEVIATION (CUMULATIVE)	PERCENT HEADS THIS SET OF TRIALS	PERCENT DEVIATION THIS SET OF TRIALS
1000	514	486	51.40	-1.40	51.40	-1.4000
2000	1030	970	51.50	-1.50	51.60	-1.6000
3000	1545	1455	51.50	-1.50	51.50	-1.5000
4000	2052	1948	51.30	-1.30	50.70	-0.7000
5000	2530	2470	50.60	-0.60	47.80	2.2000
6000	3025	2975	50.42	-0.42	49.50	0.5000
7000	3496	3504	49.94	0.06	47.10	2.9000
8000	4036	3964	50.45	-0.45	54.00	-4.0000
9000	4546	4454	50.51	-0.51	51.00	-1.0000
10000	5051	4949	50.51	-0.51	50.50	-0.5000
11000	5543	5457	50.39	-0.39	49.20	0.8000
12000	6017	5983	50.14	-0.14	47.40	2.6000
13000	6528	6472	50.22	-0.22	51.10	-1.1000
14000	7010	6990	50.07	-0.07	48.20	1.8000
15000	7506	7494	50.04	-0.04	49.60	0.4000
16000	8003	7997	50.02	-0.02	49.70	0.3000
17000	8536	8464	50.21	-0.21	53.30	-3.3000
18000	9050	8950	50.28	-0.28	51.40	-1.4000
19000	9551	9449	50.27	-0.27	50.10	-0.1000
20000	10046	9954	50.23	-0.23	49.50	0.5000

Program 15. Development of Gaussian Distribution Curve

The Gaussian, or Normal, curve arises repeatedly in statistical mathematics. Its form is

$$y = \frac{1}{\sqrt{2\pi}} e^{-1/2x^2}. \tag{1}$$

A graph of this function is the familiar bell-shaped curve with a mean of zero and standard deviation of one. This problem consists of a program that develops actual examples of Gaussian curves by utilizing a random number generator and the central limit theorem and that plots the results.

The central limit theorem states, in one form, that the average of a set of numbers ϵ_i drawn from a rectangular distribution is normally distributed. That is,

$$x_j = \left[\sum_{i=0}^{i=L} \epsilon_i - \frac{L}{2} \right] \Big/ \sqrt{L/12}, \tag{2}$$

the set of numbers x_j will be normally distributed. This program experimentally develops Gaussian curves utilizing Equation (2).

The program consists of a main program and two subroutines. The main program can handle any number of independent cases, determined by the input parameter KN. For each independent case, the variables N, L, XMEAN, and SIGMA are input. N is the total number of points that are to be used in forming the Gaussian curve. L is the number of random numbers, ϵ_i, to be used to develop each Gaussian point x_i; it corresponds to the L in Equation (2). XMEAN is a real variable that will be used as the mean in developing the Gaussian distribution, and SIGMA will be used as the distribution's standard deviation.

Initial values are set for JPOS, JNEG, BOUND, XMIN, XMAX and XUNIT. JPOS will contain the number of points developed greater than or equal to XMEAN+2.5*SIGMA; JNEG, the number of points less than or equal to XMEAN−2.5*SIGMA. XUNIT is the width of one unit along the X-axis.

The array NX, which will contain the total number of points generated for each unit along the X-axis, is initialized to zero. Next, the N points forming the curve are developed. The major loop, using I as its index variable, loops N times. The inner loop, using J as its index variable, accumulates the sum of L uniformly distributed random numbers by calling RANDU L times. The value of x_j is calculated according to Equation (2) and stored in X. X is then transformed by multiplying by SIGMA and adding this product to XMEAN.

The transformed X is tested against XMIN and XMAX. If it should exceed either bound, the appropriate accumulator is incremented and control passes to statement number 50, the terminator of the outer loop. If the point is within the bounds, control transfers to statement number 44 where the proper interval along the X-axis is computed and 1 is added to this location within the NX array.

Upon completion of the "I" loop, summary statistics including the total number of points generated, the number of calls to RANDU for producing each point, the number of points out of range positively and negatively, and the array of points to be graphed are output.

The NX array is floated and stored in the array Y. The subroutine BRGRF, discussed earlier, is called. The Y array is graphed with 50 units along the perpendicular axis and 100 along the horizontal axis. The major loop in KK is completed, and if another set of input values are expected, the program continues.

The program has been run twice with sets of example data: the first run used an L value of 12 to develop 1000 points; the second run used an L value of 24 to develop 1000 points. The two Gaussian curves generated are shown in the output.

SOURCE PROGRAM

```
C       PROGRAM 15   DEVELOPMENT OF GAUSSIAN DISTRIBUTION CURVE
        DIMENSION NX(100),Y(100)
        DATA SYMBL/'#'/
        READ(5,9) KN,IX
        DO 100 KK=1,KN
        READ(5,19) N,L,XMEAN,SIGMA
        JPOS=0
        JNEG=0
        BOUND=2.5*SIGMA
        XMIN=XMEAN-BOUND
        XMAX=XMEAN+BOUND
        XUNIT=(XMAX-XMIN)/100.0
        DO 10 I=1,100
    10  NX(I)=0
        DO 50 I=1,N
        XSUM=0.0
        DO 40 J=1,L
        CALL RANDU(IX,IY,RAND)
        IX=IY
    40  XSUM=XSUM+RAND
        X=(XSUM-FLOAT(L)/2.0)/SQRT(FLOAT(L)/12.0)
        X=X*SIGMA+XMEAN
        IF(XMIN-X) 42,41,41
    41  JNEG=JNEG+1
        GO TO 50
    42  IF(XMAX-X) 43,43,44
    43  JPOS=JPOS+1
        GO TO 50
    44  J=IFIX((X-XMIN)/XUNIT+0.5)
        NX(J)=NX(J)+1
```

SOURCE PROGRAM (continued)

```
   50 CONTINUE
      WRITE(6,29)  N,L,JPOS,JNEG,NX
      DO 60 I=1,100
   60 Y(I)=NX(I)
      CALL BRGRF(50,100,Y,SYMBL)
  100 CONTINUE
      STOP
    9 FORMAT(2I10)
   19 FORMAT(2I5,2F10.2)
   29 FORMAT('1NUMBER OF POINTS=',I6/' EACH POINT CREATED BY',I3,' CALLS
     1 TO RECTANGULAR RANDOM NUMBER GENERATOR'/' NUMBER OF POINTS EQUAL
     2TO OR GREATER THAN MEAN+2.5*SIGMA =',I6/' NUMBER CF POINTS EQUAL T
     30 OR LESS THAN MEAN-2.5*SIGMA   =',I7//' NUMBER CF POINTS PER SUB
     4INTERVAL, BEGINNING WITH SUBINTERVAL ONE:'/(' ',20I6/))
      END
```

SUBROUTINE BARGRAPH

```
C        BARGRAPH SUBROUTINE
         SUBROUTINE BRGRF(NVY,NVX,FOFX,SYMBL)
         DIMENSION FOFX(100),VEC(100),POINT(102)
         DATA POINT,BLANK/102*'.',' '/
         YMAX=0.0
         DO 10 I=1,NVX
         VEC(I)=BLANK
         IF(FOFX(I)-YMAX) 10,10,5
    5    YMAX=FOFX(I)
   10    CONTINUE
         YUNIT=YMAX/FLOAT(NVY)
         K=NVX+2
         WRITE(6,9)  (POINT(I),I=1,K)
         DO 40 I=1,NVY
         DO 30 J=1,NVX
         IF(FOFX(J)-FLOAT(NVY+1-I)*YUNIT) 30,30,25
   25    VEC(J)=SYMBL
   30    CONTINUE
   40    WRITE(6,19)  POINT(1),(VEC(J),J=1,NVX),POINT(1)
         WRITE(6,19)  (PCINT(I),I=1,K)
         WRITE(6,29)  YUNIT
         RETURN
    9    FORMAT('1',10X,102A1)
   19    FORMAT(11X,102A1)
   29    FORMAT(//'  EACH UNIT ON THE Y-AXIS REPRESENTS ',F15.4)
         END
```

INPUT DATA

```
CARD COLUMNS:
         1         2         3         4         5         6         7         8
1234567890123456789012345678901234567890123456789012345678901234567890123456789 0

           2     5596773
1000      12       0.0          1.0
1000      24       0.0          1.0
```

Page 1 of OUTPUT DATA

```
NUMBER OF POINTS=  1000
EACH POINT CREATED BY 12 CALLS TO RECTANGULAR RANDOM NUMBER GENERATOR
NUMBER OF POINTS EQUAL TO OR GREATER THAN MEAN+2.5*SIGMA =   6
NUMBER OF POINTS EQUAL TO OR LESS THAN MEAN-2.5*SIGMA  =   3

NUMBER OF POINTS PER SUBINTERVAL, BEGINNING WITH SUBINTERVAL ONE:
 2    0    1    1    2    3    4    3    3    1    4    3    2    1    3    2    3    5    3    2    1    1    2    1    4    7    4
 9   12    9    9    6   12    4    6   17   18   16   23   15    8   16   21    9   14   22   15   22   10   12    7   15
20   16    8   15   26   25   16   26   29   12   13   16   22   17   14   17   20    6   26    9   22   22   15   22    5
11   22   17   12   22   11   21   10    7   11   12    9    8    4    9    9    6    3   12   12   12    6    5
10    1    7    3    8    4    1    3    2    3    2    2    5    2    1    1    1    1    1    1    3
```

Page 2 of OUTPUT DATA

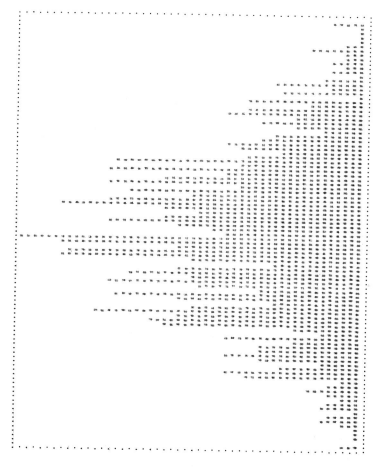

EACH UNIT ON THE Y-AXIS REPRESENTS   0.5600

Page 3 of OUTPUT DATA

```
NUMBER OF POINTS= 1000
EACH POINT CREATED BY 24 CALLS TO RECTANGULAR RANDOM NUMBER GENERATOR
NUMBER OF POINTS EQUAL TO OR GREATER THAN MEAN+2.5*SIGMA =   4
NUMBER OF POINTS EQUAL TO OR LESS THAN MEAN-2.5*SIGMA =   9

NUMBER OF POINTS PER SUBINTERVAL, BEGINNING WITH SUBINTERVAL ONE:
   3    1    3    0    2    1    1    4    5

   7    5   10    8   10   10    4   20    1    8    6   12
  14   21   18   24   16   15   18   22   13   11   21   21   17
  17   13   18   16    9    3   17   13   11   11   14   17
   3    4    5   11    3    1    3    2    4    4    2    4

   2    5    6    3    3    6    5    4    8
  13    8   18    9   14   16   21   13   21
  19   19   20   15   22   22   19   19   10
  14    8   13   18    7    9    9    5    6
   2    4    2    3    2    1    0    0    0
```

Page 4 of OUTPUT DATA

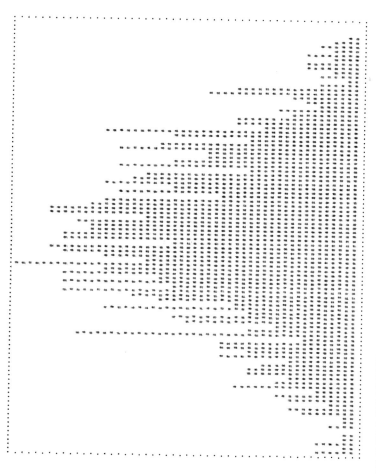

EACH UNIT ON THE Y-AXIS REPRESENTS   0.4800

Program 16.   Truth Table Generator

This program is a simple truth table generator. It introduces the use of logical variables and logical constants. As written it will produce a truth table with up to 10 logical variables.

The vector K is dimensioned 10. The vector L is declared to be logical and it is also dimensioned 10. The order of the truth table, N, is input. The components of K are initialized to the powers of 2 from 2^0 through 2^{N-1}. The components of L are all initialized to the value .TRUE.. NN is set to 2^N, the possible different truth combinations of N variables.

The major DO 20 loop, along with the DO 30 loop, controls the determination and output of the NN possible different truth values for N logical variables. Study statement 20 carefully. The MOD(M,K(I)) subprogram statement function, where M is equal to $J - 1$, controls the oscillation between .TRUE. and .FALSE. as the N logical variables making up the truth table are considered. The MOD, or modulo, function returns the remainder of the division of its first component variable by its second component variable. If for a particular K(I) this value is zero, the logical variable L(I) will have its logical value reversed. Assure yourself that this code will produce efficiently, and without duplication, all possible combinations of truth values for N logical variables.

Statement 20 writes under control of FORMAT 19 the N truth values for L for each of NN loops. FORMAT 19 introduces the use of the L format specification for logical variables. If a logical variable has .TRUE. as its stored value, T will be printed. If its stored value is .FALSE., then an F will be printed.

SOURCE PROGRAM

```
C       PROGRAM 16 TRUTH TABLE GENERATOR
        DIMENSION K(10)
        LOGICAL L(10)
        WRITE(6,29)
        READ(5,9)  N
        DO 10 I=1,N
        K(I)=2**(I-1)
 10     L(I)=.TRUE.
        NN=2**N
        DO 20 J=1,NN
        M=J-1
        DO 30 I=1,N
 30     IF(MOD(M,K(I)).EQ.0)  L(I)=.NOT.L(I)
 20     WRITE(6,19)  (L(I),I=1,N)
        STOP
  9     FORMAT(I5)
 19     FORMAT(' ',20L5)
 29     FORMAT('1')
        END
```

INPUT DATA

CARD COLUMNS:
```
          1         2         3         4         5         6         7         8
1234567890123456789012345678901234567890123456789012345678901234567890123456789 0

     4
```

OUTPUT DATA

```
F     F     F     F
T     F     F     F
F     T     F     F
T     T     F     F
F     F     T     F
T     F     T     F
F     T     T     F
T     T     T     F
F     F     F     T
T     F     F     T
F     T     F     T
T     T     F     T
F     F     T     T
T     F     T     T
F     T     T     T
T     T     T     T
```

Program 17.   Logical Expression Evaluating Program

This program continues the discussion of logical variables introduced in the previous program. It differs somewhat from other programs in this book in that for each run, in addition to data read in from the card reader, one statement in SUBROUTINE LOGIC must be changed.

This program will evaluate any logical expression containing up to 10 logical variables. All combinations of the values for the expression's component logical variables are output along with the appropriate logical value for the expression itself.

The user must prepare a logical statement to be tested. This statement must follow the FORTRAN rules for logical expressions. Each logical operator, AND, OR, or NOT, must be bounded by periods. Levels of parentheses may be as deep as the FORTRAN available to the user permits. All variables used in the expression, in addition to the variable to the left of the equal sign must be declared logical. As written this program requires the user to reference in the logical expression only the variables A through J. This expression must be set equal to the logical variable M. These names may, of course, be changed by appropriate changes to the COMMON, LOGICAL, and SUBROUTINE statements in the subroutine LOGIC. If the user wishes to evaluate a logical statement containing more than 10 variables, he must change the DIMEN–SION, LOGICAL, DATA, and FORMAT statements 19, 29, and 39 in the main program as well as the above noted statements in the subroutine.

The main program inputs one value, N, which is the number of variables in the logical expression to be evaluated. The logical statement containing the logical expression to be evaluated is assumed to have been inserted in SUBROUTINE LOGIC. Output heading information is written to Output Unit 6, assumed to be a line printer, according to FORMATs 29 and 39. A vector K is initialized to powers of 2 as in the previous program, and the logical vector L is initialized to the logical value .TRUE.. NN is set to 2 raised to the N power. NN then is the number of possible values for a logical expression containing N members. The generation of the various truth values for the expression under evaluation is performed by the DO 20 and the DO 30 loops. The DO 30 loop controls the oscillation of truth values for each of the L(I) logical variables making up the logical expression. This code is virtually identical to that used in Program 16.

SUBROUTINE LOGIC is called NN times, each time evaluating a different combination of logical values for the L(N) logical variables. The expression's logical value is returned in MM. The last WRITE statement, statement number 20, outputs the expression's value, and the string of values for its component parts for this call to LOGIC. The last executable statement of the program is the STOP.

SOURCE PROGRAM

```
C       PROGRAM 17    LOGICAL EXPRESSION EVALUATING PROGRAM
        DIMENSION K(10)
        DIMENSION BAR(10)
        LOGICAL L(10),MM
        DATA BAR/10*'66'/
        COMMON L
        READ(5,9) N
        WRITE(6,29) (I,I=1,N)
        WRITE(6,39) (BAR(I),I=1,N)
        DO 10 I=1,N
        K(I)=2**(I-1)
     10 L(I)=.TRUE.
        NN=2**N
        DO 20 J=1,NN
        DO 30 I=1,N
        M=J-1
```

SOURCE PROGRAM (continued)

```
  30 IF(MOD(M,K(I)),EQ,0) L(I)=.NOT.L(I)
     CALL LOGIC(MM)
  20 WRITE(6,19) MM,(L(I),I=1,N)
     STOP
   9 FORMAT(I5)
  19 FORMAT(3X,L5,20X,10L5)
  29 FORMAT('1','THE EXPRESSION',T30,' IF ITS COMPONENTS ARE'/T7,'IS',
    1 T21,'COMPONENT: ',10(I2,3X))
  39 FORMAT('+',7('66'),T21,5('66'),1X,10(A2,3X))
     END
```

SUBROUTINE LOGIC

```
     SUBROUTINE LOGIC(M)
     COMMON A,B,C,D,E,F,G,H,I,J
     LOGICAL A,B,C,D,E,F,G,H,I,J,M
C    ******      INSERT LOGICAL STATEMENT HERE      ******
     M=A.AND.B.AND.(C.OR.D).OR.(.NOT.E)
     RETURN
     END
```

INPUT DATA

```
DATA FOR PROGRAM 17    LOGICAL EXPRESSION EVALUATING PROGRAM
CARD COLUMNS:
          1         2         3         4         5         6         7         8
1234567890123456789012345678901234567890123456789012345678901234567890123456789 0
    5
```

OUTPUT DATA

THE EXPRESSION	IF ITS COMPONENTS ARE				
-----15-------	COMPONENT: _1	_2	_3	_4	_5
T	F	F	F	F	F
T	T	F	F	F	F
T	F	T	F	F	F
T	T	T	F	F	F
T	F	F	T	F	F
T	T	F	T	F	F
T	F	T	T	F	F
T	T	T	T	F	F
T	F	F	F	T	F
T	T	F	F	T	F
T	F	T	F	T	F
T	T	T	F	T	F
T	F	F	T	T	F
T	T	F	T	T	F
T	F	T	T	T	F
T	T	T	T	T	F
F	F	F	F	F	T
F	T	F	F	F	T
F	F	T	F	F	T
F	T	T	F	F	T
F	F	F	T	F	T
F	T	F	T	F	T
F	F	T	T	F	T

OUTPUT DATA (continued)

```
T                    T    T    T    F    T
F                    F    F    F    T    T
F                    T    F    F    T    T
F                    F    T    F    T    T
T                    T    T    F    T    T
F                    F    F    T    T    T
F                    T    F    T    T    T
F                    F    T    T    T    T
T                    T    T    T    T    T
```

Program 18.   Last Move Loses

This program simulates a simple zero-sum, two player game known as Last Move Loses. A complete description of the game can be found in an article by Block.[1] The program acts as two competing players whereby one player plays randomly and the other remembers his mistakes and does not repeat them. The program serves as a very simple illustration of a non-biological learning system.

In this game a number between 1 and 12 is randomly selected as a starting value. (Dice would be used for parlor game play.) The players alternately subtract 1, 2 or 3 from the starting value to obtain a new total. The player who arrives at a total of zero (or a negative number) loses. In a stricter way of defining the game, each player is allowed to subtract up to the number remaining with a maximum subtracting value of 3 imposed. Hence the player who makes the last subtraction (or move) loses.

The program represents the "smart" player (A) through the use of the subroutine PLAYER. The other player (B) is unintelligent—his playing is represented by a random number generator. Totals are printed along with the actual order of each game.

After initiating the random number generator and reading the number of games to be played, we call PLAYER with the first constant in the argument list being zero to indicate that A's memory is to be initialized. The memory matrix (MA) contains four entries for each possible number in the game, 1 through 12. The first three entries are initialized to the values 1, 2 and 3 in order to give possible numbers to be used in the subtraction. The fourth entry is the number of possible guesses and is set to 3 for all values except 1 and 2, where it is respectively 1 and 2.

---

[1] H. D. Block, "Learning in Some Simple Non-Biological Systems", *American Scientist*, 53, 59 (1965).

Control is returned to the main program and loop 10 proceeds over all games. KT is used to count the number of steps in the game. The K array accumulates the actual totals for each step in the game. A random number between 1 and 12 is chosen for K(1). Note that the random number generator, RANDU, is called from a function RAND. RAND is passed IX, the familiar odd, positive integer for RANDU; and it returns as the value for YFL, the rectangularly distributed random number in the range of 0.0 to 1.0 produced by RANDU.

PLAYER is called with its first argument equal to 1, indicating it is to make a move. The other entries in the argument list are the present total, the move to be returned, and the memory matrix. PLAYER uses the fourth entry for the given total to determine how many guesses are possible, and then randomly chooses among the possible ones by returning either the first, second or third entry. If the number of entries, however, has been reduced to zero, A has learned he can be beaten with any move from that point on, and he resigns from the game by returning a zero guess as M. In the main program, M is tested and if it is zero or negative, A has lost. If it is positive, B then makes a random move. This alternating procedure continues until one of the players loses, at which point the totals are updated and the summary of the game is printed.

In the case in which A loses (except on the first move, if he resigns), PLAYER is called again with the initial argument in the call list equal to 2. This indicates to the subroutine that the memory matrix must be altered. KA indicates the move which lead to A's loss. This is the last move if A returned 1 through 3, or the next to the last move if zero was returned. (A's memory is also to be purged of moves that lead to resignation. In this manner the unsuccessful experiences are propagated through the memory matrix). A remembers which entry was used as the variable J. If J is 1, PLAYER shifts entry 2 to 1 and 3 to 2. If J is 2, just 3 is shifted to 2. Finally, whether or not J is 1, 2, or 3, the number of possible guesses, entry 4, is reduced by 1. The student should study how this process removes the unsuccessful guess from future selection.

After all the specified games have been played, the "learned" memory is printed. The test example shows a memory which has come to play the optimum game. A will win every game—his advantage lying in the first move—that starts at 2, 3, 4, 6, 7, 8, 10, 11, or 12; A will resign immediately in every game that starts with 1, 5, or 9. An interesting modification of the program would be that which would permit A to continue playing in games starting with 1, 5, or 9 under the assumption that his opponent will make a mistake (draw a "bad" random number) which would permit A to win.

SOURCE PROGRAM

```
C     PROGRAM 18   LAST MOVE LOSES
      DIMENSION MA(12,4),K(12)
      DATA NA,NB/2*0/
      CCMMON IX
      READ(5,9) IX,N
      X=RAND(IX)
      CALL PLAYER (0,0,0,MA)
      WRITE(6,19) ((MA(II,JJ),II=1,12),JJ=1,4)
      WRITE(6,29) N
      DO 10 I=1,N
      KA=0
      X=RAND(IX)
      KT=1
      K(1)=IFIX(11.0*X+1.5)
    4 CALL PLAYER(1,K(KT),M,MA)
      IF(M)7,7,5
    5 KA=K(KT)
      KT=KT+1
      K(KT)=K(KT-1)-M
      IF(K(KT))22,22,2
    7 IF(KA)17,17,22
   22 CALL PLAYER (2,KA,0,MA)
   17 NB=NB+1
      A=FLOAT(NA)/FLOAT(I)
      B=1.0-A
      WRITE(6,39) I,(K(J),J=1,KT)
      WRITE(6,49) A,B
      GO TO 10
    2 M=IFIX(3.0*RAND(IX)+0.5)
      IF(M)24,24,23
   23 KT=KT+1
      K(KT)=K(KT-1)-M
      IF(K(KT))24,24,4
   24 NA=NA+1
      A=FLOAT(NA)/FLCAT(I)
      B=1.0-A
      WRITE(6,59) I,(K(J),J=1,KT)
      WRITE(6,49) A,B
   10 CONTINUE
      WRITE(6,69) ((MA(II,JJ),II=1,12),JJ=1,4)
      STOP
    9 FCRMAT(I6,I4)
   19 FORMAT('1INITIAL CHOICE MATRIX:'/4(10X,12I5/))
   29 FORMAT('1FOR ',I4,' GAMES',T92,'CUMULATIVE VICTORY PERCENTAGE'/
      1 '+',13('_')/' GAME WINNER   STARTING VALUE',6('    A    B'),T99,
      2 'FOR A',T109,'FOR B'/'+____ _____',T16,14('_'),12(4X,'_'),T99,
      3 5('_'),T109,5('_'))
   39 FORMAT(1X,I3,T10,' B',T23,I3,T30,11I5)
   49 FORMAT('+',T94,2F10.5)
   59 FORMAT(1X,I3,T10,'A',T23,I3,T3C,11I5)
   69 FORMAT('1FINAL CHOICE MATRIX:'/4(10X,12I5/))
      END
```

SUBROUTINE PLAYER

```
      SUBROUTINE PLAYER (IX,N,K,M)
      DIMENSION M(12,4)
      COMMON IIX
      IF(IX-1) 1,2,15
    1 DC 10 I=1,12
      DO 20 J=1,3
   20 M(I,J)=J
   10 M(I,4)=3
      M(1,4)=1
      M(2,4)=2
```

SUBROUTINE PLAYER (continued)

```
      RETURN
    2 IF (M (N,4)) 3,3,4
    3 K=C
      RETURN
    4 IF (M (N,4)-1) 6,6,7
    6 J=1
      GO TO 5
    7 X=RAND(IIX)
      IF (M (N,4)-2) 8,8,11
    8 IF (X-0.5) 6,6,12
   12 J=2
      GO TO 5
   11 IF (X-0.3334) 6,13,13
   13 IF (X-0.6667) 12,12,14
   14 J=3
    5 K=M (N,J)
      RETURN
   15 GO TO (16,17,18),J
   16 M (N,1) =M (N,2)
   17 M (N,2) =M (N,3)
   18 M (N,4) =M (N,4) -1
      RETURN
      END
```

FUNCTION *RAND*

```
      FUNCTION RAND(IX)
      CALL RANDU(IX,IY,YFL)
      RAND=YFL
      IX=IY
      RETURN
      END
```

SUBROUTINE RANDU

```
      SUBROUTINE RANDU(IX,IY,YFL)
      IY=IX*65539
      IF(IY) 5,6,6
    5 IY=IY + 2147483647 + 1
    6 YFL=FLOAT(IY)
      YFL=YFL * 0.4656613E-9
      RETURN
      END
```

INPUT DATA

```
CARD COLUMNS:
         1         2         3         4         5         6         7         8
 1234567890123456789012345678901234567890123456789012345678901234567890123456789 0

123457 100
```

Page 1 of OUTPUT DATA

```
INITIAL CHOICE MATRIX:
          1    1    1    1    1    1    1    1    1    1    1    1
          2    2    2    2    2    2    2    2    2    2    2    2
          3    3    3    3    3    3    3    3    3    3    3    3
          1    2    3    3    3    3    3    3    3    3    3    3
```

Page 2 of OUTPUT DATA

FOR 100 GAMES

GAME	WINNER	STARTING_VALUE	A	B	CUMULATIVE VICTORY PERCENTAGE FOR_A	FOR_B
1		8	5	2	0.0	1.00000
2	B	3	2	1	0.0	1.00000
3	A	8	5	2	0.33333	0.66667
4	A	10	8	0	0.50000	0.50000
5	A	2	1	4	0.60000	0.40000
6		6	5	7	0.66667	0.33333
7	B	11	8	1	0.71429	0.28571
8	A	5	4	4	0.62500	0.37500
9	A	6	3	0	0.66667	0.33333
10	A	8	6	4	0.70000	0.30000
11	A	4	1	0	0.72727	0.27273
12	A	6	5	9	0.75000	0.25000
13	A	2	1	6	0.76923	0.23077
14	A	11	10	1	0.78571	0.21429
15	A	10	9	2	0.80000	0.20000
16	A	3	2	6	0.81250	0.18750
17	A	4	1	4	0.82353	0.17647
18	A	9	7	3	0.83333	0.16667
19	A	10	9	1	0.84211	0.15789
20	B	7	6	5	0.80000	0.20000
21	A	6	5	0	0.80952	0.19048
22	B	5	2	4	0.77273	0.22727
23	A	9	6	0	0.78261	0.21739
24	A	4	2	0	0.79167	0.20833
25	A	12	11	6	0.80000	0.20000
26	A	8	6	3	0.80769	0.19231
27	A	2	1	9	0.81481	0.18519
28	A	10	7	4	0.82143	0.17857
29	A	9	6	2	0.82759	0.17241
30	A	11	8		0.83333	0.16667
31	A	12	11	9	0.83871	0.16129
32	A	3	1	4	0.84375	0.15625
33	B	7	6	2	0.81818	0.18182
34	A	2	1		0.82353	0.17647
35	A	10	9		0.82857	0.17143
36	A	6	4		0.83333	0.16667
37	A				0.83784	0.16216

0.84211	0.15789
0.82051	0.17949
0.82500	0.17500
0.82927	0.17073
0.80952	0.19048
0.81395	0.18605
0.79545	0.20455
0.80000	0.20000
0.78261	0.21739
0.78723	0.21277
0.77083	0.22917
0.75510	0.24490
0.76000	0.24000
0.76471	0.23529
0.76923	0.23077
0.75472	0.24528
0.75926	0.24074
0.76364	0.23636
0.76786	0.23214
0.77193	0.22807
0.77586	0.22414
0.77966	0.22034
0.78333	0.21667
0.78689	0.21311

0.79032	0.20968
0.77778	0.22222
0.78125	0.21875
0.76923	0.23077
0.75758	0.24242
0.76119	0.23881
0.76471	0.23529
0.76812	0.23188
0.75714	0.24286

Page 2 of OUTPUT DATA (continued)

#	Player								
38	A	5	3	2	1				
39	B	5	3	1					
40	A	7	5						
41	A	3	2	−1					
42	B	5							
43	A	4	1	0					
44	B	9	8	5					
45	A	12	11	10	6	3	2	1	−2
46	B	9	6	4	1				
47	A	7	5	3					
48	B	9	6	5	1				
49	B	9	7	6					
50	A	2	1	−1					
51	A	12	9	8	3	2	1	0	
52	A	3	1	0					
53	B	9	7	5					
54	A	11	9	6	5	2	1	0	
55	A	4	1	−2					
56	A	10	7						
57	A	8	6						
58	A	4	1	0					
59	A	8	5						
60	A	3	2						
61	A	12	9	7	4	2	0		

Page 3 of OUTPUT DATA (continued)

#	Player							
62	A	12	10					
63	B	5						
64	A	7	6	4	1			
65	B	9						
66	B	5						
67	A	11	8	7	6	3	2	1
68	A	8	5	2	1	0		
69	A	7	6	4	−1			
70	B	10	9	6	5	3	2	

Page 3 of OUTPUT DATA (continued)

Row								
71		7	4		1			0.74648	0.25352
72	B	4	1				-1	0.75000	0.25000
73	A	2	1		-1		-2	0.75342	0.24658
74	A	3	1	0	6			0.75676	0.24324
75	A	8	7	6			0	0.76000	0.24000
76	A	12	9	6				0.76316	0.23684
77	A	3	1	0	3			0.76623	0.23377
78	A	8	6	5	2	1		0.76923	0.23077
79	A	6	5	9	7			0.77215	0.22785
80	A	10	9		-1	1	-1	0.77500	0.22500
81	A	3	1		-1			0.77778	0.22222
82	A	2	5	4	4			0.78049	0.21951
83	A	7	1	0	0			0.78313	0.21687
84	A	2		6	6	1		0.78571	0.21429
85	B	9	8	8	3			0.77647	0.22353
86		11	6	11	3	-1	-1	0.77907	0.22093
87	A	5	9	9	7			0.77011	0.22989
88	A	7	6	1	5	1		0.77273	0.22727
89	A	12	1	6	-1			0.77528	0.22472
90	B	11						0.77778	0.22222
91	B	7	5	1	5	1		0.76923	0.23077
92	A	3		2	-1	1		0.76087	0.23913
93	B	5	6	-2	2			0.76344	0.23656
94	A	6	4		1		-2	0.75532	0.24468
95	B	4	5	11	10	8		0.75789	0.24211
96	A	5	12	1				0.76042	0.23958
97	B	2	5	1				0.75258	0.24742
98	A							0.75510	0.24490
99	B							0.74747	0.25253
100	A							0.75000	0.25000

Page 4 of OUTPUT DATA

FINAL CHOICE MATRIX:

2	1	3	1
3	3	3	1
	3	3	0

Program 19.   The Draft Problem

A probability problem of some interest in circles other than academic is the random selection of men to be drafted into the Armed Services. If we ignore any consideration for selection other than date of birth, this program demonstrates that a single random selection of birth dates will very likely result in overrepresentation and underrepresentation of identifiable subpopulations, unless all identifiable subpopulations have exactly the same distributions of birth dates. While it is true that an infinite number of random samples will result in no bias in selection, any single sample of birth dates will not necessarily produce equal proportions of subpopulations in filling a quota.

To simplify the problem, one hundred birth dates for four subpopulations are assumed. The array P(I,J) will initially contain the frequency of each subpopulation J born on day I. S is the grand total of the subpopulations, T(J), the total population for each J subpopulation. The first READ statement inputs the number of "drafts" to be run, N; the total number to be "drafted", QUOTA; and a starter value, IX, for the random number generator, SUBROUTINE RANDU.

N and QUOTA are output according to FORMAT 19. The second READ inputs the frequency born on each day for the four subpopulations—all 100 values for subpopulation one are read first followed by the 100 values for subpopulation two, etc. according to FORMAT 29.

The first two nested DO loops accumulate the total population for each subpopulation, T(J), and the grand total population, S. The next DO loop computes the percentage of the grand total population comprised by each subpopulation and stores these results in the array F. The major DO loop, ending with statement number 80, is then initiated. This loop, using K as its index variable, will be performed N times. The array M is set equal to 1 through 100. NN is set to 100, Q to 0.0, and the array R is set to 0.0. NN is then floated and the result is stored in XN.

RANDU is called, returning a random real number between 0.0 and 1.0 in YFL. YFL is multiplied by XN, the product rounded to the nearest integer, and this value is stored in L. If L is less than or equal to 0, it is set equal to XN. L is now the first birth date to be chosen.

The next DO loop accumulates the number drafted from each subpopulation (on birth date L) in R(J), and the total number drafted is stored in Q. The array value M(L) is used as the first subscript of P. As a birth date, L, is selected, it is no longer available for later selection. Consequently, the next four statements take the last available birth date in the array M, switch M(L) with this value, and reduce the available members of the array, M, by 1.

The total chosen so far, Q, is tested against the total to be "drafted", stored in QUOTA. If QUOTA has not been equaled or exceeded, control transfers to statement number 1, and another birth date is selected. As soon as QUOTA is reached or exceeded, control passes to statement number 4.

The DO loop at statement number 4 computes R(J)/Q, the percentage of each subpopulation chosen, and G(J)/F(J), the relative percentage chosen from each subpopulation. The last statement of the major DO loop outputs Q, J, T(J), F(J), R(J), G(J), and RF(J).

Upon completion of the major DO loop, the percentage distribution of birth dates for each subpopulation is computed and these percentages are output according to FORMAT 59. The last executable statement of the program is the STOP.

SOURCE PROGRAM

```
C       PROGRAM 19   THE DRAFT PROBLEM
        DIMENSION P(100,4),T(4),F(4),R(4),G(4),RF(4),M(100)
        DATA S,T/5*0.0/
        READ(5,9) N,QUOTA,IX
        WRITE(6,19) N,QUOTA
        READ(5,29) ((P(I,J),I=1,100),J=1,4)
        DO 20 J=1,4
        DO 10 I=1,100
10      T(J)=T(J)+P(I,J)
20      S=S+T(J)
        DO 30 J=1,4
30      F(J)=T(J)/S
        DO 80 K=1,N
        DO 40 L=1,100
40      M(L)=L
        NN=100
        Q=0.0
        DO 50 J=1,4
50      R(J)=0.0
1       XN=FLOAT(NN)
        CALL RANDU(IX,IY,YFL)
        IX=IY
        YFL=YFL*XN
        L=IFIX(YFL+0.5)
        IF(L) 2,2,3
2       L=IFIX(XN)
3       DO 60 J=1,4
        R(J)=R(J)+P(M(L),J)
60      Q=Q+P(M(L),J)
        KK=M(L)
        M(L)=M(NN)
        M(NN)=KK
        NN=NN-1
        IF(Q-QUOTA) 1,4,4
4       DO 70 J=1,4
        G(J)=R(J)/Q
70      RF(J)=G(J)/F(J)
80      WRITE(6,39) Q,(J,T(J),F(J),R(J),G(J),RF(J),J=1,4)
        DO 90 I=1,100
        DO 90 J=1,4
```

SOURCE PROGRAM (continued)

```
90 P(I,J)=(P(I,J)/T(J))*100.0
   WRITE(6,49) (J,J=1,4)
   WRITE(6,59) (I,(P(I,J),J=1,4),I=1,100)
   STOP
 9 FORMAT(I5,F10.0,I10)
19 FORMAT('1 NUMBER OF RUNS=',I4/T40,'QUOTE NEEDED=',F10.0)
29 FORMAT(10F8.0)
39 FORMAT('0TOTAL THAT WILL BE DRAWN IN THIS DRAWING:',F10.0//
  1 T2,'CLASS',T10,'POPULATION',T25,'% OF TOTAL',T40,'NUMBER',
  2 T55,'% OF QUOTA',T70,'PERCENT CLASS'/T25,'POPULATION',T44,
  3 'DRAWN',T53,'IN THIS CLASS',T69,'REPRESENTATION',//
  4 (T2,I3,T10,F10.0,T25,F10.4,T40,F8.0,T55,F10.4,T70,F10.4/))
49 FORMAT('1DISTRIBUTION OF % BIRTH FREQUENCY BY CLASS FOR 100 BIRTHD
  1AYS'/T2,'DAY',T10,4(I5,3X))
59 FORMAT(I4,T8,4F8.2)
   END
```

INPUT DATA

```
CARD COLUMNS:
        1         2         3         4         5         6         7         8
12345678901234567890123456789012345678901234567890123456789012345678901234567890
    2      500.    9876543
       1.       2.       3.       4.       5.       6.       7.       8.       9.      10.
       1.       2.       3.       4.       5.       6.       7.       8.       9.      10.
       1.       2.       3.       4.       5.       6.       7.       8.       9.      10.
       1.       2.       3.       4.       5.       6.       7.       8.       9.      10.
       1.       2.       3.       4.       5.       6.       7.       8.       9.      10.
       1.       2.       3.       4.       5.       6.       7.       8.       9.      10.
       1.       2.       3.       4.       5.       6.       7.       8.       9.      10.
       1.       2.       3.       4.       5.       6.       7.       8.       9.      10.
       1.       2.       3.       4.       5.       6.       7.       8.       9.      10.
       5.       5.       5.       5.       5.       5.       5.       5.       5.       5.
       5.       5.       5.       5.       5.       5.       5.       5.       5.       5.
       5.       5.       5.       5.       5.       5.       5.       5.       5.       5.
       5.       5.       5.       5.       5.       5.       5.       5.       5.       5.
       5.       5.       5.       5.       5.       5.       5.       5.       5.       5.
       5.       5.       5.       5.       5.       5.       5.       5.       5.       5.
       5.       5.       5.       5.       5.       5.       5.       5.       5.       5.
       5.       5.       5.       5.       5.       5.       5.       5.       5.       5.
       5.       5.       5.       5.       5.       5.       5.       5.       5.       5.
      10.       9.       8.       7.       6.       5.       4.       3.       2.       1.
      10.       9.       8.       7.       6.       5.       4.       3.       2.       1.
      10.       9.       8.       7.       6.       5.       4.       3.       2.       1.
      10.       9.       8.       7.       6.       5.       4.       3.       2.       1.
      10.       9.       8.       7.       6.       5.       4.       3.       2.       1.
      10.       9.       8.       7.       6.       5.       4.       3.       2.       1.
      10.       9.       8.       7.       6.       5.       4.       3.       2.       1.
      10.       9.       8.       7.       6.       5.       4.       3.       2.       1.
      10.       9.       8.       7.       6.       5.       4.       3.       2.       1.
       2.       5.       2.       5.       2.       5.       2.       5.       2.       5.
       2.       5.       2.       5.       2.       5.       2.       5.       2.       5.
       2.       5.       2.       5.       2.       5.       2.       5.       2.       5.
       2.       5.       2.       5.       2.       5.       2.       5.       2.       5.
       2.       5.       2.       5.       2.       5.       2.       5.       2.       5.
       2.       5.       2.       5.       2.       5.       2.       5.       2.       5.
       2.       5.       2.       5.       2.       5.       2.       5.       2.       5.
       2.       5.       2.       5.       2.       5.       2.       5.       2.       5.
       2.       5.       2.       5.       2.       5.       2.       5.       2.       5.
```

Page 1 of OUTPUT DATA

```
NUMBER OF RUNS=   2
                                     QUOTE NEEDED=      500.

TOTAL THAT WILL BE DRAWN IN THIS DRAWING:      513.
```

CLASS	POPULATION	% OF TOTAL POPULATION	NUMBER DRAWN	% OF QUOTA IN THIS CLASS	PERCENT CLASS REPRESENTATION
1	550.	0.2821	120.	0.2339	0.8293
2	500.	0.2564	135.	0.2632	1.0263
3	550.	0.2821	177.	0.3450	1.2233
4	350.	0.1795	81.	0.1579	0.8797

```
TOTAL THAT WILL BE DRAWN IN THIS DRAWING:      510.
```

CLASS	POPULATION	% OF TOTAL POPULATION	NUMBER DRAWN	% OF QUOTA IN THIS CLASS	PERCENT CLASS REPRESENTATION
1	550.	0.2821	146.	0.2863	1.0150
2	500.	0.2564	130.	0.2549	0.9941
3	550.	0.2821	140.	0.2745	0.9733
4	350.	0.1795	94.	0.1843	1.0269

Page 2 of OUTPUT DATA

```
DISTRIBUTION OF % BIRTH FREQUENCY BY CLASS FOR 100 BIRTHDAYS
DAY        1         2         3         4
  1       0.18      1.00      1.82      0.57
  2       0.36      1.00      1.64      1.43
  3       0.55      1.00      1.45      0.57
  4       0.73      1.00      1.27      1.43
  5       0.91      1.00      1.09      0.57
  6       1.09      1.00      0.91      1.43
  7       1.27      1.00      0.73      0.57
  8       1.45      1.00      0.55      1.43
  9       1.64      1.00      0.36      0.57
 10       1.82      1.00      0.18      1.43
 11       0.18      1.00      1.82      0.57
 12       0.36      1.00      1.64      1.43
 13       0.55      1.00      1.45      0.57
 14       0.73      1.00      1.27      1.43
 15       0.91      1.00      1.09      0.57
 16       1.09      1.00      0.91      1.43
 17       1.27      1.00      0.73      0.57
 18       1.45      1.00      0.55      1.43
 19       1.64      1.00      0.36      0.57
 20       1.82      1.00      0.18      1.43
 21       0.18      1.00      1.82      0.57
 22       0.36      1.00      1.64      1.43
 23       0.55      1.00      1.45      0.57
 24       0.73      1.00      1.27      1.43
 25       0.91      1.00      1.09      0.57
 26       1.09      1.00      0.91      1.43
 27       1.27      1.00      0.73      0.57
 28       1.45      1.00      0.55      1.43
 29       1.64      1.00      0.36      0.57
```

30	1.82	1.00	0.18	1.43
31	0.18	1.00	1.82	0.57
32	0.36	1.00	1.64	1.43
33	0.55	1.00	1.45	0.57
34	0.73	1.00	1.27	1.43
35	0.91	1.00	1.09	0.57
36	1.09	1.00	0.91	1.43
37	1.27	1.00	0.73	0.57
38	1.45	1.00	0.55	1.43
39	1.64	1.00	0.36	0.57
40	1.82	1.00	0.18	1.43
41	0.18	1.00	1.82	0.57
42	0.36	1.00	1.64	1.43
43	0.55	1.00	1.45	0.57
44	0.73	1.00	1.27	1.43
45	0.91	1.00	1.09	0.57
46	1.09	1.00	0.91	1.43
47	1.27	1.00	0.73	0.57
48	1.45	1.00	0.55	1.43
49	1.64	1.00	0.36	0.57
50	1.82	1.00	0.18	1.43
51	0.18	1.00	1.82	0.57
52	0.36	1.00	1.64	1.43
53	0.55	1.00	1.45	0.57
54	0.73	1.00	1.27	1.43
55	0.91	1.00	1.09	0.57
56	1.09	1.00	0.91	1.43
57	1.27	1.00	0.73	0.57
58	1.45	1.00	0.55	1.43
59	1.64	1.00	0.36	0.57
60	1.82	1.00	0.18	1.43
61	0.18	1.00	1.82	0.57

Page 3 of OUTPUT DATA

62	0.36	1.00	1.64	1.43
63	0.55	1.00	1.45	0.57
64	0.73	1.00	1.27	1.43
65	0.91	1.00	1.09	0.57
66	1.09	1.00	0.91	1.43
67	1.27	1.00	0.73	0.57
68	1.45	1.00	0.55	1.43
69	1.64	1.00	0.36	0.57
70	1.82	1.00	0.18	1.43
71	0.18	1.00	1.82	0.57
72	0.36	1.00	1.64	1.43
73	0.55	1.00	1.45	0.57
74	0.73	1.00	1.27	1.43
75	0.91	1.00	1.09	0.57
76	1.09	1.00	0.91	1.43
77	1.27	1.00	0.73	0.57
78	1.45	1.00	0.55	1.43
79	1.64	1.00	0.36	0.57
80	1.82	1.00	0.18	1.43
81	0.18	1.00	1.82	0.57
82	0.36	1.00	1.64	1.43
83	0.55	1.00	1.45	0.57
84	0.73	1.00	1.27	1.43
85	0.91	1.00	1.09	0.57
86	1.09	1.00	0.91	1.43
87	1.27	1.00	0.73	0.57
88	1.45	1.00	0.55	1.43
89	1.64	1.00	0.36	0.57
90	1.82	1.00	0.18	1.43
91	0.18	1.00	1.82	0.57
92	0.36	1.00	1.64	1.43
93	0.55	1.00	1.45	0.57
94	0.73	1.00	1.27	1.43
95	0.91	1.00	1.09	0.57

Page 3 of OUTPUT DATA (continued)

96	1.09	1.00	0.91	1.43
97	1.27	1.00	0.73	0.57
98	1.45	1.00	0.55	1.43
99	1.64	1.00	0.36	0.57
100	1.82	1.00	0.18	1.43

Program 20.　Redistricting *

This is a simple redistricting program for allocating subunits (counties) of a population (state) into districts solely on the basis of population. A population matrix is input, with a population value for each subunit, and each subunit is assigned to a district starting from the most widely separated peripheral locations and working inward on the population matrix. No guarantee is made that boundaries of districts will not overlap. Indeed, in examples with a large number of districts, this will almost always be the case. This program vastly oversimplifies the difficulties of redistricting, and it should be studied with that understanding.

The state to be "districted" is laid out as a rectangular array of subunits (counties). Each cell in the array is assigned a population value. Although a rectangular representation will fit many states, there are several whose shape simply does not come close to it. A zero population value should be assigned to those array locations which do not represent a county. The population distribution, then, will be represented by an NX by NY matrix. ND is the number of districts the counties are to be divided among.

LP and LH are both matrices initially containing the populations of the counties. The DO 110 and DO 120 loops input the population matrix,

---

* There exists a considerable and growing (especially following a national census) literature on computer aided redistricting. A small sample of such works includes:

Hess, S. W., Weaver, J. B., Siegfeldt, H. J., and Zitlan, P. A. "Nonpartisan Political Redistricting by Computer", *Operations Research*, Volume 13, 1965, pp. 998–1006.

Gerhart, B. C. and Littschwager, J. M., "Legislative Districting by Computer", *Behavioral Science*, September, 1969, Volume 14, pp. 404–417.

Beyle, T. L., Harkins, P. B., Lathrop, G. T., and Thyken, R. "Four Men and a Computer and a Redistricting Exercise", *We The People Of North Carolina*, Volume XXIX, No. 3, March, 1971.

For a glimmer of the complexity of a functioning redistricting program, see:

REDIST, Version 3.3, Program Description and User Manual, Revised January 1969. CROND, Inc. (Available from the National Municipal League, 47 East 68th Street, New York, N.Y. 10021) and output it as a reference. Note that the example output gives an approximate picture of the state being districted. At three of the four corners of this example matrix, zeros predominate. Due to the necessary warpage in forcing a rectangular shape upon the test data, some array members within the state shape do not correspond to counties, and they are therefore set to zero.

The number of counties to be worked with (including those with zero population) is computed as NC. NP is calculated as the number of peripheral counties that exist for an NX by NY state. The next four loops determine the coordinates of the counties around the periphery.

The DO 50 loop initializes the population of each district as zero and calculates the number of the peripheral position (LS) to give the most widely separated counties as starting points for the districts. For example, for a square state of 16 counties there will be 10 counties on the periphery. If there are to be 4 districts, then the values of LS would be 1, 4, 7 and 10. Coordinates as defined by (NPX(LS),NPY(LS)) will be (1,1), (4,1), (4,4) and (1,4). (The reader should convince himself how loops 10 through 50 accomplish this calculation.)

The DO 60 loop assigns each county, one at a time, to a district with the two criteria of adding to the district with the lowest population and always adding the next county with the shortest euclidian distance from the starting point of the district. The DO 70 loop determines which district has the lowest population and stores that district number in K. LLD is defined as one more than the square of the greatest possible distance, i.e., the diagonal distance of the rectangle. Squares of distances are used throughout the program as these fall in the same order as long as all distances are greater than one, and this procedure saves repeated calculations of square roots. The DO 80 loop then determines the coordinates of the closest county that has not been assigned to another district and stores these coordinates in LJ and LL. After a county has been assigned to a district, its population value in the LP matrix is set to -1 to avoid future assignment. The population of the (LJ,LL) county is added to the district and the LC matrix location is assigned the district number. The LC matrix will contain the district map. The DO 90, DO 100 loops assign the district number 0 to every "county" that started out with a zero population. Finally the district map, contained in LC, is output according to FORMAT 29.

In the example, actual population figures from the 1970 Census for the state of North Carolina were used. This is a rather irregular state in its physical distribution of 100 counties. The 11 districts do overlap on several occasions. The population of the computed districts is only slightly uniform, ranging from 3879 to 6388 (population was input in 100's of people). It may be expected that the output for a state whose counties are more uniformly distributed physically than North Carolina will be more nearly uniform itself.

As a more than trivial problem, the student may consider modifying this program in such a fashion that population deviations of no more than plus or minus 5% from the "perfect" district size are to be permitted, and that all districts must contain contiguous counties.

SOURCE PROGRAM

```
C      PROGRAM 20    REDISTRICTING
       DIMENSION LP(25,25),NPX(96),NPY(96),LS(25),LC(25,25),LPD(25)
       DIMENSION LH(25,25)
       READ(5,9)NX,NY,ND
       WRITE(6,19) NX,NY,ND
       DO 110 L=1,NY
       READ(5,9)     (LP(J,L),J=1,NX)
       DO 120 J=1,NX
  120  LH(J,L)=LP(J,L)
  110  WRITE(6,29) (LP(J,L),J=1,NX)
       NC=NX*NY
       NP=2*NX+2*NY-4
       J=0
       DO 10 I=1,NX
       J=J+1
       NPX(J)=I
   10  NPY(J)=1
       DO 20 I=2,NY
       J=J+1
       NPX(J)=NX
   20  NPY(J)=I
       M=NX-1
       DO 30 I=1,M
       J=J+1
       NPX(J)=M-I+1
   30  NPY(J)=NY
       M=NY-1
       DO 40 I=2,M
       J=J+1
       NPX(J)=1
   40  NPY(J)=M-I+2
       DO 50 I=1,ND
       LPD(I)=0
   50  LS(I)=1+(I-1)*((NP/ND))
       DO 60 I=1,NC
       K=1
       DO 70 J=2,ND
       IF(LPD(J)-LPD(K))1,70,70
    1  K=J
   70  CONTINUE
       LLD=2*NX*NY+1
       DO 80 J=1,NX
       DO 80 L=1,NY
       IF(LP(J,L))80,3,3
    3  LD=(NPX(LS(K))-J)**2+(NPY(LS(K))-L)**2
       IF(LD-LLD)2,80,80
    2  LLD=LD
       LJ=J
       LL=L
   80  CONTINUE
       LPD(K)=LPD(K)+LP(LJ,LL)
       LC(LJ,LL)=K
       LP(LJ,LL)=-1
```

SOURCE PROGRAM (continued)

```
   60 CONTINUE
      WRITE(6,39) (I,LPD(I),I=1,ND)
      WRITE(6,49)
      DO 90 L=1,NY
      DO 100 I=1,NX
      IF(LH(I,L)) 87,87,100
   87 LC(I,L)=0
  100 CONTINUE
   90 WRITE(6,29) (LC(J,L),J=1,NX)
      STOP
    9 FCRMAT(16I5)
   19 FORMAT('1NUMBER COLUMNS=',I5/' NUMBER ROWS=',3X,I5/' NUMBER DISTS=
     1',2X,I5/'0THE INPUT POPULATION MATRIX:'/)
   29 FORMAT(25(' ',25I4/))
   39 FORMAT('1DISTRICT   POPULATION'/25(T4,I2,T15,I6/))
   49 FORMAT(//T30,'THE STATE DISTRICT MAP AS A MATRIX'/)
      END
```

INPUT DATA

```
CARD COLUMNS:
         1          2          3          4          5          6          7          8
1234567890123456789012345678901234567890123456789012345678901234567890123456789012345678901234567890

   23       9      11
    0       0      0       0       0       0       0  196    81   514   238   724   190   259   328   327
  158     539    240     235      85      55      70
    0       0      0      .0       0     134     127  234   495   246  2143  2886   964   577  1327     0
  268     591      0     205     108      84     268
    0       0      0       0     160     129       0  567   195   722   189   956   764   296     0  2285
    0       0    523     247     140      38      70
    0      66     79     417    1451     428     307  604   909     0   900     0     0   305   497   617
  575     150    739       0     360      56       0
  163      52    159     216     197     117     473  726   325     0   909   428   190   390     0     0
    0     854    552     626      95       0       0
    0       0      0       0       0       0       0    0  1484  3547   547   235   399   164  2120   450
    0     380      0      98     316       0       0
    0       0      0       0       0       0       0    0     0     0     0     0     0   269   848   265
    0     181      0    1031       0       0       0
    0       0      0       0       0       0       0    0     0     0     0     0     0     0     0   469
    0     830      0       0       0       0       0
    0       0      0       0       0       0       0    0     0     0     0     0     0     0     0     0
  242       0      0       0       0       0       0
```

Page 1 of OUTPUT DATA

```
NUMBER COLUMNS=    23
NUMBER ROWS=        9
NUMBER DISTS=      11

THE INPUT POPULATION MATRIX:

    0    0    0    0    0    0    0  196   81  514  238  724  190  259  328  327  158  539  240  235   85   55   70
    0    0    0    0    0  134  127  234  495 2462 1432 886  964  577 1327    0  268  591    0  205  108   84  268
    0    0    0  160  129    0  567  195  722  189  956  764  296    0 2285    0    0  523  247  140   38   70
    0   66   79  417 1451  428  307  604  909    0  900    0    0  305  497  617  575  150  739    0  360   56    0
  163   52  159  216  197  117  473  726  325    0  909  428  190  390    0    0    0  854  552  626   95    0    0
    0    0    0    0    0    0    0    0 1484 3547  547  235  399  164 2120  450    0  380    0   98  316    0    0
    0    0    0    0    0    0    0    0    0    0    0    0    0  269  848  265    0  181    0 1031    0    0    0
    0    0    0    0    0    0    0    0    0    0    0    0    0    0    0  469    0  830    0    0    0    0    0
    0    0    0    0    0    0    0    0    0    0    0    0    0    0    0    0  242    0    0    0    0    0    0
```

Page 2 of OUTPUT DATA

```
DISTRICT  POPULATION
   1         6398
   2         3960
   3         4773
   4         4952
   5         4176
   6         3879
   7         4401
   8         4487
   9         4379
  10         5031
  11         4558
```

Page 3 of OUTPUT DATA

THE STATE DISTRICT MAP AS A MATRIX

```
0   0   0   0   0   0   0   2   2   3   3   3   3   4   4   4   4   5   5   5   5   5   5
0   0   0   0   0   2   2   2   2   2   3   1   3   5   4   0   4   5   0   5   5   5   6
0   0   0   0   2   2   0   2   2   1   2   11  7   0   0   4   0   0   5   5   6   6   6
0   1   1   1   1   11  2   1   11  0   2   0   0   7   6   5   7   6   6   0   6   6   0
1   11  11  11  11  11  11  11  11  0   9   9   0   0   0   0   0   6   7   7   6   0   0
0   0   0   0   0   0   0   0   10  10  9   9   9   9   8   7   0   8   0   7   6   0   0
0   0   0   0   0   0   0   0   0   0   0   0   0   9   9   8   0   8   0   7   0   0   0
0   0   0   0   0   0   0   0   0   0   0   0   0   0   0   8   0   8   0   0   0   0   0
0   0   0   0   0   0   0   0   0   0   0   0   0   0   0   0   8   0   0   0   0   0   0
```

Program 21.   A Maze Learning Program

This program illustrates FORTRAN coding which is organized in such a way as to simulate learning. The program will be discussed in terms of the maze shown in Fig. 21.1, although the algorithm is in no way limited to this maze. The approach could be applied to any maze; however, some coding changes would be required if more than nine gates were to be considered. The program simulates the behavior of a rat that is allowed to learn from past mistakes and remember those paths which lead to the final gate.

The maze, illustrated in Fig. 21.1, has a starting point, Gate 1, a terminal point, Gate 9, and seven intermediate gates. Gates 1, 2, 6, 7, and 8 have as one alternate exit path a *cul de sac*. The paths from each gate are implicitly assumed to be distinguishable so that an intelligent animal, motivated to reach Gate 9, should learn an optimum or near optimum route with repeated attempts. The hypothetical animal is provided with a "memory" for each gate containing the relative proba-

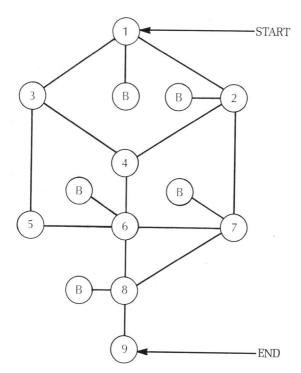

FIGURE 21.1   *Example Maze for Maze Learning Program.*

bility for each of the possible exits. Initially, all possible exits from each gate will be equally probable. As experience is gained, these probabilities will be changed so that the probability of more desirable choices will increase at the expense of the less desirable choices. The user of the program can specify: how fast the learning is to take place, the likelihood that a *cul de sac* will be re-entered, and the probability that return to the gate just left will occur.

The program consists of a main program and the use of the familiar RANDU subroutine to generate a random number between 0.0 and 1.0. RANDU must be initialized by using an argument which is an odd, positive integer. This starting value is read into IX. After each call to RANDU, the value of IX is replaced by the odd, positive integer, IY, which is returned by the subroutine.

The program uses five dimensioned variables. IC stores the record of gates entered; P stores the probabilities that serve as the memory for each gate; PTN is used to store information for output; IP contains the descriptive information about each gate; and ITGAT contains the "unpacked" representation of this descriptive information. The coding strategy should be apparent from the following table.

TABLE 21–1.   Initial Parameters for Maze in Fig. 21.1.

Gate (I)	Gate Information IP(I)	Initial Path Probabilities P(I,J)
1	3203	1/3,1/3,1/3
2	74104	1/4,1/4,1/4,1/4
3	5413	1/3,1/3,1/3
4	6323	1/3,1/3,1/3
5	632	1/2,1/2
6	875405	1/5,1/5,1/5,1/5,1/5
7	86204	1/4,1/4,1/4,1/4
8	97604	1/4,1/4,1/4,1/4
9	—	

The contents of IP represent the alternative paths from each gate using a "packed" word for each gate. For example, Gate 1 has three pathways available (3 is the right or low order digit), which lead to 0, a *cul de sac*, and to Gates 2 and 3. Gate 2 has four pathways, 0, a *cul de sac*, and Gates 1, 4 and 7. The reader should rationalize the remaining values input for IP with Fig. 21.1.

The initial probabilities that a pathway will be taken are stored in P(I,J). The second subscript designates which of the paths is described. For example, P(1,1) is the probability that the path to 0 will be taken from Gate 1, P(1,2) is the probability that the path to Gate 2 will be taken, and P(1,3), the probability of going to Gate 3. As noted above, the probabilities are initially equal, but they will be adjusted as "learning" occurs. The selection of a specific pathway from a gate is based on the value of a random number. For example, the choice of the first path from Gate 1 would be made as illustrated in Table 21–2.

TABLE 21–2.   Path Selection from First Gate on First Pass

Random Number Drawn, Z	Path Selected Leading to Gate
$Z < 0.33$	0
$0.33 \leq Z < 0.66$	2
$0.66 \leq Z \leq 1.00$	3

The manner in which learning is simulated is simply to adjust the contents of P(I,J). After several passes, P(1,1), P(1,2) and P(1,3) may contain 0.1, 0.6 and 0.3. In this case Path 2 is twice as probable as Path 3 and six times as probable as Path 0.

The executable statements begin by inputting values for N, the total number of gates from which exits are allowed; NSTOP, the number of gates in the minimum or optimum path; and IX, the starter for RANDU. A test is performed on N to determine whether or not to continue execution. If execution continues, a feed to a new page on the printer is performed. The gate descriptions are next input into IP. The following executable statement places in INN the number of the final gate. Values are then input for BL, the level of feedback against paths leading to *cul de sacs;* SL, the level of reinforcements given to successful pathways through the maze; and BKW, the probability that a return along the same path will occur. These three values are all in the range 0.0 to 1.0 with the first value negative so that the feedback will lessen the possibility that the path will be taken.

After a series of initializations, the DO 10 loop loads the initial probabilities into P and unpacks each IP(I) into ITGAT(I,J). Starting with statement 4, the first trip through the maze begins. M is the present values of the gate, NZ is a counter to total the zero branches, and MM is the number of trips through the maze. IFLGP is a flag used to control output. Statement number 2 starts the "inner loop" of the learning process. Control cycles between this statement and one of the two unconditional GO TO 2 statements found in the statements down to statement number 13. Control will remain within this area until Gate 9 is reached and control transfers to statement number 13 for appropriate output. After output, control returns to statement number 4 if the learning is not complete and another pass is started.

Special note should be taken of the DO 20 loop and the two statements immediately following it, these combine to select and place in L the gate chosen to be next. The statements above statement number 903 treat the problem of return along the same path. The counter IDED keeps track of the number of consecutive attempts to return along the same path and allows the return if twenty consecutive attempts are made. In other words, a disastrous series of random numbers will not put the program in an endless loop. When control passes to statement number 903, the present gate location plus the number of alternate paths from the gate are packed into IC(M). The next several statements determine if the gate transfered to is a *cul de sac* or the final gate. If it is neither, control passes back to statement 2 to move onto the next gate. Alternately, control transfers to statement 11 and the DO 40 loop system gains control.

The DO 40 loop system is the brain of the program. The coding used to reinforce a successful pass or to learn that blind alleys should be avoided is based on the premise that memory will fall off exponentially back through the path just taken and that learning will propagate more strongly through gates already well learned. The adjusted probabilities are then renormalized. The authors certainly do not presume that this is an adequate model for real memory, but it seems to give interesting and almost believable results. When control passes from the DO 40 loop, control returns to statement 2 if a feedback against a *cul de sac* has taken place, and statement 13 gains control if the animal has arrived at Gate 9.

Statement 13 and the statements following supervise the output options of the program. The reader should follow the coding of this section carefully with reference to the example output included. The program terminates a given experiment under three possible circumstances. First, 150 trials have been made; second, the last 10 trials have all followed a path with a minimum number of gates; and finally, the last 20 trials have involved the same number of gates. In this latter case, a less than optimum path has been learned.

The output included as an example shows the gate sequence of each trip through the maze, and prints the average number of gates for each 10 passes and the contents of the memory every 50 passes. The contents of the memory and the input parameters are also printed when a given case terminates. The program will continue to evaluate new mazes until a blank card is input when attempting to input new values for N, NSTOP, and IX.

NOTE: This program will not run on some computers that limit integer size to a maximum of 32767. This is because the array IP may contain integers of larger magnitude. A suggested project for the reader might be to recode the program so that IP is a two-dimensional array. (This would be a major coding change.)

SOURCE PROGRAM

```
C       PROGRAM 21   A MAZE LEARNING PROGRAM
        DIMENSION IC(1000),P(10,10),PTN(10)
        DIMENSION IP(10)
        DIMENSION ITGAT(9,10)
   998 READ(5,39) N,NSTOP,IX
        IHOLD=IX
        IF(N.EQ.0) GO TO 200
        WRITE(6,99)
        READ(5,9)(IP(I),I=1,N)
        INN=IP(N)/(10**(IP(N)-(IP(N)/10)*10))
        READ(5,19)BL,SL,BKW
        XTOT=0.
        DO 80 KP=1,10
    80 PTN(KP)=0.
        ITN=1
        III=2
        MM=0
        FC=0.0
        DO 10 I=1,N
        K=IP(I)-(IP(I)/10)*10
        ITGAT(I,1)=K
        PR=1.0/FLOAT(K)
        ITEMP=IP(I)/10
```

SOURCE PROGRAM (continued)

```
       DO 10 J=1,K
       ITGAT (I,J+1)=ITEMP-(ITEMP/10)*10
       ITEMP=ITEMP/10
   10  P(I,J)=PR
    4  M=1
       IFLGP=1
       NZ=0
       MM=MM+1
       IC(1)=1
       I=1
       IDED=0
    2  CALL RANDU(IX,IY,Z)
       IX=IY
       IT=I
       K=IP(I)-(IP(I)/10)*10
       PR=0.0
       DO 20 J=1,K
       PR=PR+P(I,J)
       IF(Z.LT.PR) GO TO 1
   20  CONTINUE
       J=K
    1  L=ITGAT(I,J+1)
       IF(M.EQ.1)GO TO 903
       IF(L.NE.(MOD(IC(M-1),10)))GO TO 903
       CALL RANDU(IX,IY,Z)
       IX=IY
       IF(Z.GT.BKW)GO TO 903
       IDED=IDED+1
       IF(IDED.GT.20)GO TO 903
       GO TO 2
  903  IC(M)=IC(M)+J*10+K*100
       IDED=0
       M=M+1
       IC(M)=L
       IF(IC(M).EQ.0) IC(M)=MOD(IC(M-1),10)
       IF(L) 6,6,7
    6  FL=ABS(BL)
       SSL=BL/ABS(BL)
       NZ=NZ+1
       GO TO 11
    7  IF(L-INN)12,3,12
    3  FI=ABS(SL)
       SSL=SL/ABS(SL)
   11  DO 40 I=2,M
       IK=IC(M-I+1)
       K=IK/100
       J=IK/10-K*10
       IK=MOD(IK,10)
       PPT=P(IK,J)
       P(IK,J)=P(IK,J)*(1.+SSL*FL)
       IF(FL.LE.0.0) GO TO 46
       TEST=ALOG(FL)/PPT
       IF(TEST.GT.-78.0) GO TO 45
       FI=0.0
       GO TO 46
   45  FI=FL**(1.0/PPT)
   46  PR=0.0
       DO 50 J=1,K
   50  PR=PR+P(IK,J)
       DO 60 J=1,K
   60  P(IK,J)=P(IK,J)/PR
   40  CONTINUE
       I=IT
       IF(L-INN)2,13,2
   12  I=L
       GO TO 2
   13  DO 70 J=1,M
```

SOURCE PROGRAM (continued)

```
 70 IC(J)=MOD(IC(J),10)
    WRITE(6,29)(IC(J),J=1,M)
    FC=FC+FLOAT(M)
    DC=FC/FLOAT(MM)
    WRITE(6,59) M,NZ,DC
    PTN(ITN)=M
    ITN=ITN+1
    IF(MM.EQ.1)GO TO 8
    IF(MOD(ITN,11).NE.0)GO TO 8
    ITN=1
    TOT=0.
    DC 90 JX=1,10
 90 TCT=TOT+PTN(JX)
    TOT=TOT/10.
    WRITE(6,69)TOT,MM
    IF(IFIX(TOT)-NSTOP.EQ.0) GO TO 5
    IF(XTOT.EQ.TOT)GO TO 5
    XTOT=TOT
  8 IF(MM.EQ.150)GC TC 5
    IF(MOD(MM,50).NE.0)GO TO 4
    WRITE(6,89)
    IFLGP=-1
    GO TO 96
  5 FC=FC/FLOAT(MM)
    WRITE(6,49)FC,MM,BL,SL,IHOLD,BKW
 96 DC 100 I=1,N
    K=ITGAT(I,1)
100 WRITE(6,79) I,(P(I,J),ITGAT(I,J+1),J=1,K)
    WRITE(6,109)
    IF(IFLGP.LT.0)GO TO 4
    GO TO 998
  9 FORMAT(I10)
 19 FCRMAT(8F10.3)
 29 FORMAT(' ',10I5)
 39 FORMAT(3I5)
 49 FORMAT('1    GENERAL STATISTICS AND MEMORY FOR THIS TRIAL:'/
   1 ' AVERAGE =',F10.3,'  CUT OF ',I4,' PASSES WITH BL =',
   2 F10.3,'  SL=',F10.3/' RANDOM NUMBER GENERATOR STARTING VALUE=',
   3 I12,'  BKW=',F10.3//)
 59 FORMAT('+',55('_'),'**',I5,'**',5X,'ZERO BRANCHES =',I3,
   1 '  AVE PASS. =',F10.3)
 69 FORMAT(/30X,'AVERAGE OF PAST TEN =',F10.3,10X,'** PASS #',I5/)
 79 FORMAT(' GATE',I3,8X,10(F10.3,'  (',I2,')'))
 89 FORMAT('1 MEMORY AT 50 PASSES:')
 99 FORMAT('1')
109 FCRMAT(////)
200 STOP
    END
```

INPUT DATA

```
CARD COLUMNS:
         1         2         3         4         5         6         7         8
1234567890123456789012345678901234567890123456789012345678901234567890123456789Q
    8    512345
     3203
     74104
     5413
     6323
      632
     875405
     86204
     97604
  -.2       .2        .5
                                    <--- ELANK CARD
```

Page 1 of OUTPUT DATA

18**	ZERO BRANCHES =	3	AVE PASS. =	18.000
43**	ZERO BRANCHES =	7	AVE PASS. =	30.500
26**	ZERO BRANCHES =	6	AVE PASS. =	29.000
8**	ZERO BRANCHES =	0	AVE PASS. =	23.750
52**	ZERO BRANCHES =	7	AVE PASS. =	29.400
47**	ZERO BRANCHES =	5	AVE PASS. =	32.333
72**	ZERO BRANCHES =	4	AVE PASS. =	38.000
24**	ZERO BRANCHES =	0	AVE PASS. =	36.250
11**	ZERO BRANCHES =	2	AVE PASS. =	33.444
32**	ZERO BRANCHES =	0	AVE PASS. =	33.300

** PASS # 10

AVERAGE OF PAST TEN = 33.300

Page 1 of OUTPUT DATA (continued)

```
  5**   ZERO BRANCHES = 0   AVE PASS. =   30.727

 23**   ZERO BRANCHES = 0   AVE PASS. =   30.083
 15**   ZERO BRANCHES = 0   AVE PASS. =   28.923
 17**   ZERO BRANCHES = 0   AVE PASS. =   28.071

 33**   ZERO BRANCHES = 0   AVE PASS. =   28.400

 22**   ZERO BRANCHES = 1   AVE PASS. =   28.000
  7**   ZERO BRANCHES = 0   AVE PASS. =   26.765
  7**   ZERO BRANCHES = 0   AVE PASS. =   25.667

 22**   ZERO BRANCHES = 2   AVE PASS. =   25.474
```

Page 2 of OUTPUT DATA

```
                                          ZERO BRANCHES = 0   AVE PASS. = 24.650
                  ** 13**                 ** PASS # = 20
AVERAGE OF PAST TEN = 16.400

                  ** 16**                 ZERO BRANCHES = 0   AVE PASS. = 24.429
                  **  5**                 ZERO BRANCHES = 0   AVE PASS. = 23.545
                  ** 13**                 ZERO BRANCHES = 1   AVE PASS. = 23.087
                  ** 29**                 ZERO BRANCHES = 0   AVE PASS. = 23.333
                  **  9**                 ZERO BRANCHES = 0   AVE PASS. = 22.760
                  ** 20**                 ZERO BRANCHES = 0   AVE PASS. = 22.654
                  **  8**                 ZERO BRANCHES = 0   AVE PASS. = 22.111
                  ** 15**                 ZERO BRANCHES = 3   AVE PASS. = 21.857
                  **  5**                 ZERO BRANCHES = 0   AVE PASS. = 21.276
                  **  5**                 ZERO BRANCHES = 0   AVE PASS. = 20.733
AVERAGE OF PAST TEN = 12.500              ** PASS # = 30

                  **  6**                 ZERO BRANCHES = 0   AVE PASS. = 20.258
                  **  5**                 ZERO BRANCHES = 0   AVE PASS. = 19.781
                  **  9**                 ZERO BRANCHES = 0   AVE PASS. = 19.455
                  ** 13**                 ZERO BRANCHES = 0   AVE PASS. = 19.265
                  **  5**                 ZERO BRANCHES = 0   AVE PASS. = 18.857
                  **  6**                 ZERO BRANCHES = 0   AVE PASS. = 18.500
                  **  5**                 ZERO BRANCHES = 0   AVE PASS. = 18.135
                  **  6**                 ZERO BRANCHES = 1   AVE PASS. = 17.816
                  **  5**                 ZERO BRANCHES = 0   AVE PASS. = 17.487
                  ** 10**                 ZERO BRANCHES = 0   AVE PASS. = 17.300
AVERAGE OF PAST TEN = 7.000               ** PASS # = 40
```

Page 2 of OUTPUT DATA (continued)

```
1----2----7----8----9                              **   5**  ZERO BRANCHES = 0   AVE PASS. = 17.000
1----2----7----8----9                              **   5**  ZERO BRANCHES = 0   AVE PASS. = 16.714
1----3                    4    2    7    8          **  11**  ZERO BRANCHES = 0   AVE PASS. = 16.581
9----5
1----2----4----7----6----5----3----8----9          **   9**  ZERO BRANCHES = 0   AVE PASS. = 16.409
1----2----7----9----8                              **   7**  ZERO BRANCHES = 0   AVE PASS. = 16.200
1----3----6----8----9                              **   5**  ZERO BRANCHES = 0   AVE PASS. = 15.957
1----3----8----9                                   **   8**  ZERO BRANCHES = 0   AVE PASS. = 15.787
1----2----7----6----8----9                         **   7**  ZERO BRANCHES = 0   AVE PASS. = 15.604
1----2----7----8----9                              **   5**  ZERO BRANCHES = 0   AVE PASS. = 15.388
1----2----7----8----9                              **   5**  ZERO BRANCHES = 0   AVE PASS. = 15.180
```

AVERAGE OF PAST TEN =   6.700   ** PASS #   50

Page 3 of OUTPUT DATA

```
MEMORY AT 50 PASSES:
GATE 1   0.019 ( 0)   0.710 ( 2)   0.271 ( 3)
GATE 2   0.005 ( 0)   0.057 ( 1)   0.057 ( 4)
GATE 3   0.346 ( 1)   0.326 ( 4)   0.327 ( 5)
GATE 4   0.343 ( 2)   0.313 ( 3)   0.344 ( 6)
GATE 5   0.484 ( 3)   0.516 ( 6)   0.881 ( 7)
GATE 6   0.026 ( 0)   0.099 ( 4)   0.099 ( 5)   0.156 ( 7)
GATE 7   0.001 ( 0)   0.005 ( 2)   0.005 ( 6)   0.989 ( 8)
GATE 8   0.000 ( 0)   0.000 ( 6)   0.000 ( 7)   1.000 ( 9)   0.620 ( 8)
```

```
1----3----4----7----9                              **   7**  ZERO BRANCHES = 0   AVE PASS. = 15.029
1----2----7----8----9                              **   5**  ZERO BRANCHES = 0   AVE PASS. = 14.827
1----2----7----9----8                              **   5**  ZERO BRANCHES = 0   AVE PASS. = 14.642
1----2----7----8----9                              **   5**  ZERO BRANCHES = 0   AVE PASS. = 14.463
```

Page 3 of OUTPUT DATA (continued)

```
1 | 2 | 7 |   | 8 | 9 |                    **  5**  ZERO BRANCHES = 0  AVE PASS. =  14.291
1 | 2 | 7 |   | 8 | 9 |                    **  5**  ZERO BRANCHES = 0  AVE PASS. =  14.125
1 | 2 | 7 |   | 8 | 9 |                    **  5**  ZERO BRANCHES = 0  AVE PASS. =  13.965
1 | 2 | 7 |   | 8 | 9 |                    **  5**  ZERO BRANCHES = 0  AVE PASS. =  13.810
1 | 2 | 7 |   | 8 | 9 |                    **  5**  ZERO BRANCHES = 0  AVE PASS. =  13.661
1 | 2 | 7 |   | 8 | 9 |                    **  5**  ZERO BRANCHES = 0  AVE PASS. =  13.517
```

AVERAGE OF PAST TEN = 5.200   ** PASS #   60

Page 4 of OUTPUT DATA

```
     GENERAL STATISTICS AND MEMORY FOR THIS TRIAL:
AVERAGE =    13.517  OUT OF   60 PASSES WITH BL =    -0.200   SL=    0.200
RANDOM NUMBER GENERATOR STARTING VALUE=    12345   BKW=    0.500

GATE  1    0.006 (  0)   0.914 (  2)   0.081 (  3)
GATE  2    0.001 (  0)   0.012 (  1)   0.012 (  4)
GATE  3    0.346 (  1)   0.326 (  4)   0.327 (  5)   0.974 (  7)
GATE  4    0.343 (  2)   0.313 (  3)   0.344 (  6)
GATE  5    0.484 (  3)   0.516 (  6)
GATE  6    0.026 (  0)   0.096 (  4)   0.096 (  5)   0.181 (  7)   0.601 (  8)
GATE  7    0.000 (  0)   0.001 (  2)   0.001 (  6)   0.998 (  8)
GATE  8    0.000 (  0)   0.000 (  6)   0.000 (  7)   1.000 (  9)
```

Program 22.   An Ecosystem Model

This program presents a model of a simple ecosystem with three trophic levels. While the model is limited in terms of species number, the approach is general and could easily be expanded to more complex systems. The example system consists of a specified area (assumed to be closed to imigration and emigration) containing plants, herbivores and carnivores. Initial population levels and space requirements are input for the three species along with estimates of the probabilities for the various mechanisms affecting population levels. The mechanisms included in this model are natural death, reproduction, starvation, and predation. These mechanisms are controled by the input probabilities which are, in most cases, modified by population density functions. The random number generator, RANDU, is used to impose a random perturbation on population changes; and the number of each species that is born, that dies, etc., is computed using the binomial theorem.

The way in which each change in each population is computed is worthy of special mention. Consider the case of the herbivores. There are B herbivores living in an area of AREA units with an optimum space requirement of SB units per individual. The changes in the herbivore population per unit time depend upon the population density and the input values for: BN, the probability of natural death; BB, the probability of birth; BE, the probability of eating a plant; and BS, the number of time units without food required for starvation. Analogous notation is used for the plants where A, AN, AB and SA are defined, and for the carnivores where C, CN, CB, CE, CS and SC are defined. These probabilities are for a single event per time period with the exception of the starvation parameters BS and CS. The input probabilities are used when optimum population levels exist. These values are modified by the program at other population levels. For each process, birth, natural death, etc., the kinetic order is defined. Reproduction among the herbivores and carnivores, for example, is a second-order process, the probability for which is modified by the respective population density. The development of appropriate relationships to describe such poorly understood phenomena as the effect of crowding on birth rate is a matter of guessing. However, the use of the computer places a modest price on being wrong and trying again.

Assuming that reasonable functions can be developed to modify the probabilities that pertain to optimum population levels, we may calculate a probability that a given event will happen to an individual in a given time period. The question of how many events will occur within the entire population must now be considered. The method used here involves a random number generator and the binomial theorem. Consider, as an example, a process that has a probability of occurrence of 0.5 per individual and a population of two individuals. This means there are three possible results — no events, one event, and two events. In this case the binomial coefficients predict a probability of 0.25 that no events or two events will occur and a probability of 0.50 that only a single event will occur. Note that 0.25, 0.50 and 0.25 are the normalized coefficients of a three term binomial expansion reflecting the fact that three possible outcomes are possible. This may be generalized to a population of any size. In this program, SUBROUTINE PR accepts the probability of a single event, P, a random number R(I) and the number of individuals, X. It accumulates the normalized coefficients of the binomial expansion and checks each sum against the random number. When the accumulated sum of the binomial coefficients is equal to or greater than the random number, the number of events is taken as the number of binomial coefficients accumulated less one (first term is for zero events). The reader should examine the coding of SUBROUTINE PR carefully, seeing how this calculation is accomplished. This approach reflects the finite nature of population dynamics. In other words, the herbivore who has just watched his brother devoured by a carnivore can derive little comfort from the fact that the probability of two such events in a given time period is only one in a thousand — especially when he turns around and finds himself eyeball-to-eyeball with another carnivore.

The details of the coding presented below are not intended to represent any real system. The density-dependent functional relationships are simply illustrative, and no particular biological significance should be attached to them. The significance of this program lies in the flexibility of the approach and the ability of the digital computer to do system simulations whose credibility is limited only by the ability of the programmer.

The program begins by declaring R a dimensioned variable and reading and printing the initial populations and related probability factors. Statement 13 inputs values for N, the number of time intervals to be evaluated; NP, the frequency with which the population levels are to be printed; NDIM, the number of space units along one side of the square area considered; and IX, the "seed number" for the random number generator. The significance of the variables in the remaining READ statement lists has been noted above. After the input parameters have been printed, the area in the environment is computed and BS and CS are set to fixed-point variables.

The DO 10 loop cycles over the number of time periods, N, requested. The DO 20 loop sets 10 random numbers into R for the 10 regulatory mechanisms to be evaluated in the current time period. Note that each of the 10 regulatory mechanisms are set off by comment cards in the program. The rationale behind the coding will be illustrated by discussion of 3 of the 10 regulatory processes — the number of new plants that occur, the number of herbivores born, and the number of carnivores that starve. The reader should carefully evaluate the coding of all the mechanisms presented.

The probability, P, that a new plant will result from an existing plant is based on AB and is equal to AB in cases where the plant population is optimum or less than optimum. At greater than optimum populations, AB is modified by dividing by $(A*SA/AREA)**5$ to account for crowding. The calculated value of P is then passed to subroutine PR, which calculates the number of new plants using a random number as described above. Note that the probability that new plants will occur is a first order process up to the point that crowding occurs, in which case the number of events is a second order process.

The number of herbivores born is a second order process at any population density. Statement 62 defines the probability that a birth will occur to a given herbivore. Note that both overcrowding and low population density will tend to lower the calculated probability. Subroutine PR again computes the specific number of events to occur based on a random number and the binomial theorem. Note that P is equal to BB, the input birth probability, at the optimum population density.

The number of carnivores that starve is a second order process in that it depends on both the number of carnivores and the number of herbivores available to eat. If the number of herbivores present is equal to or greater than the optimum for the area, it is assumed that no carnivore starves. Otherwise the probability that a carnivore *does not eat* $(1.-B*SB/AREA)$ is raised to the power of the number of intervals (ICS) required for the carnivore to starve. Subroutine PR uses this compounded probability with the number of carnivores (C) to determine how many starve.

Three sets of example data are included with the program. The first two illustrate the random nature of the model. The two cases are identical except for the seed number passed to the random number generator. The initial populations for these two cases were 2500 plants, 1000 herbivores and 100 carnivores. Both the herbivores and the carnivores are above their respective optimum populations of 500 and 50. Both cases indicate an oscillatory behavior. Both outputs seem to indicate that all three populations are doing quite well, although at time period 150 for the first case and 360 for the second the herbivore population seems dangerously low. In fact it may have been lower, but results are printed only every ten time periods.

The third example calculation resulted in a disaster for the carnivores. The initial input values were 1700 plants, 1000 herbivores and

100 carnivores. These are not very close to the optimum values of 2500, 500 and 50. Initially, the lack of food supply caused a sharp drop in the herbivore population. This was reflected by a sharp drop in the carnivore population. Around time period 70 to 80, things indeed looked bleak except for the fact that the plants seemed to be recovering nicely. The herbivores required an extended period of time to recover, even in the face of a large food supply. This is attributable to a "bad" series of random numbers. During the period of substantially reduced herbivore numbers, the carnivores die out. The inability of the herbivores to recover until quite late in the time frame clearly indicates the random nature of the model. Another seed number for the random number generator might well yield a completely different result.

Two suggested changes to the program are as follows:

1. Make appropriate modifications to the coding so that the output produces a tabular summary of the number of individuals in each population that are born, die, starve, etc. A careful study of such output may well suggest some coding changes in some of the functional dependence relations given.
2. Revise the coding so that the population level of each species at the end of each time period is stored, and at the end of each calculation, pass this information to one of the plotting subroutines found in the earlier programs.

SOURCE PROGRAM

```
C       PROGRAM 22   AN ECOSYSTEM MODEL
        DIMENSION R(20)
     13 READ(5,19) N,NP,NDIM,IX
        IF(N) 101,101,12
     12 READ(5,9)A,AN,AB,SA
        READ(5,9)B,BN,BB,BE,BS,SB
        READ(5,9)C,CN,CB,CE,CS,SC
        WRITE(6,39) N,NP,NDIM,IX
        WRITE(6,49)
        WRITE(6,59) A,AN,AB,SA
        WRITE(6,69) B,BN,BB,SB,BS,BE
        WRITE(6,79) C,CN,CB,SC,CS,CE
        AREA=NDIM**2
        IES=BS
        ICS=CS
        DO 10 I=1,N
        DO 20 J=1,10
        CALL RANDU(IX,IY,YFL)
        IX=IY
        R(J)=YFL
        IF(R(J).GT.0.9999)R(J)=0.
     20 CONTINUE
C**** NUMBER OF PLANTS THAT DIE
        P=AN*(A*SA)/AREA
        P=AMAX1(P,AN)
```

SOURCE PROGRAM (continued)

```
        CALL PE(P,R(1),A,Y)
        A=A-Y
C****  NUMBER OF NEW PLANTS
        P=AB/(((A*SA)/AREA)**5)
        P=AMIN1(P,AB)
        CALL PE(P,R(2),A,Y)
        A=A+Y
C****  NUMBER OF PLANTS EATEN
        P=BE*A*SA/AREA
        P=AMIN1(P,BE)
        CALL PR(P,R(3),B,Y)
        A=A-Y
C****  NUMBER OF HERBIVORES THAT STARVE
        IF(A*SA-AREA)6,7,7
     6  P=(1.-A*SA/AREA)**IBS
        CALL PR(P,R(4),B,Y)
        B=B-Y
C****  NUMBER OF HERBIVCRES THAT DIE
     7  CALL PR(BN,R(5),B,Y)
        B=B-Y
C****  NUMBER OF HERBIVORES BCRN
        IF(IFIX(B))61,61,62
    62  P=(B*BB/(AREA/SB))*AMIN1(1.,((AREA/(B*SB))**5))
        CALL PE(P,R(6),E,Y)
        B=B+Y
C****  NUMBER OF HERBIVORES EATEN
    61  P=CE*B*SB/AREA
        P=AMIN1(P,CE)
        CALL PR(P,R(7),C,Y)
        B=B-Y
C****  NUMBER OF CARNIVORES THAT STARVE
        IF(B*SB-AREA)8,11,11
     8  P=(1.-B*SB/AREA)**ICS
        CALL PR(P,R(8),C,Y)
        C=C-Y
C****  NUMBER OF CARNIVORES THAT DIE
    11  CALL ER(CN,R(9),C,Y)
        C=C-Y
C****  NUMBER OF CARNIVORES BORN
        IF(IFIX(C))71,71,72
    72  P=(C*CB/(AREA/SC))*AMIN1(1.,((AREA/(C*SC))**5))
        CALL PR(P,R(10),C,Y)
        C=C+Y
    71  IF(I-(I/NP)*NP)10,34,10
    34  WRITE(6,29) A,B,C,I
    10  CONTINUE
        GO TO 13
     9  FORMAT(8F10.3)
    19  FORMAT(3I5,I7)
    29  FORMAT(' PLANTS=',F10.0,'  HERBIVORES=',F10.0,'  CARNIVORES=',
       1 F10.0,'    TIME PERIOD IS ',I5)
    39  FORMAT('1 INPUT PARAMETERS ARE'/' TIME INTERVALS=',I5,'  PRINT EVE
       1RY ',I3,' INTERVALS'/ ' ORDER OF THE SPACE MATRIX=',I5,'  RANDUM S
       2TARTER=',I12/)
    49  FORMAT(T16,'STARTING',T28,'PROBABILITY',T43,'PRCBABILITY',T57,
       1 'SPACE NEEDED',T72,'STARVATION'/T15,'POPULATION   NATURAL DEATH   R
       2EPRODUCTION   PER INDIVIDUAL     TIME'/'+',T15,10(' '),2X,13('_'),
       3 2X,12('_'),2X,14('_'),2X,10('_')/)
    59  FORMAT(' PLANTS......',T15,F8.0,T28,F9.3,T45,F9.3,T57,F9.2,T72,
       1 F9.2)
    69  FORMAT(' HERBIVORES..',T15,F8.0,T28,F9.3,T45,F9.3,T57,F9.2,T72,
       1 F9.2,T85,'PROB EATING PLANT',T108,F6.2)
    79  FCRMAT(' CARNIVORES..',T15,F8.C,T28,F9.3,T45,F9.3,T57,F9.2,T72,
       1 F9.2,T85,'PROB EATING HERBIVORE',T108,F6.2/'+',100('_')/)
   101  CALL EXIT
        END
```

SUBROUTINE PR

```
   SUBROUTINE PR(P,R,X,Y)
   IF(X.LT.1.)GO TO 6
   IF(P)6,6,7
6  Y=0.
   RETURN
7  IF(1.-P)4,4,5
4  Y=X
   RETURN
5  TT=0.
   Q=1.-P
   PQ=ALOG(P/Q)/2.303
   T=X*ALOG(Q)/2.303
   Y=0.
3  TT=TT+EXP(2.303*T)
   IF(TT-R)1,2,2
1  Y=Y+1.
   IF((X-Y).LE.0.)GO TO 2
   T=T+ALOG((X+1.-Y)/Y)/2.303+PQ
   GO TO 3
2  RETURN
   END
```

INPUT DATA

```
DATA FOR PROGRAM 22    AN ECOSYSTEM MODEL
CARD COLUMNS:
        1          2          3          4          5          6          7          8
1234567890123456789012345678901234567890123456789012345678901234567890123456789012345678 90

   500    10    50 137925
2500.     .001       .01        1.0
1000.     .005       .04        .05        3.0        5.0
 100.     .005       .02        .02        9.0       50.0
   500    10    50 372491
2500.     .001       .01        1.0
1000.     .005       .04        .05        3.0        5.0
 100.     .005       .02        .02        9.0       50.0
   500    10    50 27853
1700.     .001       .01        1.0
1000.     .005       .02        .04        3.0        5.0
 100.     .005       .02        .02        9.0       50.0
```

Page 1 of OUTPUT DATA

INPUT PARAMETERS ARE
TIME INTERVALS= 500 PRINT EVERY 10 INTERVALS
ORDER OF THE SPACE MATRIX= 50 RANDOM STARTER= 137925

	STARTING POPULATION	PROBABILITY NATURAL DEATH	PROBABILITY REPRODUCTION	SPACE NEEDED PER INDIVIDUAL	STARVATION TIME	PROB EATING PLANT	PROB EATING HERBIVORE
PLANTS.....	2500.	0.001	0.010	1.00			0.05
HERBIVORES..	1000.	0.005	0.040	5.00	3.00		0.02
CARNIVORES..	100.	0.005	0.020	50.00	9.00		

PLANTS= 2209.	HERBIVORES= 945.	CARNIVORES= 91.	TIME PERIOD IS 10
PLANTS= 2008.	HERBIVORES= 895.	CARNIVORES= 91.	TIME PERIOD IS 20
PLANTS= 1852.	HERBIVORES= 745.	CARNIVORES= 90.	TIME PERIOD IS 30
PLANTS= 1742.	HERBIVORES= 610.	CARNIVORES= 87.	TIME PERIOD IS 40
PLANTS= 1729.	HERBIVORES= 562.	CARNIVORES= 84.	TIME PERIOD IS 50
PLANTS= 1705.	HERBIVORES= 527.	CARNIVORES= 81.	TIME PERIOD IS 60
PLANTS= 1653.	HERBIVORES= 478.	CARNIVORES= 78.	TIME PERIOD IS 70
PLANTS= 1660.	HERBIVORES= 384.	CARNIVORES= 77.	TIME PERIOD IS 80
PLANTS= 1693.	HERBIVORES= 341.	CARNIVORES= 77.	TIME PERIOD IS 90
PLANTS= 1715.	HERBIVORES= 293.	CARNIVORES= 76.	TIME PERIOD IS 100
PLANTS= 1757.	HERBIVORES= 273.	CARNIVORES= 74.	TIME PERIOD IS 110
PLANTS= 1835.	HERBIVORES= 239.	CARNIVORES= 72.	TIME PERIOD IS 120
PLANTS= 1917.	HERBIVORES= 209.	CARNIVORES= 72.	TIME PERIOD IS 130
PLANTS= 1992.	HERBIVORES= 200.	CARNIVORES= 71.	TIME PERIOD IS 140
PLANTS= 2095.	HERBIVORES= 196.	CARNIVORES= 63.	TIME PERIOD IS 150
PLANTS= 2216.	HERBIVORES= 204.	CARNIVORES= 60.	TIME PERIOD IS 160
PLANTS= 2299.	HERBIVORES= 225.	CARNIVORES= 58.	TIME PERIOD IS 170
PLANTS= 2412.	HERBIVORES= 246.	CARNIVORES= 60.	TIME PERIOD IS 180
PLANTS= 2487.	HERBIVORES= 274.	CARNIVORES= 57.	TIME PERIOD IS 190
PLANTS= 2559.	HERBIVORES= 305.	CARNIVORES= 61.	TIME PERIOD IS 200
PLANTS= 2599.	HERBIVORES= 362.	CARNIVORES= 61.	TIME PERIOD IS 210
PLANTS= 2567.	HERBIVORES= 454.	CARNIVORES= 60.	TIME PERIOD IS 220
PLANTS= 2554.	HERBIVORES= 580.	CARNIVORES= 63.	TIME PERIOD IS 230
PLANTS= 2420.	HERBIVORES= 646.	CARNIVORES= 69.	TIME PERIOD IS 240
PLANTS= 2302.	HERBIVORES= 685.	CARNIVORES= 68.	TIME PERIOD IS 250
PLANTS= 2216.	HERBIVORES= 723.	CARNIVORES= 71.	TIME PERIOD IS 260
PLANTS= 2045.	HERBIVORES= 722.	CARNIVORES= 71.	TIME PERIOD IS 270
PLANTS= 1903.	HERBIVORES= 684.	CARNIVORES= 72.	TIME PERIOD IS 280

Page 1 of OUTPUT DATA (continued)

PLANTS= 1855.	HERBIVORES= 628.	CARNIVORES= 73.	TIME PERIOD IS 290
PLANTS= 1807.	HERBIVORES= 573.	CARNIVORES= 73.	TIME PERIOD IS 300
PLANTS= 1718.	HERBIVORES= 541.	CARNIVORES= 72.	TIME PERIOD IS 310
PLANTS= 1671.	HERBIVORES= 505.	CARNIVORES= 66.	TIME PERIOD IS 320
PLANTS= 1655.	HERBIVORES= 482.	CARNIVORES= 67.	TIME PERIOD IS 330
PLANTS= 1658.	HERBIVORES= 401.	CARNIVORES= 68.	TIME PERIOD IS 340
PLANTS= 1690.	HERBIVORES= 339.	CARNIVORES= 72.	TIME PERIOD IS 350
PLANTS= 1708.	HERBIVORES= 286.	CARNIVORES= 75.	TIME PERIOD IS 360
PLANTS= 1800.	HERBIVORES= 246.	CARNIVORES= 77.	TIME PERIOD IS 370
PLANTS= 1870.	HERBIVORES= 227.	CARNIVORES= 73.	TIME PERIOD IS 380
PLANTS= 1971.	HERBIVORES= 223.	CARNIVORES= 71.	TIME PERIOD IS 390
PLANTS= 2029.	HERBIVORES= 232.	CARNIVORES= 72.	TIME PERIOD IS 400
PLANTS= 2124.	HERBIVORES= 255.	CARNIVORES= 69.	TIME PERIOD IS 410
PLANTS= 2151.	HERBIVORES= 272.	CARNIVORES= 70.	TIME PERIOD IS 420
PLANTS= 2253.	HERBIVORES= 317.	CARNIVORES= 67.	TIME PERIOD IS 430
PLANTS= 2287.	HERBIVORES= 376.	CARNIVORES= 68.	TIME PERIOD IS 440
PLANTS= 2318.	HERBIVORES= 459.	CARNIVORES= 67.	TIME PERIOD IS 450
PLANTS= 2295.	HERBIVORES= 569.	CARNIVORES= 65.	TIME PERIOD IS 460
PLANTS= 2200.	HERBIVORES= 642.	CARNIVORES= 64.	TIME PERIOD IS 470
PLANTS= 2110.	HERBIVORES= 667.	CARNIVORES= 64.	TIME PERIOD IS 480
PLANTS= 2003.	HERBIVORES= 657.	CARNIVORES= 63.	TIME PERIOD IS 490
PLANTS= 1933.	HERBIVORES= 647.	CARNIVORES= 67.	TIME PERIOD IS 500

Page 2 of OUTPUT DATA

INPUT PARAMETERS ARE
TIME INTERVALS= 500   PRINT EVERY 10 INTERVALS
ORDER OF THE SPACE MATRIX= 50   RANDOM STARTER= 372491

	STARTING POPULATION	PROBABILITY NATURAL DEATH	PROBABILITY REPRODUCTION	SPACE NEEDED PER INDIVIDUAL	STARVATION TIME	PROB EATING PLANT	PROB EATING HERBIVORE
PLANTS.......:	2500.	0.001	0.010	1.00			
HERBIVORES=	1000.	0.005	0.040	5.00	3.00	0.95	
CARNIVORES..:	100.	0.005	0.020	50.00	0.00		0.92

PLANTS= 2235.	HERBIVORES= 957.	CARNIVORES= 95.	TIME PERIOD IS 10
PLANTS= 2048.	HERBIVORES= 911.	CARNIVORES= 91.	TIME PERIOD IS 20
PLANTS= 1891.	HERBIVORES= 791.	CARNIVORES= 87.	TIME PERIOD IS 30

TIME PERIOD IS	CARNIVORES=	HERBIVORES=	PLANTS=
40	87.	691.	1808.
50	87.	578.	1727.
60	82.	532.	1711.
70	77.	510.	1673.
80	83.	423.	1652.
90	81.	329.	1687.
100	79.	288.	1751.
110	75.	266.	1832.
120	73.	241.	1905.
130	70.	245.	1996.
140	72.	262.	2125.
150	73.	288.	2202.
160	71.	330.	2229.
170	69.	398.	2306.
180	73.	554.	2283.
190	74.	632.	2229.
200	77.	668.	2121.
210	73.	672.	2017.
220	76.	641.	1910.
230	77.	592.	1812.
240	75.	544.	1760.
250	70.	536.	1732.
260	72.	517.	1711.
270	72.	519.	1662.
280	69.	505.	1647.
290	69.	480.	1667.
300	55.	410.	1704.
310	51.	325.	1787.
320	55.	276.	1841.
330	60.	245.	1904.
340	64.	219.	2019.
350	65.	265.	2119.
360	62.	202.	2232.
370	66.	214.	2328.
380	66.	234.	2417.
390	67.	273.	2465.
400	65.	302.	2472.
410	67.	365.	2372.
420	66.	471.	2313.
430	65.	599.	2221.
440		684.	2147.
450		677.	2041.
460		680.	1932.
470		650.	1859.
480		605.	1825.
490		577.	
500			

Page 3 of OUTPUT DATA

```
INPUT PARAMETERS ARE
TIME INTERVALS= 500 PRINT EVERY 10 INTERVALS
ORDER OF THE SPACE MATRIX= 50 RANDOM STARTER= 27853
```

	STARTING POPULATION	PROBABILITY NATURAL DEATH	PROBABILITY REPRODUCTION	SPACE NEEDED PER INDIVIDUAL	STARVATION TIME	PROB EATING PLANT	PROB EATING HERBIVORE
PLANTS.....:	1700.	0.001	0.010	1.00			
HERBIVORES..:	1000.	0.005	0.020	5.00	3.00	0.04	
CARNIVORES..:	100.	0.005	0.020	50.00	9.00		0.02

PLANTS=	HERBIVORES=	CARNIVORES=	TIME PERIOD IS
1610.	610.	95.	10
1622.	425.	92.	20
1673.	289.	90.	30
1767.	210.	85.	40
1887.	151.	65.	50
2025.	149.	57.	60
2148.	149.	38.	70
2262.	150.	29.	80
2407.	157.	19.	90
2566.	158.	17.	100
2674.	155.	11.	110
2794.	156.	8.	120
2842.	154.	4.	130
2896.	158.	4.	140
2943.	155.	2.	150
2974.	155.	0.	160
3016.	153.	0.	170
3009.	160.	0.	180
3014.	157.	0.	190
3021.	160.	0.	200
3029.	152.	0.	210
3040.	157.	0.	220
3059.	158.	0.	230
3059.	163.	0.	240
3057.	168.	0.	250
3076.	176.	0.	260
3063.	176.	0.	270
3059.			280
3091.			290
3113.			

Page 3 of OUTPUT DATA (continued)

```
PLANTS=  3119.   HERBIVORES=  173.   CARNIVORES=   .   TIME PERIOD IS  300
PLANTS=  3133.   HERBIVORES=  185.   CARNIVORES=   .   TIME PERIOD IS  310
PLANTS=  3144.   HERBIVORES=  185.   CARNIVORES=   .   TIME PERIOD IS  320
PLANTS=  3142.   HERBIVORES=  200.   CARNIVORES=   .   TIME PERIOD IS  330
PLANTS=  3114.   HERBIVORES=  204.   CARNIVORES=   .   TIME PERIOD IS  340
PLANTS=  3088.   HERBIVORES=  208.   CARNIVORES=   .   TIME PERIOD IS  350
PLANTS=  3074.   HERBIVORES=  212.   CARNIVORES=   .   TIME PERIOD IS  360
PLANTS=  3040.   HERBIVORES=  222.   CARNIVORES=   .   TIME PERIOD IS  370
PLANTS=  3005.   HERBIVORES=  235.   CARNIVORES=   .   TIME PERIOD IS  380
PLANTS=  2986.   HERBIVORES=  249.   CARNIVORES=   .   TIME PERIOD IS  390
PLANTS=  2961.   HERBIVORES=  266.   CARNIVORES=   .   TIME PERIOD IS  400
PLANTS=  2931.   HERBIVORES=  283.   CARNIVORES=   .   TIME PERIOD IS  410
PLANTS=  2880.   HERBIVORES=  301.   CARNIVORES=   .   TIME PERIOD IS  420
PLANTS=  2864.   HERBIVORES=  335.   CARNIVORES=   .   TIME PERIOD IS  430
PLANTS=  2822.   HERBIVORES=  361.   CARNIVORES=   .   TIME PERIOD IS  440
PLANTS=  2788.   HERBIVORES=  400.   CARNIVORES=   .   TIME PERIOD IS  450
PLANTS=  2751.   HERBIVORES=  457.   CARNIVORES=   .   TIME PERIOD IS  460
PLANTS=  2721.   HERBIVORES=  535.   CARNIVORES=   .   TIME PERIOD IS  470
PLANTS=  2648.   HERBIVORES=  582.   CARNIVORES=   .   TIME PERIOD IS  480
PLANTS=  2569.   HERBIVORES=  606.   CARNIVORES=   .   TIME PERIOD IS  490
PLANTS=  2495.   HERBIVORES=  638.   CARNIVORES=   .   TIME PERIOD IS  500
```

Program 23.   A General Purpose Data Analysis Program

This program is an example of a first step toward the development of a general purpose social science data analysis program. It makes use of execution time format specification, introduced in an earlier program, to permit its application to data sets of differing format without the need for recompilation of the program for each execution. Since we have previously discussed the contingency table and the correlation and regression code, only the "shared" statements, the "front end" of the program, will be covered here.

An array, FMT, is dimensioned 20. This array will contain the execution time format statement. Note that appropriate changes to this DIMENSION and to the input statement filling FMT will permit the input of a format specification exceeding one card in length. Through the use of a DATA statement, REGR and CONT are set equal to "REGR" and "CONT", respectively. The first executable statement of the program reads from Input Unit 5 under control of FORMAT 409 four alphabetic characters into SWT. The second executable statement reads a complete card image (20A4) into FMT. SWT is then compared to REGR. If SWT contains "REGR", control transfers to statement number 5000, the beginning of the code for the correlation and regression analysis section of the program. If SWT does not equal "REGR", its contents is compared to "CONT". If SWT equals CONT, control transfers to statement number 4000, and a contingency table analysis is performed. If SWT contains neither "REGR" nor "CONT", an error has occurred. The user is so notified by the WRITE statement using FORMAT 429, and execution stops.

Note that SWT is read from columns 10–13 of the first parameter card. This permits the user to punch the word SELECT in columns 1–6, or any other identification information, for that matter. This assists him in keeping track of his parameter cards. Of course, columns 14 through 80 of this first card may also contain any identification information the user wishes, since they are not read.

The reader may add additional functions to this program with relative ease. Care should be exercised to prevent duplicate variable names in specification statements; e.g., DIMENSION, DATA, etc., and to avoid multiple use of the same statement numbers.

The expansion of this program, as written, into a general purpose package is not recommended. The present design permits only one analysis to be performed during one execution of the program. No effort has been made to optimize the union of the code from the two programs incorporated in the present program. The correlation and regression code can accept no more than 999 cases for analysis, and only two variables, one independent and one dependent, may be analyzed per execution.

This program is meant simply to demonstrate the power of execution time format specification and to whet the appetite of the more advanced social science programmer. If there is not a general purpose data analysis package available for the reader's use, he has by now been exposed to sufficient FORTRAN to construct such a program. While such a task is truly quite large, the usefulness of the end product—both to the programmer and to the community of social science users around him—makes its accomplishment extremely rewarding.

SOURCE PROGRAM

```
C       PROGRAM 23   A GENERAL PURPOSE DATA ANALYSIS PROGRAM
C          THIS PROGRAM IS A MELD OF PROGRAM 10, CONTINGENCY TABLE ANALYSIS,
C          AND PROGRAM 12, CORRELATION AND REGRESSION WITH SCATTER PLOT.
C          IT MAKES USE OF EXECUTION TIME FORMAT SPECIFICATION FACILITIES.
C          ADDITIONAL FUNCTIONS MAY BE ADDED TO EXPAND ITS CAPABILITIES.
C
C       INPUT DATA CARDS ARE AS FOLLOWS:
C COLUMNS:      1              2
C       12345678901234567890 12345 ...
C       SELECT    PROG           WHERE 'PROG' IS EITHER 'REGR' OR 'CONT'
C       ( ... FORMAT INFORMATION FOR INPUT DATA ...)
C       **
C          **      PARAMETER CARDS REQUIRED BY EITHER REGR. OR CONT. PROGRAM
C             **
C       DD
C          DD      DATA CARDS
C             DD
C
C
C       'SHARED' SPECIFICATION STATEMENTS
C
        DIMENSION FMT(20)
        DATA REGR,CONT/'REGR','CONT'/
C
C       CORRELATION AND REGRESSION SPECIFICATION STATEMENTS
C
        DIMENSION XX(999),YY(999)
        DATA SUMX,SUMY,SUMXS,SUMYS,SUMXY/5*0.0/
C
C       CONTINGENCY TABLE SPECIFICATION STATEMENTS
C
        DIMENSION ITAB(10,10),IRTCT(10),ICTOT(10),NRV(10),NCV(10),
       1 PAD(60),LABEL(10),DASH(3)
        DATA ITAB,IRTOT,ICTOT,PAD,LABEL,DASH/120*0,60*' ','R','O','W',' ',
       1 'T','O','T','A','L','S',3*'_'/
C
C       'SHARED'   CODE SECTION
C
        READ(5,409) SWT
        READ(5,419) FMT
        IF(SWT.EQ.REGR) GO TO 5000
        IF(SWT.EQ.CONT) GO TO 4000
        WRITE(6,429) SWT,REGR,CONT
  409 FORMAT(9X,A4)
  419 FORMAT(20A4)
  429 FORMAT(' SELECT CARD IN ERROR. WAS ',A4,' SHOULD HAVE BEEN ',A4,
       1 ' OR ',A4)
        STOP
```

SOURCE PROGRAM (continued)

```
C
C       CORRELATION AND REGRESSION CODE
C
 5000 READ(5,209) NUMBR
      XN=FLOAT(NUMBR)
      INSRT=NUMBR-2
      DO 210 I=1,NUMBR
      READ(5,FMT) X,Y
      XX(I)=X
      YY(I)=Y
      SUMX=SUMX+X
      SUMY=SUMY+Y
      SUMXY=SUMXY+X*Y
      SUMXS=SUMXS+X**2
  210 SUMYS=SUMYS+Y**2
      XMEAN=SUMX/XN
      YMEAN=SUMY/XN
      STDX=(1.0/XN)*SQRT(XN*SUMXS-SUMX**2)
      STDY=(1.0/XN)*SQRT(XN*SUMYS-SUMY**2)
      B=(XN*SUMXY-SUMX*SUMY)/(XN*SUMXS-SUMX**2)
      A=(SUMY-B*SUMX)/XN
      R=(XN*SUMXY-SUMX*SUMY)/SQRT((XN*SUMXS-SUMX**2)*(XN*SUMYS-SUMY**2))
      RSQ=R**2
      F=(RSQ/(1.0-RSQ))*(XN-2.0)
      WRITE(6,219) NUMBR,XMEAN,YMEAN,STDX,STDY,R,INSRT,F,RSQ,B,A
      CALL PLOT(XX,YY,A,B,NUMBR)
      STOP
  209 FORMAT(I3)
  219 FORMAT('1',T20,'C O R R E L A T I O N   A N D   R E G R E S S I O
     1N'///T20,'SAMPLE SIZE=',I4//T30,'INDEPENDENT (X)',T50,'DEPENDENT (
     2Y)'/'+',T30,15('_'),T50,13('_')//T26,'MEAN=',T35,F9.2,T53,F9.2/
     3 T12,'STANDARD DEVIATION=',T35,F9.2,T53,F9.2//T20,'CORRELATION (R)
     4    =',F7.4,4X,'F(1,',I3,')=',F7.2/T15,'SHARED VARIATION (R**2) ='
     5 ,F7.4//T30,'SLOPE (B)=',2X,F9.4/T26,'INTERCEPT (A)=',2X,F9.2)
C
C       CONTINGENCY TABLE CODE
C
 4000 ISWCH=0
      READ(5,9) NR,NC,NCASE
      XN=FLOAT(NCASE)
      READ(5,9) (NRV(I),I=1,NR),(NCV(I),I=1,NC)
      WRITE(6,29) NCASE
      DO 5 I=1,NCASE
      READ(5,FMT) IROW,ICOI
      DO 1 J=1,NR
      IF(IROW-NRV(J)) 1,2,1
    1 CONTINUE
      GO TO 1000
    2 DO 3 K=1,NC
      IF(ICOL-NCV(K)) 3,4,3
    3 CONTINUE
 1000 XN=XN-1.0
      GO TO 5
    4 ITAB(J,K)=ITAB(J,K)+1
      IRTOT(J)=IRTOT(J)+1
      ICTOT(K)=ICTOT(K)+1
```

SOURCE PROGRAM (continued)

```
  5 CONTINUE
    IF(NR-1) 23,23,11
 11 IF(NC-1) 23,23,12
 12 IF(NR*NC-4) 23,13,20
 13 C1=ITAB(1,1)
    C1=FLOAT(ITAB(1,1))
    C2=FLOAT(ITAB(1,2))
    C3=FLOAT(ITAB(2,1))
    C4=FLOAT(ITAB(2,2))
    CHI=(XN*((C1*C4-C2*C3)**2))/((C1+C2)*(C3+C4)*(C1+C3)*(C2+C4))
    P=(FACTR(C1,C2)*FACTR(C3,C4)*FACTR(C1,C3)*FACTR(C2,C4)) /
   1(FACTR(XN,0.)*FACTR(C1,0.)*FACTR(C2,0.)*FACTR(C3,0.)*FACTR(C4,0.))
    GO TO 22
 20 SSODE=0.0
    SUMEX=0.0
    DO 21 I=1,NR
    DO 21 J=1,NC
    OBEXP=FLOAT(ICTOT(J)*IRTOT(I))/XN
    SUMEX=SUMEX+OBEXP
 21 SSODE=SSODE+FLOAT(ITAB(I,J)**2)/OBEXP
    CHI=SSODE-SUMEX
    IDF=(NR-1)*(NC-1)
 22 C=SQRT(CHI/(CHI+XN))
    PHI=CHI/XN
    NN=IFIX(XN)
    GO TO 24
 23 ISWCH=1
 24 L=6*NC
    WRITE(6,39) (PAD(I),I=1,L),LABEL
    WRITE(6,49) (NCV(I),I=1,NC)
    WRITE(6,59) ((DASH(I),I=1,3),J=1,NC)
    DO 6 IKT=1,NR
    WRITE(6,69) NRV(IKT),(ITAB(IKT,I),I=1,NC),IRTOT(IKT)
  6 WRITE(6,79) (DASH(I),I=1,3)
    WRITE(6,89) (ICTOT(I),I=1,NC)
    WRITE(6,99) NN
    IF(ISWCH) 31,31,33
 31 IF(NC*NR-4) 32,35,32
 32 WRITE(6,109) CHI,IDF,C,PHI
 33 STOP
 35 WRITE(6,119) CHI,P,C,PHI
    STOP
  9 FORMAT(20I4)
 19 FORMAT(2I4)
 29 FORMAT('1',T30,'C O N T I N G E N C Y    T A B L E    A N A L Y S I
   1S'///' FOR',I6,' CASES.')
 39 FORMAT(///T29,70A1)
 49 FORMAT(T27,10(3X,I3))
 59 FORMAT('+',T27,10(3X,3A1))
 69 FORMAT(//T25,I2,11I6)
 79 FORMAT('+',T24,3A1)
 89 FORMAT(//T8,'COLUMN TOTALS',T27,10I6)
 99 FORMAT(//T30,'TABLE TOTAL=',I6)
109 FORMAT(/T35,'CHI SQUARE=',T50,F10.2/T30,'DEGREES OF FREEDOM=',T60,
   1 I7/T30,'CONTINGENCY COEFFICIENT=',T60,F10.2/T30,'PHI SQUARED=',
   2 T60,F10.2)
119 FORMAT(/T35,'CHI SQUARE=',T50,F10.2/T30,'FISHER''S EXACT TEST=',
   1    T60,F10.4/T30,'CONTINGENCY COEFFICIENT=',T60,F10.2/T30,
   2 'PHI SQUARED=',T60,F10.2)
    END
```

SUBROUTINE PLOT

```
      SUBROUTINE PLOT(X,Y,A,B,N)
      DIMENSION X(999),Y(999),MTRX(50,90),VEC(10)
      DATA IPT,ISTAR,IO,IBLNK,MTRX/'.','*','O',' ',4500*' '/
      XMAX=ZMAX(X,N)
      YMAX=ZMAX(Y,N)
      XUNIT=(1.05*XMAX)/90.0
      YUNIT=(1.05*YMAX)/50.0
      DO 30 I=1,N
      XLEVL=0.0
      DO 10 K=1,91
      XLEVL=XUNIT*FLOAT(K)
      IF(X(I).LE.XLEVL) GO TO 15
10    CONTINUE
15    IX=K
      YLEVL=0.0
      DO 20 J=1,51
      YLEVL=YUNIT*FLOAT(J)
      IF(Y(I).LE.YLEVL) GO TO 25
20    CONTINUE
25    IY=J
      IF(MTRX(IY,IX).EQ.IPT) MTRX(IY,IX)=ISTAR
      IF(MTRX(IY,IX).EQ.IBLNK) MTRX(IY,IX)=IPT
30    CONTINUE
      K=0
      YLEVL=0.0
      DO 40 I=1,90
      YV=A+B*(XUNIT*FLOAT(I))
35    IF(YV.LE.YLEVL) GO TO 36
      K=K+1
      YLEVL=YUNIT*FLOAT(K)
      GO TO 35
36    MTRX(K,I)=IO
      YLEVL=0.0
      K=0
40    CONTINUE
      WRITE(6,9)
      DO 50 I=1,50
      K=51-I
      YV=(50.0-FLOAT(I))*YUNIT
      IF(MOD(I,5)) 45,46,45
45    WRITE(6,19) (MTRX(K,J),J=1,90)
      GO TO 50
46    WRITE(6,29) YV,(MTRX(K,J),J=1,90),YV
50    CONTINUE
      VEC(1)=0.0
      DO 60 I=2,10
60    VEC(I)=FLOAT((I-1)*10)*XUNIT
      WRITE(6,39) VEC,XUNIT,YUNIT,IPT,ISTAR,IO
      RETURN
 9    FORMAT('1',T45,'S C A T T E R   P L O T'///T2,'Y-VALUE',T106,
     1 'Y-VALUE'/'+',T2,7('_'),T106,7('_'))
19    FORMAT(T13,'I',90A1,'I')
29    FORMAT(3X,F8.0,'-I',90A1,'I-',F8.0)
39    FORMAT('+',T13,92('_')/T13,9('I',9X),'I'/T7,10(F8.1,2X)//T20,
     1 'X UNIT=',F7.2/T20,'Y UNIT=',F7.2/T10,'A POINT, (',A1,'), REPRESE
     2NTS ONE DATA VALUE.'/T10,'A STAR, (',A1,'), REPRESENTS MORE THAN O
     3NE DATA VALUE.'/T10,'THE ',A1,' CHARACTERS REPRESENT THE ACTUAL RE
     4GRESSION LINE.')
      END
```

FUNCTION ZMAX

```
      FUNCTION ZMAX(Z,N)
      DIMENSION Z(999)
      DATA ZM/-99999.9/
      DO 10 I=1,N
      IF(ZM.GT.Z(I)) GC TC 10
      ZM=Z(I)
10    CONTINUE
      ZMAX=ZM
      RETURN
      END
```

FUNCTION FACTR

```
      FUNCTION FACTR(X,Y)
      N=IFIX(X+Y)
      Z=1.0
      DO 10 I=2,N
10    Z=Z*FLOAT(I)
      FACTR=Z
      RETURN
      END
```

INPUT DATA SET ONE

```
CARD COLUMNS:
          1         2         3         4         5         6         7         8
1234567890123456789012345678901234567890123456789012345678901234567890123456789 0

SELECT    CONT
(I2,10X,I1)
   10   4  50
    1    2    3    4    5    6    7    8    9   10    1    2    3    4
    4         2
    5         4
    1         0
   10         5
   00         2
    6         4
    3         2
    5         3
    8         4
    7         5
    7         3
    2         1
    1         1
    2         1
    7         4
    9         2
    8         4
    6         3
    6         4
    5         2
    5         1
    5         4
    7         2
    4         2
    4         1
    8         4
   10         3
   10         4
   10         4
   10         3
    9         4
    8         3
    8         2
    8         4
    5         1
    5         4
    5         2
    6         2
    6         4
    7         2
    7         4
    7         3
    8         2
    8         4
    8         4
    9         3
    6         1
    2         2
    1         3
    3         2
```

INPUT DATA SET TWO

```
CARD COLUMNS:
        1         2         3         4         5         6         7         8
1234567890123456789012345678901234567890123456789012345678901234567890123456789 0

SELECT    REGR
(2F10.1)
 50
        123.5        43.5
        543.7        24.9
        124.0       421.5
       4257.1       543.3
       2468.9       954.0
         33.4       246.9
        425.8       246.8
        754.6       954.2
        426.5      9542.1
       2453.6       200.0
        789.4        43.5
       4265.3       425.6
       3246.8      4256.5
       6567.6      6447.6
       3699.9      4243.4
       2453.8       246.6
       8423.5       246.5
       2242.4       875.4
       4265.5      6654.2
       2244.5      5666.5
        246.5        24.3
       4562.2        45.7
        442.6      4424.6
        442.3      6655.4
       2411.2       445.6
        247.6        54.4
        244.6       200.4
        579.5        24.6
       1116.4       222.2
        554.4      2333.4
       4422.3       442.6
       5552.2      3665.6
       4234.3      6665.4
       7756.2      6676.4
       4432.4      4543.2
       2224.5       889.5
       4563.5       555.7
       5644.2         6.5
       4423.3      4223.3
       5422.4       423.3
       5544.3       886.5
       3556.8       579.8
       7565.7       554.3
       4565.7       243.0
       7564.4      3423.5
       7756.0       876.2
       4435.9       456.2
       8543.2       110.1
       5663.4       556.4
       8722.2       333.3
```

OUTPUT DATA SET ONE

C O N T I N G E N C Y   T A B L E   A N A L Y S I S

FOR   50 CASES.

	__1	__2	__3	__4	ROW TOTALS
__1	1	0	1	0	2
__2	2	1	0	0	3
__3	0	2	0	0	2
__4	1	2	0	0	3
__5	2	2	1	3	8
__6	1	1	1	3	6
__7	0	2	2	2	6
__8	0	2	1	6	9
__9	0	1	1	1	3
_10	0	0	2	2	4
COLUMN TOTALS	7	13	9	17	

TABLE TOTAL=   46

CHI SQUARE=	31.24
DEGREES OF FREEDOM=	27
CONTINGENCY COEFFICIENT=	0.64
PHI SQUARED=	0.68

OUTPUT DATA SET TWO

C O R R E L A T I O N   A N D   R E G R E S S I O N

SAMPLE SIZE=   50

	INDEPENDENT (X)	DEPENDENT (Y)
MEAN=	3464.99	1856.48
STANDARD DEVIATION=	2630.88	2461.51

CORRELATION (R)   = 0.0548   F(1, 48)=   0.14
SHARED VARIATION (R**2) = 0.0030

SLOPE (B)=   0.0513
INTERCEPT (A)=   1678.81

Page 2 of OUTPUT DATA SET ONE

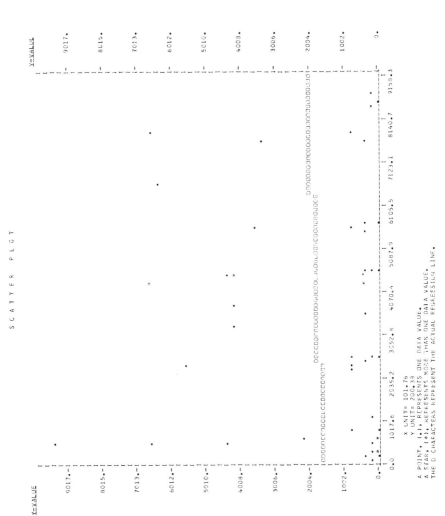

PART 3

Appendices

APPENDIX A

Number Systems

The decimal system of numbering is familiar to all of us. However, this is just one of an infinite set of numbering systems. The decimal system uses 10 as its base. The symbols in the decimal system are the digits 0, 1, 2, 3, 4, 5, 6, 7, 8 and 9. Note that there are 10 digits and that there is no single digit representing the base value, 10.

To represent a numeric quantity in the decimal system, digits are multiplied by powers of the base and these products are summed. This is not nearly as mysterious as it sounds. The quantity, 427, is simply

$$4 \times 10^2 + 2 \times 10^1 + 7 \times 10^0, \quad \text{which gives}$$
$$400 \quad + \quad 20 \quad + \quad 7 \qquad \text{or } 427.$$

Of course, any number raised to the zero power is 1.

The lowest order integer position is a digit times the base raised to the zero power. The next position to the left is a digit times the base raised to the first power, the next to the left is a digit times the base to the second power (squared), and so on.

Fractional values are given by a digit times the base raised to a negative power. For example 9297.035 is

$$9 \times 10^3 + 2 \times 10^2 + 9 \times 10^1 + 7 \times 10^0 + 0 \times 10^{-1} + 3 \times 10^{-2} + 5 \times 10^{-3}$$

or

$$9000 \;+\; 200 \;+\; 90 \;+\; 7 \;+\; .0 \;+\; .03 \;+\; .005$$

For bases greater than ten, letters are customarily assigned to represent digits greater than 9. The hexadecimal, or base 16, system has the following digits: 0, 1, 2, 3, 4, 5, 6, 7, 8, 9, A, B, C, D, E and F; where $A = 10$, $B = 11$, $C = 12$, $D = 13$, $E = 14$ and $F = 15$ in decimal notation. The hexadecimal number 7FA3 is simply

$$7 \times 16^3 + F \times 16^2 + A \times 16^1 + 3 \times 16^0$$

or

$7 \times 4096 + 15 \times 256 + 10 \times 16 + 3 \times 1 = 32675$ in decimal notation.

The binary, or base 2, number system is especially important in computer applications. It is discussed in Appendix B.

APPENDIX B

Binary Arithmetic

The binary number system uses two characters, 0 and 1, which are combined to form numbers as in the following examples.

Decimal Number	Binary Number
1	1
2	10
3	11
4	100
5	101
.	.
.	.
.	.
89	1011001

A binary number with N binary digits (bits) is approximately equivalent to a decimal number with $0.3 \, N$ digits because

$$\log_{10} 2 = 0.301$$
$$2^N = 10^N \log_{10} 2 = 10^{0.3 \, N}.$$

Thus, a five digit decimal number can be expressed by using about sixteen bits $(5/0.3 = 16.6)$.

Binary-Decimal Interconversion

Each digit of a binary number represents a power of two, so conversion of binary to decimal is done as follows: 10110.011 is equivalent to

$$2^4 + 2^2 + 2^1 + 2^{-2} + 2^{-3} = 16 + 4 + 1 + 0.25 + 0.125 = 21.375$$

The conversion of decimal to binary numbers follows the reverse process, whereby successive powers of two are subtracted from the original decimal number. Some decimal fractions cannot be represented exactly by a binary number.

Binary Addition

With two characters, binary addition rules are expressed by four laws, which are summarized in the following table.

+	0	1
0	0	1
1	1	10

$0 + 0 = 0$

$0 + 1 = 1 + 0 = 1$

$1 + 1 = 10$

The sum of the two binary numbers

$$\begin{array}{r} 110.011 \\ \underline{101.010} \\ 1011.101 \end{array}$$

is formed by the following sequence of steps (right to left):

$1 + 0 = 1$; $1 + 1 = 0$, carry 1; $1 + 0 = 1$; $0 + 1 = 1$; $1 + 0 = 1$; $1 + 1 = 0$, carry 1.

Binary Subtraction

Digital computers commonly use a method of subtraction involving complementary numbers because this allows performance of the subtraction operation by simple transformations coupled with addition.

The two's complement of a binary number is obtained operationally by inverting all the bits and then adding one to the result. For example, the quantity 65 expressed as an eight bit binary number is 01000001. Then −65 is derived as follows:

$$65 = 01000001$$
| invert | 10111110 |
| add 1 | 1 |

$$-65 = 10111111$$

Two's complement subtraction involves two steps:

1. Take the two's complement of the negative number.
2. Add the two's complement and the other number.

For example, subtraction of 5 from 16 proceeds as follows:

$$16 = 00010000$$
$$5 = 00000101 .$$

The two's complement of 5 is

$$-5 = 11111011 .$$

Then

$$
\begin{array}{r r}
16 & 00010000 \\
-5 & 11111011 \\
\hline
& 00001011
\end{array}
$$

with the last bit carried to the left ignored. The result is the binary form of eleven since

$$(1)(2^3) + (1)(2^1) + (1)(2^0) = 11 .$$

Subtraction of negative four from negative four proceeds as follows:

$$4 = 00000100$$

therefore

$$-4 = 11111100$$

and

$$
\begin{array}{r r}
-4 & 11111100 \\
-4 & 11111100 \\
\hline
& 11111000
\end{array}
$$

again ignoring the last bit carried to the left. The result is the two's complement for −8.

Binary Multiplication and Division

The binary multiplication rules are

×	0	1
0	0	0
1	0	1

$0 \times 0 = 0$

$0 \times 1 = 1 \times 0 = 0$

$1 \times 1 = 1$

Since no carrying is involved, multiplication can proceed either from right to left or left to right. Multiplication can also be done by repeated addition with shifts.

Division in binary requires the same trial and error approach used in decimal arithmetic. Repeated subtraction can also be used.

Computer Implementation of Binary Arithmetic

By going through several steps of logic, all binary arithmetic can be implemented simply on a digital computer as follows:

1. Transform the operation to repeated addition or subtraction, with shifts if necessary.
2. Transform subtraction to addition using complements.
3. Express addition and complementary operations in terms of negation and conjunction.

Conjunction consists of inspecting two binary bits; the result is 1 if both are 1, otherwise the result is 0. Negation consists of replacing a 1 by a 0 or a 0 by a 1. These logical steps form the link between the symbolic arithmetic operations and the physical capabilities of a digital computer to manipulate physical representations of zeroes and ones.

APPENDIX C

Job Processing

All large digital computers have resident in them large, sophisticated software packages called *operating systems* or executive systems, which control the computer's hardware at all time. These systems also control the flow of jobs through the computer. A sub-unit of the general systems software is the *monitor*. It is a large program (usually written in assembler language for efficiency) which consists of many subprograms such as (a) input/output routines, (b) compilers, (c) assemblers, (d) the subroutine libraries, and (e) the loader programs and others.

The *compiler* is a program that converts a FORTRAN (or other high-level language) program into computer-compatible form by changing the higher-level language statements into machine language. Compilers exist in two forms, as shown in Fig. C.1; on the left is a flow chart for the sequence of steps taken in executing a FORTRAN source program when using a two-step compiler. The compiler software translates the FOR-TRAN statements into machine language and punches them into a deck of cards called the *object deck*, which must be reloaded into the computer (using the loader programs) in order to be executed.

The second type of compiler is the one-pass type, shown on the right side of Fig. C.1. In this case, the compiler translates the FORTRAN into machine language and stores the program internally (in memory, or on tape, or on disk) and then proceeds to execute the instructions, all in one pass. This is the type of compiler most often found in large computers, and is certainly the most convenient for users. (Such compilers generally do have the capability of punching the object deck on cards if that is desirable; this is useful for programs that are to be run many times in identical form where the FORTRAN source program need not be re-compiled repeatedly.)

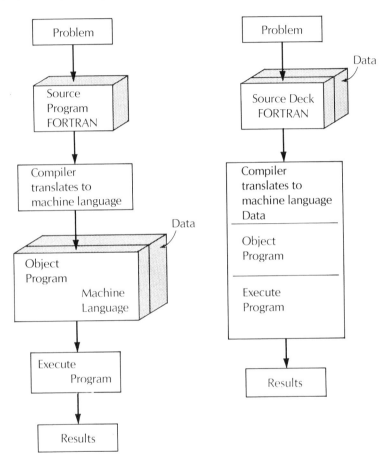

FIGURE C.1. *Compilers*

Both the monitors and the compilers in digital computers need "control cards" which are added to the deck of cards containing the source program and data cards. For example, for the IBM System/360 computers, an entire language, called Job Control Language (JCL) has been developed for these control purposes. Typically, then, several cards would be added to the source deck to tell the monitor that the program deck is in FORTRAN (and therefore needs the FORTRAN compiler) and to set up the correspondances between logical unit numbers for input and output in the program and the actual pieces of I/O hardware available for use with the computer and peripheral equipment. Other cards would be necessary to tell the FORTRAN compiler to compile the deck into an object deck, whether or not to punch an object deck, whether or not to execute the program. Because the number and format of these cards is dependent on the particular computer being used, and the particular computation center conventions, they will not be discussed here. These conventions must be learned anew for each computation center.

Many computer systems run just one program at a time and in a sequential manner, this is called batch processing. Other systems are capable of handling more than one program at a time, a method known as multiprogramming—normally confined to larger computers where it allows their capabilities to be more efficiently utilized. Some digital computers can handle users from many remote terminals at the same time by dividing time between the various users, a system known as *time-sharing*. Time-sharing works because human response is about six orders of magnitude slower than computer response.

APPENDIX D

Comparison of FORTRAN II *and* FORTRAN IV *Input/Output Statements*

I/O Operation	FORTRAN IV	FORTRAN II
Read from card reader	READ (i,n) list	READ n,list
Read from magnetic tape (formatted) (may be disk or drum on larger systems)	READ (m,n) list	READ INPUT TAPE m,n,list
Read from magnetic tape (binary)	READ (m) list	READ TAPE m,list
Write on printer	WRITE (j,n) list	PRINT n,list
Punch on cards	WRITE (k,n) list	PUNCH n,list
Write on magnetic tape (formatted) (may be disk or drum on larger systems)	WRITE (m,n) list	WRITE OUTPUT TAPE m,n,list
Write on magnetic tape (binary) (may be disk or drum on larger systems)	WRITE (m) list	WRITE TAPE m,list

m — logical unit number for I/O device
n — FORMAT statement number
i — input device number, frequently 5
j — line printer number, frequently 6
k — card punch number, frequently 7

APPENDIX E

Frequently Available Library Subprogram Statement Functions of FORTRAN IV

Name	Entry Name	Type	Comment
exponential	EXP	REAL * 4	
natural logarithm	ALOG	REAL * 4	
log base 10	ALGO10	REAL * 4	
arcsine	ARSIN	REAL * 4	
arccosine	ARCOS	REAL * 4	
arctangent	ATAN	REAL * 4	
sine	SIN	REAL * 4	Argument in radians.
cosine	COS	REAL * 4	Argument in radians.
tangent	TAN	REAL * 4	Argument in radians.
cotangent	COTAN	REAL * 4	Argument in radians.
square root	SQRT	REAL * 4	
hyperbolic tangent	TANH	REAL * 4	
hyperbolic sine	SINH	REAL * 4	
hyperbolic cosine	COSH	REAL * 4	
error function	ERFC	REAL * 4	
gamma function	GAMMA	REAL * 4	
modular arithmetic	MOD	INTEGER * 4	Two arguments: Arg_1 (mod Arg_2)
absolute value	IABS	INTEGER * 4	
	ABS	REAL * 4	

221

Name	Entry Name	Type	Comment
truncation	INT	REAL * 4 INTEGER * 4	
float	FLOAT	INTEGER * 4 REAL * 4	
fix	IFIX	REAL * 4 INTEGER * 4	

The functions given above for REAL * 4 type can be converted to REAL * 8 type by putting a D in front of the entry name for the REAL * 4 function; i.e., the REAL * 8 function for taking the cosine is DCOS.

The REAL * 4, INTEGER * 4, etc., notation is specific to the IBM System/360. Other conventions occur for other systems.

APPENDIX F

Glossary of Computer Terms

absolute address. The number permanently assigned to a particular word in the memory.

AC or **ACC.** See *register.*

access time. The time interval between the instant at which the arithmetic unit requires information from core and the instant at which the information is delivered to the arithmetic unit.

accumulator. A special section of memory in the arithmetic-logic unit of the CPU where arithmetic operations are performed.

accuracy. Degree of closeness of an approximate value to the true value.

ACM. Association for Computing Machinery.

address. A label, name, number or symbol identifying a register, location, or a device where information is stored.

add-time. Time required to perform one addition, exclusive of the time required to obtain the quantities from storage or return results to storage.

algorithm. A finite set of rules that unambiguously specifies a sequence of operations for solving a specific type of problem.

arithmetic unit. The section of the hardware of a computer where arithmetical and logical operations are performed.

assembler. A machine language program which operates on a source program of symbolic instructions to produce an executable machine language object program.

batch processing. Running a series of jobs successively on a computer system with little or no human intervention.

BCDIC *(Binary Coded Decimal Interchange Code).* A code system for representing numbers in a binary form wherein each digital number is represented by six binary bits. Frequently simply BCD.

bit. A binary digit. The basic unit in a digital computer's logic or memory. The basic unit of information.

bootstrap. A process whereby the manual introduction of a very limited set of instructions provides the capacity for the computer to read in further instructions, which add to its ability to do so, etc., until a complete set of instructions have been input.

branch. The point in a program at which the computer will proceed along a single one of two or more alternative paths according to existing conditions and instructions.

buffer. A special place (usually a section of core) set aside for storing information in transit from one part of the computer system to another until it is needed or can be accommodated at its destination. Widely used for reasons of efficiency.

byte. A group of eight bits.

clock pulse. The basic unit of time in a computer system is determined by the frequency of the clock pulses coming from the computer's clock.

closed loop. A system that is entirely self-sufficient and requires no outside intervention by the operator.

collating. The process of combining two sequences of data so that the sequence of the final data set is the same as that used in the individual data sets.

compiler. A digital computer program that accepts source programs written in a higher-level language (compiler language) and produces an executable object program.

control unit. The part of the hardware that directs the sequence of operations, interprets the coded instructions, and initiates the proper signals to execute the instructions.

core. One type of computer memory.

CPU. The central processing unit. The section of the hardware that directs and coordinates the overall functioning of the computer; it contains as subunits the arithmetic-logic unit, the registers, and the control unit.

cybernetics. The comparative study of the control and internal communication of information handling machines and the central nervous system of animals and men, in order to understand better the functioning of the brain and communication.

data. Any information, numeric or non-numeric, coded or literal.

debugging. The methods of eliminating errors from programs.

decision. The operation of determining, at a certain time, if a certain condition exists, and selecting alternative operations accordingly.

dedicated. A machine which is physically a part of a larger system and which functions as an integral part of that system.

diagnostic. A program or subprogram built into a program that is used in locating a given type of error in programming or hardware malfunction, etc.

direct couple. A computer system formed from two smaller computers which are combined into one, with one normally doing the actual computing and the other performing executive functions.

disk. A random-access auxiliary memory device on which information is stored on rotating magnetic disks.

down time. That portion of time during which a computer is not operating because of malfunctions, maintenance, errors, etc.

drum. A random-access, auxiliary device wherein information is stored on a revolving drum which is coated with magnetic material.

dump. The process of transmitting all or part of the memory, registers, etc. of a computer to some output device for inspection.

EBCDIC. *(Extended Binary Coded Decimal Interchange Code).* A code system for representing numbers in a binary form wherein each digital number is represented by eight binary bits or one byte (see **BCDIC**).

executable instruction. An instruction which, during execution, causes the computer to perform an actual operation in the machine itself.

ferrite. A magnetic chemical mixture of iron oxide and other metallic oxides included in ceramic material.

fixed point. A mode of expressing numbers such that the number is stored as a fixed number of digits.

flip-flop. An electronic circuit having two stable states, which can store one bit of information.

floating point. A mode of expressing numbers in terms of a fraction and exponent of a given base number so that numbers of any magnitude are stored with the same precision.

hardware. The informational components of a computer system.

hexadecimal. Referring to the base 16 number system.

IBM. International Business Machines Corporation.

information retrieval. A series of computer techniques for searching, recognizing, and printing data selected from a large library file.

input unit. A unit through which data is brought into the computer.

I/O. The general symbols for the process of inputting or outputting information or for the information itself.

I/O bound. A job in which the actual processing time is sufficiently brief that the overall rate of execution of the job is determined by the speed of the peripheral devices employed.

instruction. A machine word or set of characters in machine language which specifies that the computer take a certain action.

interpreter. A machine that reads punched cards and prints what is contained in the card across its top.

interrecord gap. A section of recording medium (may be tape, disk or drum) upon which no data are stored. This gap is recognized by the recording device in order to permit separation of physical blocks of information.

iteration. One cycle through a set of program statements — repeatable. One execution of a loop.

keypunch. A keyboard machine with which information can be put manually onto punch cards.

library. A collection of standard and fully tested programs, routines, and subroutines available for use by the programmer.

line printer. An output device which prints an entire line at a time of characters on paper.

loader. A program segment that, when read into memory, equips it for reading subsequent information.

loop. Repetition of a group of instructions in a routine.

machine language. A set of coded instructions that can be executed directly without intermediate programmed translation, conversion, or other preprocessing.

memory. Any device that can store information for subsequent extraction.

monitor. A supervisory program that regulates the processing of jobs in a digital computing system.

MQ. See *register*.

multiprocessing. The execution of more than one program at a time in a given computer.

nanosecond. 1×10^{-9} seconds; one billionth of a second.

noise. Any electrical disturbance tending to interfere with the desired signal or information.

object program. The program in machine language produced by the compiler when it translates a program written in a higher level language.

octal. Base eight.

off-line. A setup in which the components of a computing system or the input mechanism and the computer are not directly linked and cannot communicate electronically.

on-line. Operating in time with and under the direct control of the central equipment.

open loop. An incomplete loop that is broken at some point to allow outside intervention in the sequence of events.

operating system. A complex of supervisory programs which include assemblers, compilers, monitors, and other executive components.

output. Information transferred from the internal storage of a computer to secondary or external storage, or to a device outside of the computer.

overflow. In a counter or register, the production of a number that is beyond the capacity of the counter.

parity bit. An extra bit carried along with the informational bits of a word, which is on or off so that the sum of the bits in the word, modulo 2, is always either even or odd. It is used for checking purposes during computational operations to reduce the number of undetected errors.

peripheral equipment. Auxiliary machines that may be placed under the control of the central computer, i.e., magnetic tape units, printers, etc.

precision. The number of significant digits attached to a value.

punched card. A card of standard dimensions containing a fixed number of places where holes that represent coded information can be punched.

queue. A waiting line, such as the input queue of jobs waiting to be executed by the computer.

random access. Access to a location in storage that is in no way dependent on the previous location accessed.

random number. A number constructed of digits that are obtained by a process in which any given digit is just as likely to appear next as any other digit.

real time. In solving a problem, a speed fast enough to give answers that can be used to control the situation or operation containing the program.

registers. Sub-units of the control unit used as temporary storage for the numbers being handled by the arithmetic circuits of the machine.

relocatable. Referring to a program or program segment that can be linked together with other program segments at execution time.

reproducer. A machine which copies an inserted card deck on another deck of cards.

rewind. To reset a reel of magnetic tape to its starting point.

rounding. The operation of shortening a number to a specified number of digits, the last one of which may be increased by 1 if the most significant dropped digit exceeds 5; e.g., 57.7 rounded to a whole number is 58.

sense switch. One of a series of binary switches on the console of the computer allows the operator to control certain portions of a program externally. These switches may exist only in a symbolic form.

serial access. Access to a location in a storage device which is dependent on the previous location accessed; e.g., magnetic tapes must be accessed serially.

software. The informational components of a computer system; i.e., compiler, library routines, systems programs, etc.

source program. A set of sequential instructions written in a higher-level language.

subprogram, subroutine. A pretested program segment, used in a larger main program, which is designed to produce a certain function or operation.

tape drive. A magnetic tape transport for recording and playing back data.

time-share. To carry out two or more functions in equipment essentially simultaneously by alloting (often in rotation) small divisions of the total time to the performance of each function.

truncation. The operation of shortening a number to a specified number of digits by dropping all digits to the right of the last one saved; e.g., 7.7 truncated to a whole number is 7.

underflow.   In a counter or register, the production of a number too small to be stored by the computer.

updating.   The process of incorporating recent information into its proper place in a file of information.

variable word length.   Computer systems can sometimes allow the number of characters which constitute a machine word, to be variable and under the control of the programmer.

WATFIV.   A student-oriented FORTRAN compiler.

word.   An ordered set of characters that has at least one meaning and which is stored and transferred by the computer circuits as a unit. It is treated by the control unit as an instruction, by the arithmetic unit as a quantity.

APPENDIX G

FORTRAN IV *Program Optimization*

Programs are usually written in three stages: planning, coding, and debugging. The planning stage refers to the operation of choosing the method to be used for the desired computation. If the problem to be solved is not understood thoroughly, or if the method of solution is inappropriate, the program will be doomed from the start.

Once a method has been chosen, then the coding of the FORTRAN source program can begin. The following is a brief list of suggestions for partially optimizing the FORTRAN coding for the purpose of increasing the execution speed of the program.

1. Carefully analyze the overall problem before programming. Often it is possible to simplify the problem and/or the numerical procedures used so as to speed up the computations.

2. Execution speed can often be gained by using more memory, i.e. storage of arrays that might otherwise have to be recomputed throughout execution of the program.

3. Avoid the use of mixed-mode expressions. On many systems they are not allowed at all. On systems where they are allowed, they should be avoided in order to avoid using library subprograms which convert types (and therefore slow execution). Also, use A = 0.0 rather than A = 0, and use I = 0 rather than I = 0.0 for the the same reason.

4. Avoid the use of SUBROUTINE subprograms and arithmetic statement functions for tasks to be repeated a large number of times.

5. Avoid using branches in program logic except when necessary.

6. Make the most probable result of logical IF statements the simple drop through rather than a branch.

7. Reduce I/O to the absolute minimum.

8. Use implied DO loops for I/O instead of ordinary DO loops wherever possible.

9. Calculate constants to be used throughout the program at the beginning of the program. Calculate quantities that remain constant within a loop before entering the loop. For example,

$$DO \ 10 \ I=1,500$$
$$10 \quad C(3*I,2*K-1)=(A(2*L)-A(2*L-1))**(J*2)$$

should be programmed as

$$KK=2*K-1$$
$$L1=2*L$$
$$L2=2*1-1$$
$$JJ=J*2$$
$$DO \ 10 \ I=1,500$$
$$10 \quad C(3*I,KK)=(A(L1)-A(L2))**JJ$$

10. Avoid the use of multiple subscripts on arrays unless absolutely necessary. Use X(1000) rather than X(10,10,10).

11. Use unconditional GO TO statements rather than computed GO TO statements.

12. To determine conditional branches of more than three labels, a computed GO TO statement is more efficient than a series of IF statements.

13. Pass variables to SUBROUTINE subprograms by using COMMON statements rather than including them in the argument list.

14. Avoid testing for equality between floating point numbers because of the possibility of round-off error. It is better to use .GT. or .LT. comparisons.

15. Use the SQRT routine rather than **0.5, because the SQRT routine is faster than the logarithmic routine which is used to evaluate expressions of the form $X**R$.

16. When raising numbers to small powers, use integer exponents. Values raised to integer powers are computed by repetitive multiplication, whereas values raised to real powers are computed by using logarithmic and exponential routines.

17. Use unformatted I/O statements whenever possible.

APPENDIX H

Trouble-Shooting

Due to the complexity of computer programming languages, and often some confusion on the part of the programmer as to what he is trying to accomplish, programs are rarely written that solve the problem for which they were designed on the first run. Not only are grammatical errors and plain mistakes sources of problems in the programming statements themselves, but the machine's obstinance in executing any syntactically correct program entered into it leads to a second level of trouble-shooting difficulties. In the first instance one is looking for errors in the construction of the FORTRAN statements. In the second instance the programmer is trying to ascertain whether the program is producing the desired results, and if not, why not. We shall distinguish between these two problems of trouble-shooting in the following discussion.

Normally, the programmer does not have direct access to the machine but must submit his job and then look at the printed results. This may be called remote debugging, and it is akin to trying to learn French by ordering from the menu in a French restaurant and waiting to see what kind of food you get. Sometimes, however, the programmer actually operates his own jobs and, therefore, has the opportunity to make modifications while the program is in progress. We shall discuss the first case in the following pages, and the second case in Appendix I on "Hands-On Operation."

FORTRAN Errors

Fortran compilers on large machines are equipped with diagnostic routines that check for various types of FORTRAN errors. For the complete interpretation of any diagnostic message, it is best to first consult the manual for the particular compiler in use and then, if necessary (and if available), the consulting service of the computer center. Smaller systems usually have diagnostics but these are often less extensive.

From the outset, it should be realized that any diagnostic message may not be complete or correct. Furthermore, the lack of a message is by no means a guarantee that no error exists. The reason for this lies in the difficulty of producing good diagnostic messages and the one-way nature of the task. (Note that if the diagnostic routine could be guaranteed successful, the compiler could just correct the statement and proceed.) For example, the following statement K=I*(M−1) might be erroneously written K=I*(M−1, by accidentally omitting the right parenthesis. Most sophisticated compilers would detect an error in this statement by the process of adding the total numbers of each kind of parenthesis and finding there was one more left than right. Hence a message, directly following the statement, such as MISSING RIGHT PARENTHESIS might appear.

If, however, the asterisk were omitted, giving K=I(M−1), several errors — or none — might be indicated. This statement looks legal to a simple compiler in view of the fact that I might be a subscripted variable. A more sophisticated compiler would find I absent in any DIMENSION statement or as a function and might give, among others, any of the following messages: ILLEGAL DIMENSION, or VARIABLE MISSING FROM DIMENSION, or MISSING FUNCTION. Another mistake for this statement would result when a "U" was punched instead of a "1" (same key on both IBM−026 and IBM−029 keypunches) giving K=I*(M−U).

In a compiler which did not allow mixed mode arithmetic, this mistake would be recognized by the fact that M and I are fixed point variables while U is a floating point variable. A message such as ILLEGAL MIXED MODE OPERATION might be produced. However, if mixed mode was allowed by this compiler, the statement would be accepted with no error indicated.

Any error that can be unambiguously associated with an individual statement is usually indicated on the line following the statement. Many errors, particularly those dealing with the flow of the program, cannot be associated with an individual statement and are listed at the end of the source program listing. If the error check shows one or more diagnostic errors, then the compilation is terminated and the job left unexecuted. Typical errors of this type are missing statement numbers and improperly nested DO loops. For example, if GO TO 38 appears in the program, but no statement number 38 exists, a likely error message would be MISSING LABEL 38. Similar messages occur when a statement number is used more than once.

The fundamental point of any detected compiler error is that a program has been presented which cannot be carried out in an un-ambiguous fashion, if at all. Therefore, the program is rejected along with messages giving as much of a hint to the difficulty as possible. Trouble-shooting such errors varies somewhat on whether remote or hands-on operation is possible.

In remote operation usually more than a negligible amount of time will pass between program runs. Under these circumstances it becomes important that the number of unsuccessful runs be minimized. Hence the programmer should be satisfied (if possible) that the source of every compiler-detected error has been corrected before resubmitting his program. Furthermore, if the turn-around time is very long, it is worth-while to make a complete survey of the program after each pass in hopes of catching potential errors before they are detected by the compiler. In addition to this, each examination of the program may help the overall familiarity of the programmer with what he is attempting to do, and give him insight when other problems arise.

Adopting certain conventions and turning these into habits is of notable use in minimizing trouble-shooting compiler errors. Throughout this book the convention of all FORMAT statement numbers ending in 9 and all of DO loop statement numbers ending in 0 has been followed. While there is nothing magic about the choice of nines and zeroes for these usages, it is useful to always have FORMAT's numbered with one easily recognizable character, and DO endings with another. Because these two operations give rise to many compiler errors including many of the most mystical or difficult to understand, it is convenient to have them readily locatable. All other transfers in the programs to statements other than the two listed above, then must end in the characters 1 through 8. By adopting habits such as these, the programmer will avoid errors such as inadvertently transferring to a FORMAT statement. Or, at least if he does not avoid them, they will be more readily apparent when he notices a statement such as GO TO 9. Another useful convention is to place all the FORMAT statements at one place in the program. The programs in this book follow the convention of placing all the FORMAT's at the end of the program. This aids in two ways: first, the FORMAT's often a source of trouble are easily locatable. Furthermore, since they are not interdispersed with other statements whose numbers may be active places to transfer, there is less likelihood of the mistake of writing a transfer to a FORMAT number.

Computational Errors

Unfortunately, once a program with no compiler errors is presented to the machine, it is left solely to the programmer to determine whether the program is producing the desired results. For complex programs the first few passes usually lead to results (if any) that are obviously in error. However, some programs complete execution or terminate in some un-scheduled fashion without producing any results at all. All such errors fall under the class of *program logic errors*, when the compiler diagnostic system is sufficiently extensive to detect any type of FORTRAN mistake. (While this may approach reality for some very large systems, it still cannot be generally assumed.) The first stage in debugging any program is to retrace the steps the program should take, with the information in hand as to what happened last. That is, if no output at all was obtained then it is ascertained that the program either executed normally, became tied up in a closed loop, or did some illegal operation within the machine, before any output statement was reached. Hence the program is isolated to those paths which cannot reach any output operation. Under other circumstances, one or more outputs may have occurred, thereby iso-lating the termination as following the last output but preceding any other in the program. In addition, there are some operating system error messages which may be of some help in this portion on debugging. For example, the message ILLEGAL INPUT RECORD may be produced when a floating-point number is read under a fixed-point FORMAT specification. In lieu of obvious errors which lead to simple corrrection, or such outputs which help isolate errors, the programmer is often faced with a seemingly insoluble situation. Under these circumstances his best option, in a great majority of cases, is to resubmit the program with additional print-out statements designed to help him find the problem. Such statements, called diagnostic prints, may be placed in the program on a temporary basis and later removed when the job is successfully running. For example, consider a program which once.loaded proceeds in a continuous loop until the machine is cut off or some systems param-eter, such as a time limit, is exceeded. The looping position may often be isolated by placing in the program a system of write statement, each of which refers to a format with a literal field such as

```
        WRITE(6,9)
    9   FORMAT ( ' PRINT 1 ' )
```

WRITE(6,19)
19 FORMAT (' PRINT 2 ')

such that the printout identifies its position in the program. If printouts are judiciously placed, one run of the program will often be sufficient to isolate that portion of the program that is in a continuous loop. In other problems, such as incorrect results from confused calculations, it is often convenient to use printout statements to give the values of inter-mediate variables. In addition, DO loop indices and other useful values may be printed out in this fashion. These intermediate numbers may allow location of control and computation errors. This approach is particularly useful where complex calculations are carried out. It is often very difficult to look at a FORTRAN statement that one has written and realize that a parenthesis is incorrectly positioned or an operator left out or replaced by another, such that the statement itself is valid in the FORTRAN sense, but the computation it is carrying out is different from the one desired. Printing out the values of the variables used before the computation and the results directly after, will allow the operation to be compared to a hand calculation. A word of caution on the use of print statements, however. If carelessly placed in often repeated loops, they may result in an inordinate number of pages of relatively useless output.

A common error, but one which leads to the most mystifying results, is the error of subscripts exceeding the values specified in a DIMENSION statement. While a variable may be dimensioned for a specific number of locations at the time of program compilation, there is no way for the compiler to realize that the programmer may later input a variable which will be used as an index and cause some subscripted variable to exceed its allowed dimension. Hence, if X is dimensioned for fifty locations, and I is read in as 100, when X(I) is referenced in some statement, the fiftieth position beyond X(50) in the memory will be used. Some operat-ing systems have sufficient diagnostic ability to detect this problem and to print out an error message such as SUBSCRIPT ERROR. However, usually this is not the case and the results may be quite puzzling. The erroneous location used may belong to another variable, or it may even contain instructions for the program, thereby writing some variable value within the set of instructions. When interpreted as an instruction this number may be valid, thereby leading to unpredictable operation; or may be invalid, thereby causing termination of the program when it is reached. Suffice to say, many of the most difficult errors to understand occur when DIMENSIONS are exceeded, and this should always be considered a possibility in any complex program.

As with remote trouble-shooting of compiler errors, remote debugging of computational problems requires the utmost care to guarantee that each run is of maximum use. For this reason it is always preferable to put in excessive print statements in the first runs of a new program, since these alone give the maximum information as to how the program executed. In addition, it is useful to choose input data whose answers are known or may be easily calculated. Also, as pointed out earlier, it is useful to consider printing out DO loop parameters at various points in the program. It is also important to remember not to place output statements where they will be executed too frequently by DO loops. Finally, even though a single error is identified, it becomes important to take advantage of the run and search for other possible errors. As an aid to this process, the programmer should thoroughly satisfy himself that the error or errors which he has found did indeed lead to the results he received. If he cannot logically convince himself that this is the expected result from a given error, then the programmer should proceed to search for other errors that may also be interacting to produce the erroneous results. It is a matter of simple economics. If the average turn-around time of a given facility is four hours, then it must certainly be worth the programmer's time to spend an extra thirty minutes in pursuit of an error which may cause an additional four hour turn-around.

Finally, if all else fails, the programmer may act as a CPU himself. With a pad of paper as "memory", the programmer can execute each instruction in the program on some sample data. Every experienced programmer, at some point in his career, has gone through this procedure at least once. As the old quip goes, those who need the most practice will be sure to get it.

APPENDIX I

Hands-On Operation

Several aspects of computer programming are drastically altered when one has the capability of running one's program in real time—being in direct control of the computer while one's program is executing. These are discussed with reference to trouble-shooting of FORTRAN errors and the trouble-shooting of computational errors.

FORTRAN Errors

The most important added feature of hands-on debugging is, of course, that the programmer has virtually instant turn-around time. This is a noteable aid in that the programmer does not have several minutes or even hours or (shudder!) days between each examination of his program. Hopefully, he can remove all the compiler errors from his program with fewer runs. However, there is a counter effect in the extreme availability of the machine, so that many programmers tend to resubmit jobs hastily without carefully looking for the sources of error. The most efficient debugging is accomplished by some compromise of carefully checking each error and still taking advantage of such rapid turn-around situations. When the programmer does not understand a compiler error message, he may modify the program in some fashion, resubmit the job, and check the response. Furthermore, the programmer not realizing whether certain operations are legal may simply try them and see the compiler response. For example, in some versions of FORTRAN, dimensions may be given in variable subscripts that are assigned by the input data. In other versions this is illegal. The programmer may test such a situation by simply writing such a DIMENSION statement, and most compilers will give an error message if it is not acceptable. This is not meant to suggest that anything which fails to give an error message is a logical operation in the machine. While it may be a valid operation or even lead to an error unpredictable by the compiler, it may not lead to the desired answers and is, therefore, illogical from the viewpoint of accomplishing the desired results.

Computational Errors

When the programmer can directly operate the machine, several options are available to facilitate hands-on trouble-shooting of computational errors. One of these is the PAUSE statement:

$$PAUSE\ XXXX$$

where XXXX is a digital message. Whenever a PAUSE statement is executed, the machine halts and the message appears on some output device. (This device may be the display lights on the console, the console typewriter, or a line printer.) The machine may then be restarted and execution of the program will proceed until it either completes or reaches the next PAUSE statement. The use of such pauses allows locating looping portions of the program and various nonscheduled exits. For example, when it is not possible to find at what point a program is going into an infinite loop, judicious placement of several PAUSE statements—each with a different message—will often facilitate such isolation. This is much like the operation of diagnostic print statements as detailed in the remote debugging discussion, but is somewhat more convenient in that no accompanying format is required to accomplish the desired result.

An additional facility, which is available on many machines, is the *sense switch*. This is a console switch, or series of switches, which may be interrogated by a statement within the FORTRAN program. The statement, having various forms in different FORTRAN versions, acts to make a transfer to one of two locations based on whether the switch(es) is (are) turned on or off. This allows the programmer to build in a variety of options not otherwise available. For example, in trouble-shooting an iterative program that makes repeated passes through the same calculation loop, a printout of current values may be controlled by a sense switch. Then as the calculation proceeds, the programmer may momentarily turn the switch on and then off again and observe the value printed out at that particular point. Thus, he may test intermediate values without having to print out an inordinate number of lines. Furthermore, the sense switch may be used for ordinary options, if hand-on operation is a routine procedure in the facility.

Finally, if all else fails, the programmer may act as a CPU himself. With a pad of paper as "memory", the programmer can execute each instruction in the program on some sample data.

APPENDIX J

Card Punching

The primary mode of communication with most computers is the punched card. This appendix outlines some basic instructions for card punching. The card punch is very flexible, and reference to the appropriate manuals for the punch available for use is strongly recommended — especially for more advanced operations.

The card punch described here is the IBM 29, shown in Fig. J.1. It consists of a typewriter-type keyboard (Fig. J.2) built into a desk and has card manipulation and punching apparatus above the desk area. There are five card positions in the card punch:

1. The *card hopper* stores the blank cards until they are fed into the card punch for processing.

2. The cards are held in the *feed position* by the lever pressure finger.

3. Cards are advanced approximately one-half inch from the feed position to the *punching station*, through which they are advanced one column at a time as data are punched or the column is skipped.

4. After being punched, the card moves to the read bed and then to the *reading station*, as a second card is being positioned in the punching station. The card in the reading station moves column by column through the reading station in concert with the card moving through the punching

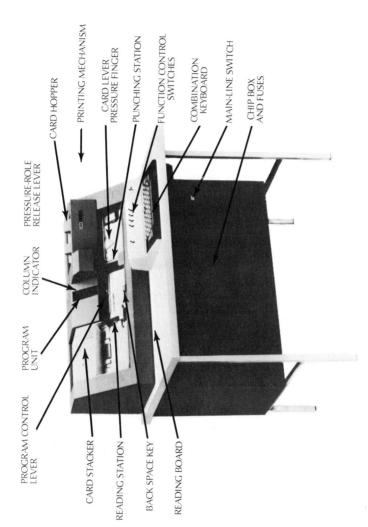

FIGURE J.1   *IBM 29 Card Punch* (Reproduced with Permission of the International Business Machines, Incorporated.)

station. If desired, the data on the card moving through the read station can be read and duplicated into the same column of the card moving through the punching station.

5. Cards complete their flow through the card punch by being stored in the *stacker position* as a deck.

All card movements, from the card hopper to the stacker, are controlled from the keyboard. Just above the read bed and behind a window is located a column indicator which tells which of the eighty columns of the card in the punching station is in place to be punched.

Punching Without Program Control

1. Turn on the card punch. The ON–OFF switch is positioned beneath the keyboard.
2. Set the function control switches. Above the keyboard there is a row of toggle switches. Rather than worry about what they are all for, simply place all but the right-most switch in the UP position. (The possible exception to this is with an interpreting keypunch. On this model the extreme switch should be down, in the PUNCH position.) Cards left in either the punch or read station can be ejected by holding the right hand switch, CLEAR, up momentarily.
3. Prepare to punch. Place the desired number of cards in the card hopper. The sliding pressure plate in the card hopper is pushed back and the cards are inserted into the hopper facing forward with the "9-edge" (bottom) down. The cards should be evenly stacked with the pressure plate holding them firmly forward. Depress the FEED key and hold it down until two cards are fed into the punch station.
4. Punching the cards. Cards are punched by typing on the keyboard. Lowercase characters are punched without shifting; the uppercase characters are obtained by pressing the left, NUMERIC, shift. When a card has been completely punched, it is released by pressing the release key, REL, which advances the punched card to the read station and moves the next blank card to the punching station. So you made a mistake. The card you have just punched is in the read station. Assume that you note an error. For example, the card below is observed in the read station.

$$9 \quad F \ O \ R \ M \ O \ T \ (\ I \ 5 \ )$$
$$\uparrow$$
$$11$$

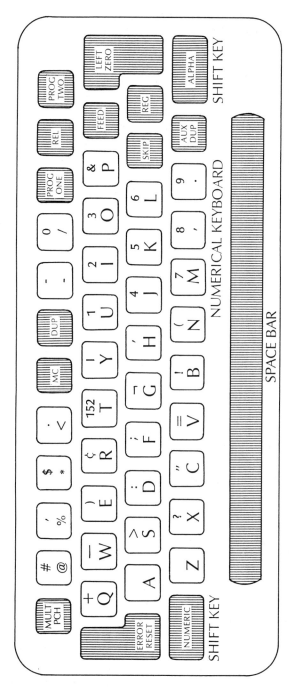

FIGURE J.2 *IBM Card Punch Keyboard* (Reproduced with Permission of the International Business Machines, Incorporated.)

Column 11 should contain an A. Rather than re-type the entire card, simply press the DUP key and hold it down or press it intermittently until the column indicator is at column 11. Now type "A" and then hold the DUP key down until all the remaining information on the card is copied. Press REL and discard the bad card as it comes into the stacker. Cards can also be manually inserted for duplication; to do so, clear the punch unit with the CLEAR switch. Insert the card to be duplicated into the read station using the slots in the center of the edge retainers of the read station. Slide this card to within about one-half inch of the extreme left edge of the read station. Insert a blank card under the metal retainers in the punch station. Push the card to the left far enough so it lays flat in the punch station, but *DO NOT* push it all the way to the punch bar. Now press the register key, REG, and proceed to duplicate as above. Both cards are moved to the stacker with the CLEAR switch. The REG key is always used to prepare a card for punching when only a single card is in the punch station.

The Program Unit

The program unit is located above the read bed. It is controlled by a drum card wrapped around the program drum, as shown in Fig. J.3. The drum card, prepared by the user for his own application, has holes punched in it to be read by the program unit, and those holes instruct the card punch to perform automatic operations such as automatically skipping or duplicating certain columns in the cards being punched. The drum is accessed by raising the hinged cover that protects it. The drum sits on a spindle inside the program unit. The program unit is activated and inactivated with the program control lever, located directly above the read bed.

Punching under Program Control

The use of a program card or drum card can take a lot of drudgery out of routine card punching. To set up a drum card, proceed as follows.

   1. *Drum removal.*   Turn the program control switch to OFF (right side of the V down) and raise the hinged cover over the drum.

   2. *Card removal.*   On the drum there is a metal strip called the clamping strip. Behind it there is a lever called the clamping strip which has three positions: clockwise, center, and counter-clockwise. To remove the old drum card, turn the clamping handle to the center position and

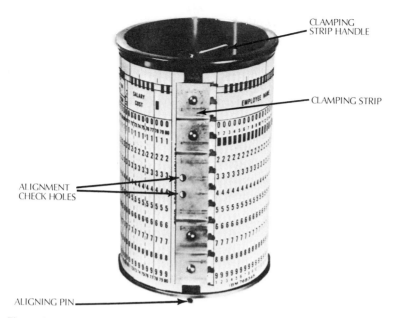

Figure J.3   *Program Drum and Drum Card* (Reproduced with Permission of the International Business Machines, Incorporated.)

slide the column 1 edge of the card from beneath the clamping strip; and then turn the clamping strip to the counter-clockwise position and slide the column 80 edge out.

    3. *Card insertion.* With the clamping strip handle in the counter-clockwise position, insert the column 80 end of the drum card under the smooth edge of the clamping strip. The card should be against the metal strip under the clamping strip. There are two small holes in this edge of the clamping strip to aid in alignment. With the card in position, turn the clamping strip handle to the center.

    Wrap the card firmly around the drum and insert the column 1 end completely under the toothed end of the clamping strip. Turn the clamping strip handle to the clockwise position. Check to insure that the card is flush with the bottom rim and is correctly positioned under both edges of the clamping strip.

    4. *Drum insertion.* With the program control switch in the OFF position, slide the drum down the shaft, making certain that the aligning shaft on the bottom of the drum is aligned with the hole in the drum mount. Close the cover and switch the program control switch on (left side of the "V" down). Press the REL key once and begin punching.

Program Card Preparation

The program card allows the card being punched to be divided into fields. In this respect it is akin to setting up a series of tabulator stops on a typewriter. To allow further discussion, zone punches must be defined. The card punch can punch in 12 rows or zones on the card. The card image in Fig. J.4 shows the location of each zone. The character assigned to each of these zones is printed above the punches.

The four types of program control punches most commonly used in making drum cards are the following.

Punch	Function
12	Field definition
11	Start automatic skip
0	Start automatic duplication
1	Alphabetic shift
none	Numeric shift

To set up a program card, start by considering the 12 zone, which is used to define the fields. As an example, assume that it is required to prepare data to be read by an 8E10.0 specification. If these numbers are to be entered in normal decimal notation (no exponential part and the decimal punched), then the numbers may start in columns 1, 11, 21, 31, ... 71. A program card for this application is shown in Fig. J. 5. Note that the start of each field is signalled by *no punch* in 12 zone and that the field is defined by consecutive 12-zone punches. With this card in position, the PROG SEL switch set to ONE, and the program control on (left side of "V" down), the keyboard is automatically in numeric shift, and the first column of the next field can be reached automatically by pressing the SKIP key. To enter a series of numbers like 13., 14., 15., 16., etc., a card is brought into punching position. The punching sequence would be **13.** SKIP **14.** SKIP etc. The values will position by the drum card in the correct fields.

Another example drum card is shown in Fig. J.6. Note that this card also defines eight ten-column fields (no 12-zone punch in 1, 11, 21, ..., 71). The 11-zone punch in columns 11, 31, 51, and 71 is the auto skip command. When this card is used with the AUTO SKIP DUP in the ON position, the PROG SEL at ONE and the program control switch ON will allow punching only in columns 1–10, 21–30, 41–50, and 61–70. Such a card would be convenient with a format such as (4(E10.0, 10X)). After it types a number in the first field, the SKIP key will cause

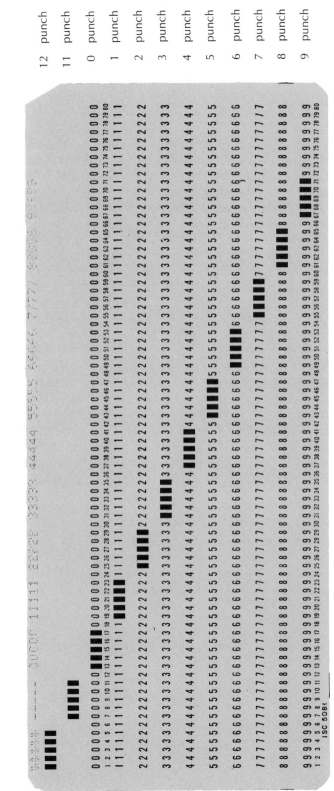

FIGURE J.4 *Zone Punches* (Courtesy of Information Supplies Corporation.)

12 punch
11 punch
0 punch
1 punch
2 punch
3 punch
4 punch
5 punch
6 punch
7 punch
8 punch
9 punch

the card to go immediately to column 21. This auto skip feature also prevents punching outside the allowed field. For example, if a character is punched in column 10, the card then will automatically skip to column 21.

The program card can also be used to advantage when punching FORTRAN programs. A generally useful drum card is shown in Fig. J.7. This card defines three fields: the first field, a numeric field from columns 1 through 6, is for statement numbers and the designation of continuation cards. The second field starts in column 7 (no 12-zone punch) and continues to column 72. Note that a 1-punch is also in each column of this field. This shifts the keyboard into the normal mode, meaning that the numeric shift must be used to punch numbers and the upper case symbols. The final field starts in column 73 and the 11-zone punch in column 73 causes this final field to be skipped. Again, for all this to happen, the V-shaped program control switch must be on or to the left, the PROG SEL to ONE, and the AUTO SKIP DUP must be ON. Note that when a card is in position for punching and no statement number is required, simply pressing the SKIP key will move the card to column 7.

Finally, the drum card shown in Fig. J.8 presents one more variation for punching FORTRAN programs with a drum card. The only change from the above card is that a 0 punch now appears in column 73. This sets the auto duplication mode. Before punching the deck of cards for the FORTRAN program, punch a leading card with the desired message in columns 73–80. This message will then be duplicated onto every card in the deck. For example, if the master card prepared contained NEUMANN in columns 73–80, then every card punched under control of the drum card in Fig. J.9 would have NEUMANN copied into these columns.

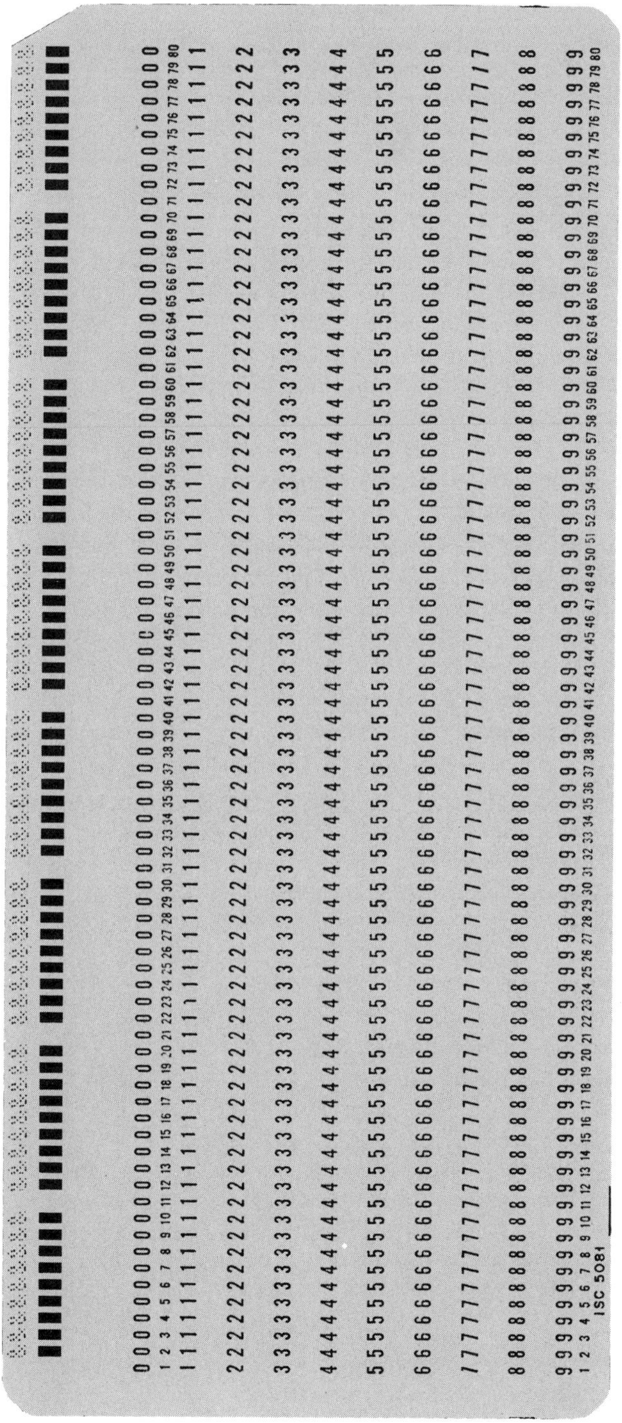

FIGURE J.5 *Program Drum Card* (Courtesy of Information Supplies Corporation.)

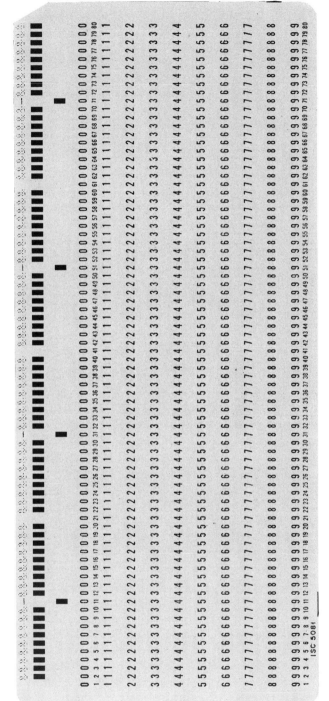

FIGURE J.6 *Program Drum Card* (Courtesy of Information Supplies Corporation.)

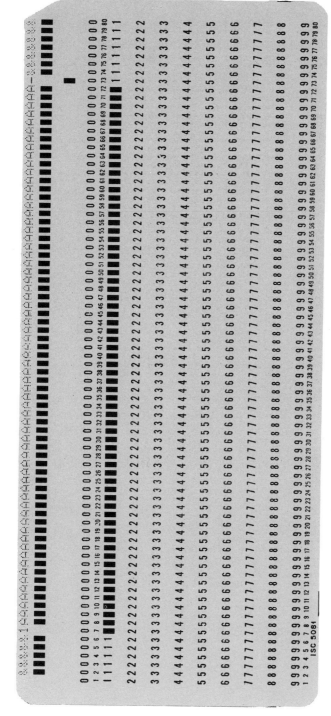

FIGURE J.7   *Program Drum Card* (Courtesy of Information Supplies Corporation.)

251

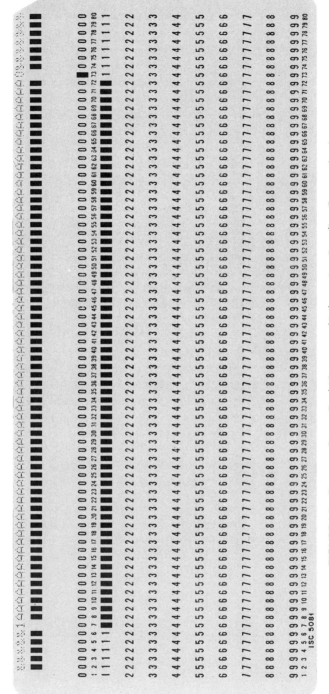

FIGURE J.8 *Program Drum Card* (Courtesy of Information Supplies Corporation.)

252

Bibliography

Chapter I

For an elementary treatment of computers in general see:

Communicating with a Computer, Bolt, A. B. and Wardle, M. E., Cambridge University Press, 1970.

A more complex discussion of the demonstration of intelligent action by computers, including Turing's classic piece, "Computing Machinery and Intelligence", is presented in *Computers and Thought*, Feigenbaum, E. A., and Feldman, J., McGraw-Hill Book Co., 1963.

An excellent advanced text, oriented toward third generation IBM systems is *Automated Data Processing, SYSTEM/360 Edition*, Brooks, Jr., F. P. and Iverson, K. E., John Wiley and Sons, Inc., 1969.

For an enlightening and frequently amusing introduction to what makes a programmer, see *The Psychology of Computer Programming*, Weinberg, G. M., Van Nostrand Reinhold Co., 1971.

Chapter II

Two college level texts oriented toward the general skills of programming are *Programming, An Introduction to Computer Languages and Techniques*, Maurer, W. D., Holden-Day, Inc., 1968.

Computer Programming, Flores, I., Prentice-Hall, Inc., 1966.

Chapter III

In addition to manuals produced by the various computer manufacturers, there are numerous books in print designed to teach the reader FORTRAN. The following are only a sample of those available.

FORTRAN Programming (Revised Edition), Stuart, F., John Wiley and Sons, Inc., 1970.

A First Course in Programming, FORTRAN IV with WATFIV, Campbell, G. M. and Singletary, W. E., Auerbach Publishers, 1971.

A Guide to FORTRAN IV Programming, McCracken, D. D., John Wiley and Sons, Inc., 1965.

Elements of FORTRAN Style: Techniques for Effective Programming, Kreitzberg, C. and Shneiderman, B., Harcourt Brace Jovanovich, Inc., 1972.

Index